Andrew Combe

The Management of Infancy Phisiological and Moral Intended

Chiefly for the Use of Parents

Andrew Combe

The Management of Infancy Phisiological and Moral Intended Chiefly for the Use of Parents

ISBN/EAN: 9783741140396

Manufactured in Europe, USA, Canada, Australia, Japa

Cover: Foto ©Thomas Meinert / pixelio.de

Manufactured and distributed by brebook publishing software
(www.brebook.com)

Andrew Combe

The Management of Infancy Phisiological and Moral Intended

Chiefly for the Use of Parents

THE

MANAGEMENT OF INFANCY,

PHYSIOLOGICAL AND MORAL.

INTENDED CHIEFLY FOR THE USE OF PARENTS.

BY

ANDREW COMBE, M.D.,

FELLOW OF THE ROYAL COLLEGE OF PHYSICIANS OF EDINBURGH, AND ONE OF THE
PHYSICIANS IN ORDINARY IN SCOTLAND TO THE QUEEN.

Ninth Edition.

REVISED AND EDITED

BY

SIR JAMES CLARK, Bart., M.D., F.R.S.,

PHYSICIAN IN ORDINARY TO THE QUEEN, & HIS ROYAL HIGHNESS THE PRINCE CONSORT.

EDINBURGH:
MACLACHLAN AND STEWART
SIMPKIN, MARSHALL, AND CO., LONDON.
MDCCCLX.

TO

HER MAJESTY

THE QUEEN.

MADAM,

In graciously accepting the Dedication of the present Revised Edition of Dr Combe's valuable work, your Majesty has given an additional proof of the interest you are known to take in the progress of Sanitary Science.

And assuredly to no one could a work, having for its object the preservation of Infant Life, and the improvement of the Moral Training and Instruction of the young, be more appropriately dedicated than to your Majesty, whose management of your own family affords a bright example to parents, and a living testimony of the wisdom of being guided, in the treatment of their offspring, by the Laws of Health, so clearly indicated by the Creator.

I have the honour to subscribe myself,

Your Majesty's

faithful and dutiful subject,

JAMES CLARK.

THE STUDY OF INFANCY, CONSIDERED EVEN AS AN ELEMENT IN
THE HISTORY AND PHILOSOPHY OF MAN, ABOUNDS IN INTEREST,
AND IS FERTILE IN TRUTHS OF THE HIGHEST PRACTICAL VALUE
AND IMPORTANCE.—COMBE.

INTRODUCTION BY THE EDITOR.

SEVERAL considerations induced me to undertake the pleasant task of revising and editing Dr Combe's valuable Treatise on the Management of Infancy. The subject is one in which I feel a deep interest, and to which I have given much attention during my professional life; a long and intimate friendship also with the enlightened Author afforded me frequent opportunities of discussing with him the subjects treated of in the following pages. I thus became well acquainted with his opinions on the causes of the frightful mortality which occurs during the earlier periods of life; and I shared with him the conviction, that the hope of diminishing the evil rested *entirely* on our being able to enlighten parents and the public generally on the causes of such mortality, and to instruct them in the means of its prevention. For these reasons, I felt that I was not unprepared for the task. Moreover, I had the feeling that I could not more usefully occupy my leisure, at the close of a long professional life, than in lending such aid as I could to carry out the benevolent intentions of the Author; while I should, at the same time, have the gratification of paying a tribute of respect to the memory of a much esteemed friend.

The work has been to me a labour of love; and it has not been a heavy one, as the last edition, which the Author himself corrected, was left so perfect that little remained for an editor to do.

In making the few alterations and additions which appeared to me necessary, I have endeavoured to identify myself with the Author, and to do merely what I believe he would himself have done, if his valuable life had been spared. In this spirit, I have gone carefully and repeatedly over the whole work. I have altered the order of some of the chapters, with the view of bringing the subjects treated of more consecutively before the reader. I have also ventured to omit some portions, chiefly in the earlier chapters, as less necessary now than during the Author's life. I have given some additional information on the causes and extent of Infant Mortality, taken

chiefly from the recent Reports of the Registrar-
General; and, lastly, I have added an APPENDIX,
in which will be found some useful matter, not so
well fitted for the body of the work.   My great
aim has been to carry out what I know was the
object of the Author; namely, to make the
work useful to young Medical Practitioners and
Teachers of youth, as well as to Parents, for
whose guidance the work was originally and
mainly designed.   To my younger Medical
brethren, entering on the anxious and responsible duties of their profession, I earnestly recommend a careful study of the work.   I know
none on the subject of Infant Hygiène, in which
is to be found so much valuable practical information, to guide young Medical Practitioners
in the management of infants and young children.   I venture to give the same advice, and
with equal earnestness, to Teachers, both male
and female, and more especially to the teachers
of Infant-Schools.

In the concluding chapters of the work,
they will find principles to guide them in conducting education in accordance with the progressive development of the Mental Faculties,
and their natural aptitude for comprehending
different subjects of study.   Until these principles, so lucidly expounded by Dr Combe, are

thoroughly understood and systematically acted
on in the management of Infant-Schools, these
very important institutions will never realise the
advantages expected of them,—and which, if
rightly conducted, they could not fail to yield,
by training and instructing the young so as to
modify their whole character, and thus promote
their welfare, their usefulness, and their happiness throughout life.

To Governesses, I consider the above advice
specially applicable. A very large proportion
of the children of the upper, and even middle
classes in this country, have no sooner left the
nursery than they are consigned to the care of
a governess, under whose direction chiefly they
remain during that plastic period of life in
which the character is very often permanently
formed. How important is it, then, that this
class of teachers should possess such a knowledge of the physical and mental constitution
of the young beings committed to their charge,
as shall enable them to cultivate and train
the moral feelings, as well as to instruct the
mind! Yet, in seminaries for the education of
young ladies intended for governesses, there is,
I believe, no such instruction given. Unfortunately, it is a kind of knowledge little understood, rarely even thought of, by either

teachers or parents; and yet it is the most important knowledge which they can possess. In my opinion, NO TEACHERS OF ANY CLASS SHOULD BE CONSIDERED COMPETENT FOR THEIR DUTIES TILL THEY HAVE GIVEN PROOF OF POSSESSING A GENERAL KNOWLEDGE OF THE STRUCTURE AND FUNCTIONS OF THE HUMAN BODY, AND OF THE LAWS OF HEALTH. Were proof required of all teachers that they possessed such knowledge, before they were intrusted with the care and education of youth, schools of all classes would be driven to make Physiology a part of their regular course of instruction.

Within the last few years, Physiology, in its application to health, has been taught with considerable success in several seminaries, more especially in the Birkbeck Schools, in London, under the enlightened direction, and by the liberal support of Mr William Ellis; and it has been invariably found, even at a very early age, to excite in a remarkable degree the interest and attention of the pupils. It is to be hoped, therefore, that the time is not far distant when Physiology will form an essential part of the course of instruction in every school.*

It is in vain to expect that education can be

* That there is no difficulty in effecting this, see APPENDIX E. for the opinion of the medical profession.

rightly and successfully conducted, until the *Educators* themselves are instructed in the nature of the physical and mental constitution of those whom they undertake to train and instruct.

As regards the instruction of young women in Physiology, I venture to suggest, for the consideration of those ladies who have gone through a systematic course of medical education with the view to qualify themselves as medical practitioners, whether devoting their time to the instruction of their own sex in the laws of health would not form an equally useful and a more appropriate profession than that of a physician or surgeon? In adopting, as their sphere of action, the *hygiène of female and infantile life*, ladies would be in their right social position; and assuredly they could have no higher vocation than that of teaching their own sex the important duties which devolve on them as mothers,—how to manage their own health and that of their offspring. If ladies, properly educated for such a duty—they need not be fully educated physicians—would devote their time and energies to this noble work, they would confer an inestimable benefit on the rising generation, and merit the lasting gratitude of posterity. They, too, will find in the present work an excellent text-book and a safe guide.

"The Ladies' National Association for the
Diffusion of Sanitary Knowledge" deserves notice in this place, its "principal object being
the preservation of the health of children."
Women are peculiarly well suited to give instruction on domestic hygiène, and to their exertions and influence chiefly must we look for the
teaching of the laws of health to the working-
classes. "It is to women that we must look
first and last," says Miss Nightingale, "for the
application of sanitary knowledge, as far as
household hygiène is concerned."* If the objects of this Association are carried out with
judgment and discretion, it cannot fail to do
much good, by enlightening the women of England on the means of preserving the health of
their families, and instructing them in the

* *Notes on Nursing*, by Florence Nightingale.
These Notes contain much most useful information, applicable both
to health and sickness,—to the private dwelling as well as to the
hospital. The work, indeed, forms a handbook of Household Hygiène
and of Nursing. It should be in the possession of every mother of a
family, and be found on the table of every sick-room and of every
hospital ward. The work may also be read with great advantage by
the medical profession, more especially the section on Ventilation.
No error in the treatment of the sick is so general,—none more injurious,—than the neglect of ventilation. It is very rare, indeed, that
one enters a sick-room in a well-ventilated state,—scarcely less so,
according to my experience, to find a medical man, of any class, who
attaches sufficient importance to thorough ventilation. If such
apathy exists among professional men, what can we expect of nurses?

management of their children. But it is not by
lectures and tracts that this can be effected.
The latter may be very useful to the members of
the Association, and to mothers in the upper and
middle classes of society, who have time to read,
and intelligence to understand them; but the
working-classes can be effectually taught only by
personal intercourse,—by visiting them at their
own homes, and there instructing them in all
that relates to the sanitary management of their
households. Personal advice, thus kindly and
delicately given on the spot, will make a deeper
and more lasting impression than many lectures
and volumes of tracts; and it will often happen
also, that, along with the mothers, the daughters
may at the same time receive a useful lesson.
By such visiting, conducted with discretion and
tact, and confined to sanitary subjects, the greatest benefit may be conferred on the working-
classes. Visitors, themselves thoroughly instructed in the principles of sanitary science,
and taking charge of defined districts, could do
much to promote the health and comfort of the
people, by making them acquainted with the
causes of disease, and the means of its prevention. There is a large field of usefulness open
to the Association, and there will, I believe, be
no want of educated, benevolent women, in all

parts of the country, ready, and even anxious, to devote their time to the fulfilment of its objects.

How strongly Dr Combe's experience impressed him with the necessity of an acquaintance with Physiology and the constitution of the infant frame being made AN ESSENTIAL PART OF FEMALE EDUCATION, appears from the following earnest appeal, which I have transferred from the body of the work, in the hope that it may attract more general attention in this place:—

" In no point of view is it possible to defend the prevailing error of leaving out what ought to constitute an essential part of female education. Till this defect be remedied, thousands of young beings, who might have been preserved, will continue to be cut off at the very outset of existence, to the lasting grief of those who would have been happy to guard them against every danger, had they only known how. Even in the best-regulated families, it is rare to meet with a mother who, before becoming such, has devoted the least attention to the study of the infant constitution, to the principles on which it ought to be treated, or to the laws by which its principal functions are regulated. She enters on her important charge with less preparation than if it were a plant or a flower, instead of a being in whose existence and happiness her whole soul is

centred. Yet to HER exclusively the infant looks
for that cherishing and affectionate care which
its delicate frame requires; to her it directs every
appeal, in the full confidence that she will be
ever watchful for its happiness and relief, and
that from her a look or a cry will procure the
requisite sympathy or aid. She it is who provides its nourishment, regulates its exercise, and
watches over its slumbers. But when we inquire to what extent her education has fitted
her for the intelligent discharge of the duties
which thus constitute the chief objects of her
social existence, we find that, in the majority of
instances, *on no one point relating to them has she
received even a little of instruction;* and that she
marries and becomes a mother without a suspicion of her deficiency in the most ordinary information concerning the nature and functions
of the infant whom she is suddenly called upon
to cherish and bring up. When her heart is
wrung by witnessing its sufferings, and she
knows not to what hand to turn to save it from
impending danger, she bitterly laments her ignorance and helplessness. But not being aware
that much of the difficulty and danger proceeds
from her defective education, the idea never occurs to her that those who come after her must,
in their turn, go through the same painful and

profitless experience with *their* children, unless, with rational foresight, they be prepared, by the requisite instruction and training, for those duties which they may soon be called on to perform.

"It is true that all women are not destined to become mothers; but how very small is the proportion of those who are unconnected by family ties, friendship, or sympathy, with the children of others! how very few are there who, at some period of their lives, would not find their usefulness and happiness increased by the possession of a kind of knowledge so intimately allied to their best feelings and affections!

"It may, indeed, be alleged, that mothers require no knowledge of the laws of the infant constitution, or of the principles of infant management, because *medical aid* is always at hand to correct their errors. According to the present habits of society, however, professional men are rarely consulted till the evil is done, and the health broken; but even if they were, intelligence and information are needed in the mother, to enable her to fulfil their instructions in a rational and beneficial spirit. On every account, therefore, it is urgently necessary that female education should be such as to fit both mind and body for the duties as well as for the embel-

lishments of life,—for the substantial happiness
of the domestic circle, at least as much as for
the light and fleeting hours of fashionable amusement,—and that, while every effort is made to
refine and elevate the mind, the solid substratum
of useful knowledge should not be neglected."

No reflecting person can read this appeal
without being impressed with the vital importance of the subject to the future welfare of the
human family.

Andrew Combe was altogether a very remarkable man. In addition to his extensive knowledge of the human constitution, the result of
close observation and deep reflection, he possessed a remarkable felicity in expressing his
views, and in explaining the application of the
physiological laws to the preservation of health
and to the direction of education according to
the age and mental development of the child.

To large intellectual endowments, and a sa-
gacity which I have never known surpassed,
were added in Dr Combe the warmest benevolence and the gentlest disposition. The good of
his fellow-creatures was ever uppermost in his
thoughts; and he omitted no occasion, and
spared no exertion within the compass of his
power, to accomplish the benevolent objects he
had in view. This spirit is evinced throughout

the whole of his writings, and in none more
than in the present—perhaps the most valuable
of his works.   Were I to enter more fully into
the excellences of Dr Combe's character, it
might be attributed to the partiality of friendship.   I shall therefore simply observe, that I
never knew a better or more truly religious
man, nor one who had the welfare of the human
race more sincerely at heart.   Unfortunately
for a large circle of friends and for mankind, his
enlightened and benevolent mind was united
to a feeble frame.   A delicacy of constitution
showed itself in his childhood; but it was not
till after he had arrived at maturity that the
delicate state of his health assumed a decided
character, and that he became the subject of
frequent attacks of pulmonary disease, which on
several occasions brought him to the brink of
the grave.   Such, indeed, was his condition that
it might be truly said of him that the greater
part of his life was one long disease.   Yet, by
judicious management of himself and frequent
changes of climate, and by a careful adaptation
of his mental and bodily labours to his powers
of endurance during the periods of comparative
health which he did possess, he contrived in
a quiet, unostentatious way to do much good
during his too short life ; and he has left behind

him writings which are of the utmost value to mankind.* Dr Combe indeed afforded, in his own person, a remarkable example of what could be effected by a very fragile constitution, acting in strict conformity with those physiological laws of which he was himself so able and lucid an exponent. His works have passed through many editions, and have had a very extensive circulation in this country, and in the United States of America. But, extended as has been their circulation, they ought to be still more generally known and studied. Every family and every teacher, from the mistress of the Infant-School to the University professor, should be familiar with Dr Combe's physiological

---

* In an admirable recent work, "Horæ Subsecivæ," by Dr John Brown of Edinburgh, will be found, graphically drawn, the character of Dr Combe's mind; but for a full knowledge of the man, the reader is referred to his "Life and Correspondence," by his brother, George Combe. He too has lately been taken from amongst us, while still earnestly engaged in the preparation of works on subjects of the highest general interest. His constitution also, during the latter portion of his life, was, like his brother's, very delicate; and it was only by the strictest attention to the laws of health that he was able to complete what is considered the ordinary term of human existence. Two better men, I believe, never lived, nor men who devoted themselves more zealously to promote the good of the human race; and the works which they have both left behind them are calculated to instruct and benefit mankind for ages yet to come. But the time is not yet arrived for estimating at their full value the whole of George Combe's works.

works;* and no medical man should commence the practice of his arduous profession
without having studied them carefully, and more
especially those on the *Hygiène* of *Infancy* and of
Youth. I deem this advice the more needful, as
Hygiène has not hitherto received the attention
which it merits as a branch of medical education. The University of London is, I believe,
the only one in this country in which Hygiène
finds a place among the prescribed subjects of
examination for degrees in medicine—a regulation mainly owing to Dr Combe's urgent recommendation.† This subject is now, however,
beginning to excite general interest; and assuredly no one has done more than Dr Combe
to press its importance on the public, and to
enlighten them on it by his published writings.

In the Army Medical School just instituted,
HYGIENE will form the most important branch
of the young medical officer's instruction. For
originating this school, we have to thank Miss
Nightingale, who, had her long and persevering
efforts effected no other improvement in the

* The Principles of Physiology applied to the Preservation of Health,
and to the Improvement of Physical and Mental Education.—The
Physiology of Digestion considered with Relation to the Principles of
Dietetics.

† See his Letter to the Editor, published in his Life and Correspondence.

army, would have conferred, by this alone, an
inestimable boon upon the British soldier, and
merited the gratitude of the country for the improved sanitary condition of the army, and the
saving of human life, which will be the result.*

When the public is made fully aware of the
extent to which health may be preserved, and
disease averted and mitigated, by a knowledge
of Physiology, the practice of Medicine will assume a very different aspect from that which it
presents in its present unsettled state.   The
physician will then be more frequently consulted
on the means of preserving and improving health
than for the treatment of disease, as is almost
solely the case at present.

Before concluding these introductory remarks,
already perhaps extended too long, I venture
to add one more extract from the Author's Pre-

* The country is indebted to the present enlightened Minister-at-
War—Mr Sidney Herbert—for the establishment of this School.   Mr
Herbert's previous inquiries into the military condition of the army,
the causes of disease, and the state of the barracks, hospitals, &c., had
fortunately impressed him with the very defective arrangements for
preserving the health of the soldier; and he could not have chosen any
means better calculated to strike at the root of the evils which he
detected, than the education of the young army medical officers for
their special duties.   The beneficial effects of this practical school,
and of the other sanitary improvements introduced by Mr Herbert,
will soon be manifest in the improved health and efficiency of the
army.

face to the last edition of the present work :—
" In taking leave of a subject which I cannot
but feel to be one of vital interest to thousands yet unborn, I would respectfully offer
one or two remarks on the spirit in which the
following pages ought to be read. . . . The
subjects treated of embrace so many important facts and principles of action, which are
comparatively new to the general reader, that it
is only by their careful and repeated study, and,
in time of need, turning again and again to the
pages in which they are explained, that a mother
can expect to become really familiar with them,
and able to apply them with ease and judgment
to the many purposes for which they are
adapted."

In this judicious advice I earnestly concur.
The work, to be really useful, must be studied
carefully, and referred to on all occasions of
doubt or difficulty. In order that mothers, and,
I take leave to add, young medical practitioners,
may derive full advantage from it, they must
have their minds thoroughly imbued with the
principles so clearly unfolded, and the practical
rules so plainly laid down in every chapter of
the work.

J. C.

London, *February* 1860.

THE AUTHOR'S DEDICATION.

TO

SIR JAMES CLARK, Bart., M.D., F.R.S.,
PHYSICIAN IN ORDINARY TO THE QUEEN, AND TO HIS ROYAL
HIGHNESS PRINCE ALBERT.

MY DEAR SIR JAMES,

Two reasons, the one of a personal and the other
of a professional nature, induce me to dedicate this treatise to you.
I gladly embrace the opportunity which it affords me of publicly expressing my regard for you, as a friend whom I have long and intimately known, and whom, during years of constant and unreserved
intercourse, I have ever found, even in the most trying circumstances,
animated by the purest integrity, and the kindliest and most benevolent dispositions.

On professional grounds, too, there is perhaps no one to whom I
could so appropriately dedicate a work intended to call attention to
that comparatively unoccupied, but most important field of medical
inquiry, which embraces the hygienic treatment of man,—as to you,
who have already laboured in it with great ability and success. For
many years, not only have you taken a deep and active interest in
the improvement of medical education, and in elevating the character, extending the scope, and increasing the usefulness of our profession; but, acting on the same principles which I have endeavoured
to enforce, you have, in your excellent works on Climate and Consumption, rendered no small service to science, by your instructive
exposition of the manner in which fatal disease of the lungs so often,
and so insidiously, originates in apparently trifling causes connected
with disregard of the ordinary laws of health. You have further

shown, that when Medicine shall be cultivated in a more liberal and comprehensive spirit, and its principles be recognised as furnishing the only solid foundation for a proper system of physical, moral, and intellectual education, it will become one of its noblest uses, and, I may add, one of its greatest privileges, to be instrumental, not more in the prevention of disease and suffering, than in contributing to the general happiness and permanent advancement of the human race.

Even as regards the special subject of the present volume, you were the first, in your treatise on Consumption, to insist strongly on the necessity of adopting a proper system of management from the very commencement of infant existence, as the only effectual means of averting that general deterioration of health in which the fatal pulmonary disease has its origin, and of procuring for the individual that measure of health and vigour without which life and its varied duties become sources of suffering rather than of enjoyment. In your volume, accordingly, are to be found many instructive details on the hygienic management of both infancy and youth ; and it affords me no small gratification to know, that, while pursuing independently the same ends, we, unknown to each other in the outset, chose nearly the same paths, and arrived together at entirely consistent and not unfrequently identical results.

To you, therefore, on both public and private grounds, I have peculiar satisfaction in dedicating this work, as a mark of esteem and regard, of which, however intrinsically unimportant and inadequate it may be, I know few in every way so worthy as yourself.

Believe me to remain always,

MY DEAR SIR JAMES,

Yours very sincerely,

ANDREW COMBE.

EDINBURGH, 10th May 1840.

THE AUTHOR'S INTRODUCTION.

MANY excellent treatises on the management of infancy already
exist; yet few of them are calculated to supply parents with the kind
of information which, in their circumstances, is especially needed.
Most of those hitherto published touch briefly upon the general
management of early childhood, merely as preliminary to an exposition of its diseases; and the perusal of them by non-professional
persons frequently leads to dangerous tampering with the lives of
the young. On this account, I cannot but consider them as improper
guides for any except medical readers. Those again which, as intended for the use of mothers, are free from this objection,—even
when abounding, as many of them do, in good sense and excellent
practical advice,—lose much of their value and usefulness from presenting their rules and admonitions as so many abstract and individual opinions, and omitting to connect them with the physiological
laws or principles on which they are based, and according to which
the effects are produced.

Sensible of these imperfections as detracting from the usefulness,
as guides for the non-professional reader, of many works in other
respects of great merit, I had almost resolved, several years before
the publication of the first edition of this book, to enter upon
the preparation of a treatise on a more comprehensive plan, and
which should, on the one hand, avoid all descriptions of disease, and,
on the other, found its precepts, at every possible point, on well ascertained physiological principles. Under the apprehension, however,
of being unable so to simplify the subject as to render it easily in-
b

telligible to the general reader, I refrained from putting together
the materials which had accumulated in my hands; till at length,
encouraged by the very favourable reception of my other works on
subjects somewhat analogous, and by the numerous testimonies I received of their practical utility, I set seriously to work, and completed the
present volume.   That it has, at least in some measure, supplied a want
extensively felt, may fairly be inferred from the very favourable reception which it has met with both at home and abroad, and also from the
spontaneous testimony of many parents and others in different ranks
of life, speaking from experience of the deepened sense of the importance of their duties which its perusal had awakened in their minds,
and of the comfort and assistance which they had derived from it in
the management of the young entrusted to their care.

Bacon has not less profoundly than felicitously remarked, that
" Man is but the servant and interpreter of nature, and is limited in
act and understanding by the extent to which he has observed the
order of nature : beyond this, neither his knowledge nor his power
can extend."   In accordance with the spirit of this aphorism, it has
been my constant endeavour, in the present, as in all my other
writings, to allow as little as possible to rest on mere human opinion,
but to show a foundation for every rule, precept, and injunction, in
the laws of the human constitution, and consequently in the will
of the Creator.   The obvious advantage of this mode of proceeding
is, that, when we once succeed in discovering any truth, that truth
will ever afterwards be regarded as an emanation of the Divine
will, and the practical rules deducible from it claim our obedience
with an authority which we cannot dispute.   Whereas, if we pass
on from subject to subject, and precept to precept, disregarding the
relations of facts to each other and to the laws of the constitution,
we may add, it is true, much information to our store, but shall often
be led to form a very erroneous estimate of its value, and be beset
with difficulties in applying it with promptitude and decision to its
proper uses, where, rightly directed, it would conduce to the happiest
results.

To illustrate this proposition, we may compare a person who under-
takes the management of the human constitution, whether in infancy

or in maturity, without any reference to the principles under which it acts, to a traveller who, without a map or a guide, wanders over a new country in search of some particular place. By some lucky chance, he may stumble at once upon the locality he is in search of, or reach it at length by some very circuitous route. But the probability is, that, after wandering about in uncertainty, he will be forced to return, weary and disappointed with the fruitlessness of his journey. He, on the contrary, who is guided by *principle*, may be likened to a traveller who, carrying with him a map in which the chief features of the country are accurately laid down, advances with comparative certainty towards his aim. If at any time, in consequence of omissions or slight inaccuracies, he chances to wander from the right course, the map itself soon warns him of the fact, and at the same time affords him the means of correcting the very error caused by its own imperfections.

It is, then, on the habitual *application of principle* to the inculcation and advancement of knowledge, more than on any novelty of detail, that the present volume rests its claim to attention. If I have been even partially successful in establishing the utility of principle in conducting inquiry, I shall not only have assisted in giving a more profitable direction to the labours of others in the same field, but have provided the best means for speedily detecting and rectifying errors inadvertently committed either by them or by myself.

In the following pages I have addressed myself chiefly to parents and to the younger and more inexperienced members of the medical profession; but it is not to them alone that the subject ought to prove attractive. The study of infancy, considered even as an element in the history and philosophy of man, abounds in interest, and is fertile in truths of the highest practical value and importance. In this point of view, it can scarcely fail to arrest the attention of any thinking and intelligent mind which is once directed to it.

In taking leave of a subject which I cannot but feel to be one of vital interest to thousands yet unborn, I would respectfully offer one or two remarks on the spirit in which the following pages ought to be read. It has *often* happened to me to hear myself quoted as the

authority for modes of infant management not only unwarranted
by, but in some instances actually opposed to, the principles I had
expounded. On inquiry, it almost invariably appeared that, instead
of the speakers being really familiar with the contents of the book
which they professed to follow, or being in the habit of frequently referring to its pages for information when wanted, they fancied they
had fulfilled their part by merely reading it once; and on this as-
sumption they proceeded thenceforth to act on their own vague recol-
lections of what it contained, as if these had been true and accurate
transcripts of the book itself. But the subjects treated of embrace so
many important facts and principles of action, which are comparatively
new to the general reader, that it is only by their careful and repeated
study, and, in time of need, turning again and again to the pages in
which they are explained, that a mother can become so familiar
with them as to be able to apply them with ease and judgment to
the many purposes for which they are adapted. Indeed, it is only
by pursuing a similar course that medical men themselves acquire
that ready command of their knowledge which enables them at once
to decide what ought to be done in any emergency; and surely the
interest of a mother in her own offspring ought to be as strong an in-
centive to her to qualify herself for her arduous task, as a love of
science or a sense of duty is to the practitioner. To read a book like
this merely as one reads a novel or a newspaper, can be of but little
solid or permanent advantage; and therefore, while I value highly
the tribute of approval implied in *endeavouring to act* upon the principles I have unfolded, I feel indifferent to even the most eloquent
and laboured eulogium, when it is not accompanied by those practical
results which are the best guarantees of its sincerity. I am the more
anxious to enforce this view, because many will, I believe, read the
work with increased interest and advantage, after their attention has
been thus directed to its true aim and character.

A. C.

EDINBURGH, *June* 1847.

CONTENTS.

CHAPTER III.

GREAT MORTALITY IN INFANCY PRODUCED BY REMOVABLE CAUSES, AND INCREASED BY PARENTAL IGNORANCE.

CHAPTER IV.

INFANT HEALTH NOT ACCIDENTAL, BUT DEPENDENT ON FIXED LAWS.

CHAPTER V.

ON THE CONSTITUTION OF THE INFANT AT BIRTH.

CONTENTS.

CONTENTS. xxxi

CONTENTS.

CONTENTS.   xxxi

CONTENTS. xxxi

CONTENTS.

xxxi

CHAPTER VIII.

CLEANLINESS, EXERCISE, AND SLEEP, IN INFANCY.

CHAPTER IX.

CHOICE AND REGIMEN OF A NURSE.

CHAPTER X.

ARTIFICIAL NURSING.

CHAPTER XIV.

MENTAL CONSTITUTION, AND PRINCIPLES OF TRAINING IN INFANCY.

CHAPTER XV.

MORAL EDUCATION IN INFANCY AND CHILDHOOD.

CHAPTER XVI.

FURTHER REMARKS ON THE MORAL MANAGEMENT OF INFANCY AND CHILDHOOD.

APPENDIX.

MANAGEMENT OF INFANCY.

CHAPTER I.

INFLUENCE OF THE CONSTITUTION OF PARENTS ON THE HEALTH OF THEIR CHILDREN.

In looking abroad upon society, we observe some
families apparently surrounded by every external advantage, yet in which it is found difficult to rear
the children to maturity. Either from convulsions,
scrofula, consumption, or some other form of disease,
one after another is carried off; and those who survive are characterised by great delicacy of constitution, and require the most assiduous care for their
preservation. In contrast to this, we meet with other
families, seemingly much less fortunate in their outward circumstances, but in which one child grows up
after another, as if no such thing as disease existed,
or as if the ordinary disorders of infancy were but
mysterious processes for the farther development of
the organism. That such remarkable differences
exist, must have been observed by all who attend to

A

what is passing around them; and the very important question occurs,—On what do they depend?

To some extent, at least, we have no difficulty in answering the inquiry. The very terms of our statement imply that the unusual susceptibility of disease in the one case, and the immunity from it in the other, arise from no peculiarity of treatment or external circumstances, but are dependent on some inherent difference of constitution derived from one or both parents. Such, accordingly, is the truth ; and so manifest is the influence of hereditary constitution upon the organism and qualities of the offspring, that from the earliest ages it has attracted the attention of mankind. Apparent exceptions occur, in which the children differ widely from their progenitors; but these are so few, and may for the most part be so easily explained, that the general principle remains unshaken.

Admitting, then, the reality of HEREDITARY INFLUENCE, the next point of practical importance is to discover what are the conditions in the parents which affect most powerfully the health of the child.

The following are the most deserving of notice:—

NATURAL INFIRMITIES OF CONSTITUTION, BODILY AND MENTAL, DERIVED FROM THEIR OWN PARENTS.

PREMATURE MARRIAGES, ESPECIALLY OF DELICATE PERSONS, AND OF THOSE STRONGLY PREDISPOSED TO HEREDITARY DISEASE.

MARRIAGES BETWEEN PERSONS TOO NEARLY ALLIED IN BLOOD, PARTICULARLY WHERE EITHER OF THEM IS DESCENDED FROM AN UNHEALTHY RACE.

MARRIAGES CONTRACTED TOO LATE IN LIFE.

GREAT DISPROPORTION IN AGE BETWEEN THE PARENTS.

THE STATE OF THE PARENTS AT THE TIME OF PRO-CREATION.

THE STATE OF HEALTH, AND CONDUCT, OF THE MOTHER DURING PREGNANCY.

Of these I shall speak in succession.

It may be thought that in a work like the present, destined chiefly for the guidance of parents and young medical practitioners, it is superfluous to treat of any of the first five heads; seeing that the child is supposed to be already in existence, and that it is no longer in our power to avert the consequences of an infirm constitution, or of an ill-assorted marriage. But this objection has little force; for the more delicate the infant is, the more necessary does it become to detect the true source of the delicacy, in order that the means of remedying it may be used with that discrimination which is essential to its correction. The same treatment, for example, which is suitable to an infant whose infirm health arises from its inheriting the constitutional tendencies of the race of either parent, may not be equally suitable to another whose delicacy is caused by disease occurring accidentally during the pregnancy of the mother. Here then, is a strong practical reason why we should not only be aware of all the sources of infant delicacy, but also be able, in every particular case, to discriminate between them.

But even supposing the children already born to be beyond the reach of benefit from the inquiry, it is certain that, by improving the health of the parents,

the *future* offspring will participate in their increased
vigour, and more easily escape the evils which afflicted the earlier born.   Nor is this the only consideration, important though it be: parents have an
advising and controlling power over the marriages of
their children, and, by convincing their understand-
ings, may call into operation in early life, before the
passions can obscure the judgment, a guiding influence which will insensibly put them on their guard
against forming an alliance with a very unhealthy or
defective race.   A kind and judicious parent may
exercise a salutary influence in this respect; and if
the young were accustomed to see their parents and
guardians acting more habitually under the guidance
of principle, they would be much less apt than they
are to follow heedlessly the bent of their passions, in
a matter so directly involving their permanent happiness.   But when nothing is done, either by example
or precept, to put the young on their guard, it is not
surprising that mere inclination, family interest, and
fortune, should be more important considerations in
forming matrimonial alliances, than family endowments of mind and body, or soundness of family
health; and so long as this shall be the case, so long
will much misery continue to be produced, which
might otherwise have been foreseen and prevented.

HEREDITARY PREDISPOSITION.

The influence of original constitution is often manifested in the almost inevitable destruction which

awaits the children of certain families about the period of adolescence. One after another drops into the grave from consumption, though every precaution has been used to ward off the fatal malady. The principle is also exemplified, in its brighter aspect, in the histories of long-lived persons, almost all of whom are found to have been descended from long-lived ancestors; in fact, nothing is more certain than that, OTHER CIRCUMSTANCES BEING FAVOURABLE, ROBUST AND HEALTHY PARENTS HAVE ROBUST AND HEALTHY CHILDREN. This law, indeed, holds good throughout animated nature. In the vegetable world, quite as much importance is attached to the quality of the seed as to a good soil and good cultivation; and in like manner, in rearing the lower animals, especially the horse, purity of race is prized above all other conditions; and so entire is the dependence placed upon the hereditary transmission of qualities, that the genealogy of the race-horse, of the hunter, and even of the farm-horse, is regarded as a sure criterion of the properties which may be expected in their progeny. In the dog, the sheep, and the different varieties of cattle, we calculate with certainty on the re-appearance of the qualities of the parents in their young. Man himself, as an organised being, is no exception to the general law; and it is a false and injurious delicacy which would try to divert attention from a truth so influential on happiness, and which has long forced itself on the notice of physiologists and physicians. In relation to this subject, the great Haller mentions a very remarkable instance of two noble ladies who were married on account of their wealth, although they were nearly idiots,—and from whom the mental defect extended for a century into several families, so that some of all their descendants continued idiots in the fourth, and even to the fifth generation.* " Parents," says Dr Gregory, " frequently live over again in their offspring; for children certainly resemble their parents, not merely in countenance and bodily conformation, but in the general features of their minds, and in both virtues and vices. Thus, the imperious Claudian family long flourished at Rome, unrelenting, cruel, and despotic; it produced the merciless and detestable tyrant Tiberius, and at length ended, after a course of six hundred years, in the bloody Caligula, Claudius, and Agrippina, and then in the monster Nero."†

The most remarkable example of the hereditary transmission of qualities with which I am acquainted, is that of a blind man called Moses Le Compte, whose *thirty-seven* children and grandchildren became similarly affected. In all of them the defect of sight began about the age of fifteen or sixteen, and lapsed into total blindness about the age of twenty-two.‡ Sir H. Holland mentions several cases of a similar kind;§ but as such facts are by no means rare, and may be observed in a more or less marked degree in ordinary society, it is needless to adduce any further instances.

* Elem. Physiol., lib. xxix., sect. 2, 8.
† Conspectus Medic. Theor., cap. 1, sect. 16.
‡ Baltimore Medical and Physical Repository.
§ Medical Notes and Reflections.

With such evidence before us, we are perfectly warranted in maintaining that the possession, by the parents, of a sound and vigorous bodily constitution, and an active and well-balanced mind, has an important influence in securing similar advantages to the offspring. If either parent inherits the feeble delicacy or mental peculiarities of an unhealthy or eccentric race, the probability is very great that the offspring will be characterised by similar qualities. But, in compensation for this, THE VERY SAME LAW BY WHICH THE LIABILITY TO GOUT, INSANITY, IMBECILITY, SCROFULA, AND CONSUMPTION, IS TRANSMITTED FROM GENERATION TO GENERATION, ENABLES US TO RECKON WITH EQUAL CERTAINTY ON THE TRANSMISSION OF HEALTH AND VIGOUR, WHEREVER THESE HAVE BEEN THE HEREDITARY FEATURES OF THE RACE.

Those, then, who desire bodily and mental soundness in their offspring, ought carefully to avoid marrying with persons who are either feeble in constitution, or strongly predisposed to any very serious disease, such as insanity, cancer, imbecility, scrofula, &c. ; and, above all, the greatest care should be taken against the occurrence of the same morbid predisposition in both father and mother. Where any peculiarity of constitution is confined to one parent, and is not very strong, it may, in some degree, be counteracted by a judicious marriage and mode of life ; but where its influence is aggravated by being common to both parents, the children can scarcely escape. I am acquainted with families in which the consequences of acting in opposition to this principle

have been deplorable,—where several of the children
have fallen victims to scrofula and consumption, and
others have survived in idiocy, occasioned evidently
by the imprudent marriage of persons nearly allied in
blood, and both strongly predisposed to the same form
of disease.

In thus insisting on the necessity of greater attention being paid to the law of hereditary predisposition, I do not mean that the actual disease
which afflicted the parent will certainly re-appear in
the children ; but only that the offspring of such
parents will be much more liable to its invasion from
the ordinary incidents of life, than those belonging to
a healthier stock, and will require unusually careful
and judicious management to protect them from it.
One of the chief advantages, indeed, of knowing the
nature and extent of the influence, is the power
which we gain of counteracting it by a system of
treatment calculated to strengthen the weaker points
of the constitution.   Thus, if a child inherits a very
scrofulous habit from both of its parents, and is
brought up under the same circumstances which
induced or maintained the disease in them, there is
the highest probability that it will fall a victim to
some form or other of scrofulous disease, or will
escape only after a long and severe struggle, to drag
on through life with a feeble constitution.   But if
timely precautions are taken—if the child is put on a
proper regimen, kept much in the open air, and perhaps transferred for a few years to a drier and warmer
climate—it may altogether escape the disease, and

even enjoy permanently a higher degree of health than had ever been experienced by either of its parents.

In other cases of family predisposition a similar result will follow. The excitable and capricious children of parents who have been insane, or are strongly predisposed to become so, will run great risk of lapsing into insanity, if brought up in circumstances tending to increase the irritability of the nervous system, and to call the feelings or passions into strong and irregular action. Whereas, if subjected from the first to a mode of treatment calculated to allay nervous irritability, to give tone to the body and composure to the mind, the danger in after life will be greatly diminished.

It is, then, the CONSTITUTIONAL PREDISPOSITION OR UNUSUAL LIABILITY, and not the actual disease, which is thus transmitted from parent to child.

MARRIAGE OF PERSONS TOO NEARLY ALLIED IN CONSANGUINITY.

Next to the direct inheritance of a family predisposition, the constitutional tendencies derived from the union of persons too nearly allied in blood, and more especially if themselves descended from a tainted stock, are perhaps the most prejudicial to infant health; and their baneful effects are nowhere more strikingly seen than in the deteriorated offspring of some of the royal and aristocratic families of Europe, in which frequent intermarriages have taken place without any regard being paid to the morbid predisposition on either side. Such intermarriages are

often observed also in private life, especially among
the Jews. "The rich Jews in this country," says Dr
Elliotson, "have the same bad custom of marrying
first cousins; and I never saw so many instances of
squinting, stammering, peculiarity of manner, imbecility, or insanity, in all their various degrees, intense
nervousness, &c., in an equal number of other persons."* When very near relations marry, who are
themselves infirm, there is usually either no issue, or
offspring characterised by unusual delicacy of constitution. The unhappy results of marriages between
blood relations, observed in the United States of
America, correspond exactly with what is seen in this
and other European countries.†

AGE AT WHICH PERSONS MARRY.

EARLY MARRIAGE.—The time of life at which persons marry, exercises a great influence on the health
and qualities of the offspring. If the parents have
married before the full development and maturity of
their own organism, the first children are generally
more deficient in stamina than those born subsequently. This, indeed, is one of the reasons why
the children of the same family often present considerable differences of constitution and character,
and why the first-born is sometimes puny in an
otherwise vigorous race. Marriage, therefore, ought
never to take place before maturity, because the

* Elliotson's Human Physiology, 5th edition, p. 1098.
† See Appendix, A.

system is not sufficiently consolidated for the important function of reproduction, and both parent and child suffer from anticipating the order of nature. In this country, it may be stated as the general rule, that women do not attain their full development before from twenty to twenty-three years of age, and men from twenty-five to thirty. But, in defiance of this rule, it is not uncommon to encourage even delicate girls to marry at seventeen, before the mental or physical powers are fully developed, and at the manifest risk of entailing infirm health on themselves and their offspring, and thus throwing away the best chance of their own permanent happiness. In the case of the lower animals the principle is well known, and, money being there at stake, especial care is taken to avoid the error so frequently committed among ourselves.

LATE MARRIAGES are scarcely less unfavourable to the health of the offspring than those contracted in very early life. Beyond a certain age, neither animals nor plants are capable of producing a vigorous progeny; and hence, the postponement of marriage beyond the period of maturity, now so common, especially among professional men suffering under the influence of strong competition for a livelihood, is not unfrequently a source of evil to their offspring. The impulse to propagate has generally lost much of its force before the age of forty, and comparatively few children are born after that age to parents who have been united soon after attaining maturity. In many

cases of late marriages, moreover, the constitution of
the parents has been impaired by mental or bodily
labour, by dissipation, and even, it may be, by that
disappointment to the domestic affections which involuntary celibacy implies.

DISPARITY OF AGE.—Another cause of infirm health
in children, which ought not to be overlooked, is great
disparity of years in the two parents.   When one of
the parents is very young and the other already advanced in life, the constitution of the offspring is very
rarely sound.

STATE OF THE PARENTS.

The next circumstance which permanently influences the health of the offspring is the state of the
parents at the time of procreation.   It is well known
that, while all the children of the same family have
a certain general resemblance, no two of them are
exactly alike.   A chief reason of this difference is the
unavoidable change in the state of the parents, induced partly by the lapse of years, and partly by external circumstances acting upon their bodily and
mental constitution ; and from numerous facts which
have been observed, it seems highly probable that the
offspring may be affected even by any temporary disturbance of health in the parents about the time at
which conception takes place.   Anxiety of mind and
unusual depression of spirits in the father, have been
found imprinted in ineffaceable characters on the con-

stitution of the child; and instances are known in
which idiocy in the offspring has appeared to bo the
result of casual intoxication on the part of a generally
temperate father.   A stronger motive to regularity of
living, and moderation in passion, can scarcely be
presented to a right-minded parent, than the knowledge of their permanent influence on his offspring.
Many a father has deplored, and perhaps resented, the
follies of an irreclaimably wayward son, without sus-
pecting that they derived their origin from some forgotten irregularity of his own.*

Another and very powerful cause of delicacy in children is a PERMANENTLY DERANGED STATE OF HEALTH IN
THE PARENTS, showing itself in a lowered tone of all
the animal functions, and a general feeling of being
unwell.   Of all the varieties of this cause, perhaps the
most frequent and the most injurious to the offspring
is *habitual indigestion*, and its consequence, *impaired
nutrition*.   Many parents pass years of their lives in
a constant state of discomfort from "bilious" and
"stomach" complaints, induced by inattention to diet,
exercise, cleanliness, ventilation, sufficiency of light,
healthiness of place of residence, and the like; and
thus unthinkingly entail a part of the penalty on
their innocent offspring.   Ignorant of the consequences of their conduct, they are without sufficient
motive to give up their habitual indulgences, or to persevere in the easy use of the means required for the

* For the effects of intemperance in the parents as a cause of
idiocy in the children, see Dr S. G. Howe's work "On the Causes of
Idiocy in Massachusetts," reprinted at Edinburgh in 1858.

improvement and preservation of their own health;
and they are surprised when assured that, while thus
trifling with their own comfort, they are sporting
with the welfare and fate of those on whom their
whole affections are one day to be centred.

It is a very common saying, that clever men generally have stupid children; and the inference has been
drawn, that the father exerts very little influence on
the constitution of his offspring. It is true that the
families of men of genius are rarely so remarkable for
talent as themselves; but I deduce an opposite conclusion from the fact, and maintain that these very
cases afford strong proofs of the reality of the father's
influence, and ought consequently to be direct warn-
ings for our guidance. Not to dwell on the circumstance that men of genius frequently marry
late, it is notorious that nothing can be farther removed from the standard of nature than their state
of health and general mode of life. Are they not,
as a class, enthusiastic, excitable, irregular in their
habits, the sport of every passing emotion, and, almost
without exception, victims to indigestion, and often
to melancholy? And are these the seeds from which
Nature has designed *healthy* vigour of mind or body
to spring up in their offspring? Take into account
also the influence of the mother, and the well-known
fact that men of genius rarely select highly-gifted
women for their wives, and then say whether high
talent can reasonably be expected to emanate from
parents, one of whom rises at best only to mediocrity,
and the other falls temporarily to or below it, from

sheer exhaustion of mind and broken health. Would it not rather be wonderful, if, in such untoward circumstances, genius were always to descend, in unabated splendour, even to the first line of the posterity? It is not from such materials that living genius has ever sprung. A genius might, in some favourable moment, be *born* to such a father; but in all probability he would die before the world could tell that a genius had lived. As might be expected, the circumstances under which the highest order of minds most frequently appears, are where the father is healthy and active, and the mother unites an energetic character with sound bodily health, or with some high and sustaining aim of life, animating her mental and bodily functions. The mother of Napoleon I. was of this description; and the mothers of most of our celebrated men will be found to have been more or less distinguished by similar characteristics;—accordingly, how often, in the biographies of men of genius, do we remark that it was the mother who first perceived and fanned in the child the flame which burst into after brightness! From all this it appears, then, that the influence of the father on the character of the child is not less powerful than that of the mother, and is overlooked only from not taking into account the tendency of broken health and irregular habits in the father to modify, and even counteract, his natural influence on the offspring.

In some circumstances, however, where, either from feelings of admiration, deep interest, or other

impressive cause, the mind of the mother is, during
gestation, strongly concentrated upon the father's
image or character, his reflex or indirect influence
on the organism and qualities of the future child is
often strikingly great. It is perhaps from some
unsuspected cause of this kind, that in some instances
all the children of a family show a strong resemblance
to one parent, and very little to the other.

The whole subject of the influence of the constitution, both physical and mental, of parents, on the
health, development, and mental character of their
offspring, merits grave consideration, and must, as
the knowledge of physiology becomes more generally
diffused, force itself upon the attention of every intelligent, thinking person. Until the various inherited,
and even acquired conditions of parents, which exercise a deteriorating influence on their children, are
generally understood, and practically recognised in
forming matrimonial alliances, and regulating the
mode of living, mankind must deteriorate, or at
least will never attain the degree of perfection of
which the human race is evidently susceptible,
and which, we cannot doubt, it is the intention of
the Creator that it should attain. We have alluded
to the well-known results of careful breeding in improving the qualities of our domestic animals ; and,
although the comparison may be considered rather
humiliating, all our knowledge of the physiology of
man leads to the conclusion, that the human race, as
far as our physical nature is concerned, is governed by
the same laws, and that the health and constitution

of the offspring depend mainly on those of the parents. Hereditary delicacy and defects may, in a great degree, be overcome by judicious management of the child from birth to maturity, although perhaps never entirely effaced. But the whole subject of hereditary descent is of such moment, and still in some respects so obscure, that it calls for the earnest attention of physiologists and philanthropists.

CHAPTER II.

INFLUENCE OF THE MOTHER'S MODE OF LIVING DURING PREGNANCY ON THE HEALTH OF THE CHILD.

THE last conditions which I shall notice as affecting the health of the future infant are, THE STATE OF MIND, HEALTH, AND CONDUCT OF THE MOTHER DURING PREGNANCY,—conditions which, though in general very little taken into account, are so vitally important, and so directly within the scope of the present work, that I have devoted a separate chapter to their consideration.

The only circumstance which can explain or excuse the indifference shown by many mothers to the state of their health during pregnancy, is their entire ignorance of the injury which they are inflicting on their offspring. Many a mother, who will not deny herself the temporary gratification of a single desire or appetite on her own account, would be the first and the firmest in resisting the temptation, if her reason were fully convinced that every transgression of the laws of health which she commits diminishes the chances of health in her child. Yet such is unquestionably the fact.

MENTAL EMOTIONS.

Some proofs of the reality of the mother's influence on the constitution of her unborn child have already been laid before the reader, and, were it necessary, many more might easily be added. Authentic cases might be adduced of mothers, agitated by distressing anxieties during pregnancy, giving birth to children who continued through life a prey to nervous, convulsive, or epileptic disease, or displayed a morbid timidity of character which no subsequent care could counteract. In regard to this class of cases, indeed, popular belief has gone beyond the reality, in ascribing the moles and purple stains with which some children are born, entirely to the working of the mother's imagination.

Times of public danger and sudden alarm furnish many examples of the influence of maternal grief and anxiety on the constitution of the offspring; and if similar results have attracted less notice during quieter times and in private life, it has not been from their non-occurrence, but from their being less attended to. For, even in private life, great and sudden changes of fortune, or accidents which have kept the mind of the parent in a state of intense anxiety or excitement during pregnancy, are sometimes observed to imprint, on a single member of a family, a distinctive character which cannot be otherwise accounted for.

The constitutional aversion to even the sight of a

drawn sword, and to every kind of danger, shown by
James I. of England, so admirably portrayed in *The
Fortunes of Nigel*, is ascribed, and apparently not
without reason, to the constant anxiety and apprehension suffered by Mary during the period of gestation.

We know that a fit of passion in a nurse vitiates
the quality of the milk to such a degree as to cause
colic and indigestion in the sucking infant. If, in
the child already born, and in so far independent of
its parent, the relation between the two is thus
intimate, surely it must be still closer when the
infant lies in its mother's womb, is nourished by its
mother's blood, and is, to all intents and purposes,
a part of her own body. Facts and reason alike
demonstrate the reality of this influence, and much
practical advantage would result to both parent and
child were the conditions and extent of its operation
better understood.

LONGINGS.—For a long time it was believed that the
mother's imagination was the sole cause of all the
local peculiarities and imperfections with which some
children are born; but more accurate inquiry has now
shown, that a real coincidence between the object
longed for and the character of the mark or deformity
is extremely rare. In the great majority of instances
the longing is followed by no local mark in the child,
and very often the mark occurs when no particular
longing has ever been experienced by the mother.
Cases, no doubt, are mentioned in which deformity of

the infant has occurred apparently in consequence
of a strong impression made by some mutilated
object on the mother during gestation; but we
have only to consider how numerous such objects
are, and how rarely the supposed consequence follows, to perceive that the true cause is generally of a
deeper kind.

While, however, such cases are so rare that the
preponderance of evidence is decidedly against the
probability of *local* deformities in the infant being
generally the results of an accidental shock given to
the feelings of the mother, there is more than enough
to establish the existence of a direct relation between
the *general* state of health and feelings of the mother
and the *general constitution* of the child.   Reason,
indeed, independently of experience, would lead us to
expect this; for whatever affects the general health
and action of the system must affect *all* its component
parts,—and the child in the mother's womb being, for
the time, virtually a part of herself, it is natural to
suppose that it should be subjected to nearly the
same influences as the rest of her organism.   If her
digestion is impaired, and the quality of her blood
deteriorated, by anxiety of mind or continued neglect
of her health, how can the infant be otherwise than
injured, seeing that it must be nourished by the same
blood which is insufficient for her own healthy nutrition ?

If vivid mental emotion in the mother during
pregnancy exerts, in extreme and exceptional cases,
a marked effect on the constitution of the child, it is

not less certain that the *habitual state* of mind, whether it be that of excitement or depression, or of tranquil or irritable temper, exerts an equally positive and constant, though of course less remarkable influence on the offspring. In this way the mental disposition of the child is often a legible transcript of the mother's condition and feelings during pregnancy; and here, as already remarked, is one of the sources of variety of character in children of the same family. The later born often differ greatly, both in mental and bodily constitution, from the earlier progeny; but then, how great also the change between the feelings, passions, and physical health of the parent of twenty or twenty-five, and those of the same parent at forty years of age, after long experience of the turmoil and vicissitudes of life !

The extent of the modifying power of the mother is seen again in the fact already referred to, that almost all great men have descended from mothers remarkable for their mental endowments and activity. Few men of eminence, on the contrary, have been blessed with distinguished children ; partly, as I have said, because they seldom married women of superior minds, and partly because few of themselves were robust, and still fewer lived in such a way as the laws of health require. The influence of the mother is probably as direct as the father's, and, from her peculiar province, continues much longer. Hence her usually greater share in the production of a gifted offspring.

When we contrast the robust constitution of a

healthy, peasant's child in the country, with the
feeble organism of the child of a delicate mother
living in the midst of the enervating dissipations of
a capital, can we imagine for a moment that *chance*
alone has given health to the one and delicacy to the
other, and that the mode of life of the parent has had
no share in the result ?   If we cannot, does not that
mother incur a heavy responsibility who thus, whether
from wilful ignorance or from the selfish pursuit
of immediate pleasure, perils the health and permanent happiness of her offspring ?   From the moment
of conception it is the paramount duty of the mother
to endeavour to maintain, by every means in her
power, the highest state of mental and bodily health
of which her constitution is susceptible ; and this is
the more binding upon her, that its performance
involves no sacrifice worthy of the name,—none
which will not be amply compensated to her by its
favourable effects, as well on her own health as on
that of her infant.

By many women pregnancy is regarded with alarm,
as a period full of danger, and doubtful in its result.
But it is a consolation to know that this period is
not naturally dangerous, and is rendered so only, or
chiefly, by neglect or mismanagement on the part of
the mother herself.   If, regardless of the future, she
neglects, as many do, the ordinary laws of health, or
gives way to indolent inactivity, to the excitement of
passion, to dissipation and the indulgence of appetite,
it cannot surprise any one that she should suffer more
seriously than if she were not pregnant.   But as

mothers often err from ignorance alone, it becomes of
the greatest importance that they should be made
acquainted with the true relation between their conduct during the period of pregnancy and the health
of their offspring, that they may better secure the
welfare of their infants by an intelligent observance
of the laws of health.

It is true that instances may be adduced, in which
even a dying mother has given birth to a well-grown
and robust-looking child; but these rare cases, even
if admitted in their broadest aspect, are very far
from neutralizing the much more frequent opposite
instances.   There are women in whom severe and
fatal disease of a local kind exerts comparatively little
effect on the general system.   There are others in
whom the disease itself is suspended in its course
during pregnancy, and the whole energies of the
body are concentrated, as it were, on the womb, to
complete the evolution of the new being; and the
moment this is effected, the malady regains its force,
and hurries even faster than before to a fatal termination.   This happens frequently in consumption.   The
infant may then be, and sometimes is, comparatively
healthy, or grows up so when carefully treated and
put to a very healthy nurse.   But, instead of dis-
proving the mother's influence, such cases establish
it more clearly.   If, when the progress of consumption is interrupted during pregnancy, the mother in
consequence enjoys a far higher degree of health and
energy than before the commencement of this condition, what stronger proof can there be of the reality

of her influence on her offspring than that the unborn
child should participate in her renewed health and
strength, and at length come into the world with a
far better chance of life than if the mother's disease
had never been suspended ?

The children of scrofulous parents are also frequently
regarded as exceptions to the principle of hereditary
influence; and it is quite true that, as children,
they often present an appearance of health which is
apt to deceive a superficial or inexperienced observer.
They may be so plump, well-grown, and rosy-com-
plexioned, as to present the very picture of health.
But beneath all this fair and promising surface lurk
too often a softness and delicacy of structure, and an
excitability of the system, which indicate the absence
of real stamina.   Such children generally shoot up,
tall, thin, and impressionable, or they become full,
heavy, and languid; falling victims, sooner or later,
to the very parental infirmity which, in their earlier
childhood, seemed least likely to attack them.

The condition of the mother being thus influential
on the well-being of her offspring, the importance of
contributing in every possible way to her health,
comfort, and cheerfulness, especially during pregnancy, is surely very obvious. This, however, must
be done by rational observance of the laws which
regulate the exercise of the various functions, and not
by the foolish indulgence of her whims.   Gloomy,
painful, or harassing impressions ought to be guarded
against, and good-natured equanimity and cheerfulness cultivated by all around her. Let it be her

B

constant aim to engage in healthful and invigorating
occupation, which shall afford a wholesome stimulus
to her intellectual and moral faculties, and withdraw
her attention from dwelling too much upon herself.
In her leisure hours, let her seek some rational and
invigorating exercise of mind and body, and be on
her guard against giving way to caprice of temper,
to the temptations of indolence, to endless novel-
reading, or to any form of social dissipation.   In
very few instances does it become advisable to cease
from engaging in the ordinary duties of the family,
or to change such habits of life as have been found
by experience to be healthful.   Among the circumstances which require attention during pregnancy,
even more than at any other time, may be mentioned breathing a free, pure air; sleeping in a well-
aired room, on a bed not so soft as to induce relaxation, and either without curtains, or with curtains
never closely drawn; regular daily exercise in the
open air; and great attention to personal cleanliness, to dress, diet, and all the ordinary conditions of
health.   Having treated of most of these in my other
works, I shall confine myself at present to such modifications of them as apply PECULIARLY TO THE STATE OF
PREGNANCY, and shall begin with the subject of DIET.

DIET.

A notion is very prevalent, that an unusual supply
of nourishing food is required during pregnancy, on
account of the rapid development of the new being

in the maternal womb. In some instances in which the general health, digestive powers, and appetite improve during gestation, an increased allowance of food becomes necessary, and is productive of much advantage. But in the great majority of cases, where no such improvement takes place, and the appetite is already more vigorous than the powers of digestion, nothing but mischief can follow from increased diet. It is true that substance is expended in the development of the child; but Nature herself has provided for that demand by the suppression of the periodical discharge to which women are at other times subject, and which ceases altogether when the age of child-bearing is past. When, therefore, during pregnancy, the health is good and the appetite natural, there is no need whatever of increasing the quantity or altering the quality of the food which is found by experience to agree with the constitution, nor can anything but harm result from attempting to " support the strength" by too nutritious a diet.

When, from mistaken views, a change is made from a plain and nourishing diet to full and generous living, and especially if the usual exercise is at the same time diminished, a state of fulness, no less dangerous to the mother than injurious to the embryo, is apt to be induced, or is prevented only by the digestive powers giving way,—which leads to much suffering from nausea, heartburn, flatulence, inordinate craving, weakening perspirations, and other unpleasant symptoms. Where digestion continues unimpaired, and the superfluity of nourish-

ment is taken into the system, a fulness with sense of
oppression ensues, which infallibly leads to mischief,
when not timeously relieved, either by nature or by
art. Occasionally, bleeding from the nose or lungs,
or from piles, removes the impending danger. At
other times it may be necessary to draw blood from a
vein to avert it; now and then it happens that
Nature seeks relief by attempting to re-establish the
customary discharge from the womb, and, in this
state, imprudence on the part of the mother may
induce miscarriage, to the risk of her life. In short,
the fulness of system thus imprudently induced must
have vent somewhere; and it will depend on the
existence of any local weakness, or some accidental
circumstance, in what organ and in what way the
relief shall be effected, and with what extent of danger it shall be accompanied. To the child, no less
t'an to the parent, its consequences are injurious, not
on'y by endangering premature birth, but by affecting the future soundness of the child's constitution;
and hence arises a solemn moral duty of the mother
not to place herself voluntarily in circumstances
which may not only defeat her fondest hopes of
happiness, and leave her a prey to broken health and
enduring regret, but also permanently impair the constitution of her offspring.

But, while avoiding one error, we must be careful
not to run into the opposite extreme, and sanction an
insufficient diet. Many women in the poorer classes
suffer grievously in this way, and, from absolute
inability to procure nourishing food in due quantity,

give birth to feeble and unhealthy children, whose whole life is a scene of suffering, but who, fortunately, do not often long survive. This, in truth, is one cause of the physical inferiority of the children of the working-classes, and the greater mortality observed amongst them; and as it almost necessarily leads to moral inferiority likewise, it eminently calls for the serious attention of philanthropic and enlightened statesmen. As reasonably may we expect fine fruit and rich harvests from an impoverished soil, as well-constituted children from parents exhausted by bodily exertion, and insufficiently nourished. It is in workhouses that the evil is seen in its most glaring form. These are peopled by the children of the lowest, most sickly, or most improvident parents. From birth, they are the worst fed and the most miserably clothed; hence their bodies are stunted and weak, their minds and morals impaired and degraded. If the children in any workhouse be contrasted with the children at even a common country-school, their physical and mental inferiority will be conspicuous, and we shall be struck with the absence from their expression of that elasticity and hilarity of spirit which distinguishes a healthful and happy childhood.

The effects of insufficient diet in impeding the development of the infant in the mother's womb are so well ascertained, that no doubt of the fact can exist in the mind of any one who has examined the subject for himself; and, were this a proper place, I might point out the risk which is incurred, by enforcing too rigid economy in this respect in workhouses, of

producing deterioration of the children, and consequently a future increase of pauperism. But I can
only allude to the existence of such a risk, and throw
out a warning which those who are interested may
afterwards turn to account.

It is naturally the children of the poor that suffer
most from inadequate nourishment of the parent during pregnancy; but those of the richer classes also
suffer from it, though in a different way. *The system
is duly nourished, only when food proper in itself is
also properly digested ;* if the digestion be imperfect,
no food, however nutritious, will afford a healthy
sustenance. From inattention to this fact, many
mothers in the higher ranks of life give birth to
feeble and imperfectly-developed children. Fond of
indulging in every luxury, they eat unseasonably,
and often largely, till the powers of the stomach are
exhausted, and digestion becomes so much impaired
that the food ceases to nourish. As regards the
infant, the result is the same whether the want of
nourishment arises from deficient food or imperfect
digestion ; and hence the duty so strongly incumbent
on the mother, to act like a rational being, for her
infant's sake, if not for her own. Morally considered,
it is as culpable on her part to starve the infant before
birth by voluntarily impairing her power of nourishing it, as by refusing it food after it is born.

In all instances, the great aim ought to be, to
act according to the laws of the human constitution,
and consequently *to adapt the kind and quantity of
nourishment to the wants of the individual and the*

state of the digestive organs. Following this rule,
we shall find that while, in general, no increase in
quantity is required during pregnancy, there are
nevertheless many women who enjoy a higher degree of health in the married state, and especially during pregnancy, than they did before, and in whom the
appetite is increased only because digestion and the
other organic functions are carried on with greater
vigour. In such cases, an improved diet is not only
safe, but natural and even necessary; care being
taken, however, not to push it so far as to impair the
amended tone of the system. By a little attention,
the proper limit can in general be easily determined.
So long as healthy activity of mind and body, aptitude for exercise, and regularity of the animal functions, continue unimpaired, there is nothing to fear;
but if oppression, languor, or other indications of
constitutional disorder, begin to show themselves.
no time should be lost in effecting the necessary
restrictions in diet.

At no period of life is it so important to observe
moderation and *simplicity* in this respect, and to
avoid the use of heating food and stimulants, as
during pregnancy. Not only is the system then unusually susceptible of impressions, and apt to be disordered by the slightest causes, but in women of a
nervous constitution the stomach is often the seat
of a peculiar irritability, accompanied by a craving
and capricious appetite, which sometimes leads to
excess in the use of both wine and food. It requires much good sense and self-denial on the part of

the mother to resist these morbid cravings. During
the latter stages of pregnancy, the risk from this
cause is *greatly* increased ; and to a long-existing intestinal derangement, produced by a redundant and
heterogeneous diet, Dr Eberle justly ascribes a peculiar and highly dangerous affection, resembling puer-
peral fever, which comes on soon after delivery, and
is often characterised by a remarkable sinking of the
vital powers.* In cases of this kind, the disordered
health previous to parturition is not so striking as
to arrest the attention of ordinary observers, though
perfectly obvious to experienced eyes ; and when,
after delivery, danger declares itself, it is viewed
with all the surprise and alarm of an unexpected
event, although it might have been foreseen, and to
a considerable extent prevented by a wise regimen
and due attention to the action of the bowels.

If the public mind were only enlightened enough
to act on the conviction that no effect can take place
without some cause, known or unknown, producing
it, many evils from which we now suffer might easily
be avoided. If women could be convinced that, as
a general rule, the danger attending confinement in
childbed is in proportion to the previous sound or
unsound condition of the system, and to good or bad
management at the time, they would be much more
anxious than they are to conform to the laws of
health, both for their own sake, and for the sake of
the child whose welfare is so largely committed to
their trust.

* Eberle on the Diseases and Physical Education of Children.

LONGINGS.

In regard to longings for extraordinary kinds of food, much caution ought to be exercised. Longings rarely occur in a healthy woman of a well-constituted mind. Indeed, they are almost peculiar to delicate, nervously irritable women, who have been accustomed to much indulgence, and have no wholesome OCCUPATION to fill up their time. Hence, the proper way to treat them is not to yield to every new desire, but to provide worthier objects of interest to the intellect and feelings, and to give the stomach the plain and mild food which alone, in its weakened state, it is able to digest. In very capricious and confirmed cases, it is sometimes prudent to yield temporarily; but even then the main object—the means of cure—ought never to be lost sight of.

During pregnancy, the great aim, for the sake of both parent and child, ought to be to sustain the general health in the highest state of efficiency. In order to attain this, the mother ought to pursue her usual avocations and mode of life, if these are in harmony with the laws of health. Regular daily exercise, cheerful occupation and society, great cleanliness, moderate diet, pure air, early hours, clothing suitable to the season, and healthy activity of the skin, are all more essential than ever, because now the permanent welfare of another being is at stake, in addition to that of the mother.

Conducted with strict attention to these rules, the

B 2

first pregnancy may become a means, not only of
improving the mother's present health and securing
that of her child, but of giving her a higher degree
of permanent health than she enjoyed before her
pregnancy. On the other hand, neglect of the laws
of health, during this period, by delicate women,
especially when they have been married young, very
often lays the foundation of increased delicacy during
the remainder of life.

DRESS.

For many years past, common-sense and science have
combined to wage war against custom and fashion
on the subject of female dress, particularly tight-lacing
and the use of stiff, unyielding corsets; but hitherto
with only partial success. Of late, however, a glim-
mering perception has begun to prevail, that the object
for which the restraint is undergone may be more
certainly attained by following the dictates of nature
and reason than by mechanical compression; and if
this important truth shall make way, fashion will ultimately be enlisted on the right side, and the beautiful
forms of nature be preferred to the ungainly deformities of misdirected art. Already, a better acquaintance with the laws of the animal economy, added to
the lamentable lessons of experience, has convinced
many mothers that the surest way to deform the
figure, and prevent gracefulness of carriage, is to prohibit exercise, and impede the free expansion of the
chest by the use of stiff and tight stays; and that the

most effectual way to improve both is to follow the opposite course. It was not by the use of tight bands and stays that the classic forms of Greece and Rome were fashioned; and if we wish to see these reproduced, we must secure freedom of action of the whole muscular system, as an indispensable preliminary. If the body be allowed fair play, the spine will grow up straight and firm, but at the same time graceful and pliant to the will, and the rest of the figure will develop itself with freedom and elegance; while the additional advantage will be gained, of the highest degree of health and vigour compatible with the nature of the original constitution. Hence, it ought to be the first duty of the young wife who has reason to believe herself pregnant, to take special care so to arrange her dress as to avoid the slightest compression of the chest or abdomen, and thus secure the utmost freedom of respiration. I need only add, that the evils of tight-lacing do not end with the birth of the child. The compression, by preventing the full development of the breasts and nipples, renders them unfit to furnish that nourishment on which the life of the infant may entirely depend; and yet it is only when absolutely compelled to give way as pregnancy advances, that many mothers loosen their corsets sufficiently to admit of common breathing space, and remove the unnatural obstacles of steel or whalebone, which experience has shown to be so injurious.

While I strongly advocate the propriety of bringing up young girls without the use of such ill-judged support, I by no means recommend that delicate mothers,

to whom long custom has rendered corsets necessary,
should at once lay them aside, although I have known
this done with manifest advantage. They ought,
however, to substitute thin whalebone blades for the
stiff steel in common use, and be very careful to wear
them sufficiently loose to admit of the free enlargement and ascent of the womb. If this precaution be
neglected, both mother and infant may be seriously
injured, and even the labour rendered more difficult,
and ruptures or other ailments induced. To afford
the necessary support during the latter months of
pregnancy, a broad elastic bandage worn round the
body will often be of great service ; but every approach to absolute pressure should be scrupulously
avoided.

EXERCISE.

Nothing contributes more effectually than exercise to
a sound state of health during gestation, and to a safe
and easy recovery after delivery. With ordinary care,
walking may be continued almost to the last hour,
and with excellent effect upon all the functions. In
this respect, the Queen has set an example to her
subjects ; and her easy labours and rapid recoveries
have been in a great measure owing to her systematic
observance of daily active exercise in the open air,
during the whole period of gestation. The early part
of the day ought to be selected for exercise, especially
in winter. Riding in an open carriage is a very
useful addition to walking, but ought never to super-

sede it. Many evidences, indeed, prove that the degree of danger attending pregnancy depends very much on the mother herself. Child-bearing is a natural and not a morbid process; and in the facility with which healthy regular-living women pass through it, we have abundant evidence that the Creator did not design it to be necessarily a time of great suffering and danger. Where the mode of life and the habitual occupations of the mother are rational, the more closely she can adhere to them during pregnancy the better will it be for herself, and consequently also for her infant.

BATHING.

Cleanliness and fresh air are important aids to health at all times, but doubly necessary during gestation. Hence the propriety of having recourse to tepid bathing, especially in the case of women in whom the nervous system is unusually excitable. It promotes the healthy action of the skin, abates nervous excitement, tends to prevent internal congestion, and is in every way conducive to health. A bath, at the temperature of 94° to 96° Fahrenheit, once a week during pregnancy, will in most cases be found very beneficial. A quarter of an hour, as a general rule, is sufficiently long to remain in the bath; and it should never be taken soon after a meal.

Other circumstances might be mentioned as influencing the mother's health, and indirectly that of the child; but as they affect her only in common with other people, and so come under the head of the

general laws of health, I need not now enlarge upon
them. Sensible people, who have never thought on
the subject, may be surprised at the earnestness with
which I have recommended attention to the mother's
state, as the surest way of securing the health of the
child; but if they will observe and reflect upon what
is passing around them, they will see many proofs of
the principle which I have been enforcing, and find
reason to admit the importance of its practical results.

Before quitting this part of the subject, I think it
proper to direct attention to the MANAGEMENT OF THE
BREASTS towards the end of pregnancy. All undue
pressure, by stays or otherwise, should be carefully
avoided, especially over the nipples, as the skin covering them is extremely delicate and sensitive. The
breasts should also be carefully examined by a medical
man, a month or longer before the termination of a
first pregnancy, as it occasionally happens that one or
both nipples are compressed and flattened, and artificial means may be necessary to develop them sufficiently to enable the child to suck. Neglect of this
precaution may prevent an otherwise healthy mother
from suckling her child, and also give rise to inflam-
mations, often ending in painful abscesses of the
breast.

CHAPTER III.

WHEN we learn from incontestable evidence that between one-third and a half of all the children ushered into the world die within the first *five* years after birth, the conclusion naturally come to is, that such a frightful result can arise only from some great and wide-spread errors in the ordinary management of the young; and this inference is confirmed when we farther consider that among those animals which most nearly resemble man in their general structure, but which differ from him in being guided by a natural instinct in the treatment of their offspring, no such mortality is to be met with. Did it occur in wild and barbarous regions only, it might seem a natural consequence of the hardships by which even infancy is there surrounded. But the startling circumstance is, that it happens in the midst of comfort and civilization, precisely where knowledge and the means of protection are supposed to abound; and it is only from our being so much accustomed to its occurrence

that it excites so little surprise, and comes, in fact, to
be virtually considered as a part of the established
order of nature, which we can neither alter nor avert.
But as the first efficient step towards preventing an
evil, or providing a remedy for it, is to obtain a clear
idea of its existence and nature, I think it advisable to adduce such evidence as may satisfy even the
most sceptical, that the rate of infant mortality is both
excessive in amount, and capable of being greatly
reduced by careful and judicious management. If
these points be satisfactorily established, we shall then
be enabled to resume our inquiry into the means of
improvement with increased interest, and a greater
probability of success.

To show the great mortality which at present occurs
in infancy, I need only refer to the unquestionable
authority of the statistical returns contained in the
Annual Reports of Births, Deaths, and Marriages in
England, presented to Parliament by the Registrar-
General. In the very first of these reports, it is re-
corded that, of the total deaths which took place in
England and Wales in 1838, nearly ONE-THIRD occurred under two years of age! This, be it remarked,
was not a year selected for any unusual fatality, but
was merely the first in which registration was established; and its general results are confirmed by the
experience of subsequent years, and also of other
countries. Thus, on consulting the English returns
for 1841, we find a mortality under two years of age,
of 101,478 out of a total of 343,847 deaths, being
rather more than 29 per cent. In Belgium, again,

whore the returns are made with equal accuracy, and
the population enjoys a high degree of domestic comfort and general intelligence, *one* in every *ten* infants
born alive dies *within the first month ;* while *at the
end of five years,* only 5733 out of every 10,000, or
little more than one-half, are still alive.* In Manchester and Salford, indeed, matters are still worse ;
for it appears from the Registrar-General's Second
Report, that out of 9276 deaths which occurred in that
city in the year ending June 30th 1839, 2384, or about
one-fourth, were of infants under one year ; 3680, or
more than one-third, under two years ; and 5145, or
considerably more than a half, under five years of
age !

In these returns, however, it must be kept in mind,
the deaths in infancy are compared with the total
deaths at all ages. But as the proportion of children
to adults varies very much in different communities,
this is obviously a fluctuating standard. To estimate
fairly the actual rate of mortality in infancy, we must
compare the number of children dying, with the total
number alive, at the same age. This, Dr Farr, of the
Registrar-General's office, has kindly enabled us to do,
by constructing the following table. He has estimated
the numbers born alive, and the numbers dying, in
each of the first five years of life, in sixty-three healthy
districts of England ; and, for the sake of comparison,
he has done the same for Manchester.

* Quetelet sur l'Homme et le Développement de ses Facultés, vol. i.
pp. 161-167.   Paris, 1835.

Of 100,000 Children born alive, the numbers alive and the numbers dying, in each of Five subsequent Years, in England, in Sixty-three healthy Districts of England, and in Manchester, are as follows:—

	In England, from 1838-44.		In Sixty-three healthy districts of England, from 1849-53.		In Manchester, 1838-44.	
Ages.	Out of 100,000 children born, the numbers living at each age under 5 years.	Numbers dying in each year of age.	Out of 100,000 children born, the numbers living at each age under 5 years.	Numbers dying in each year of age.	Out of 100,000 children born, the numbers living at each age under 5 years.	Numbers dying in each year of age.
Year. 0	100,000	14.588	100,000	10,295	100,000	26,892
1	85,412	5,378	89,705	3,005	73,118	11,468
2	80,034	2,914	86,700	1,885	61,632	4,680
3	77,120	1,944	84,815	1,305	56,952	3,236
4	75,176	1,407	83,510	1,051	53,716	2,267
Total No. dying in the first five years of age,	20,231		Total No. dying in the first five yrs. of age, 17,541		Total No. dying in the first five yrs. of age, 48,561	

Thus, supposing 100,000 of the children belonging to 1838, born in England on the 1st of January of that year, it will be seen, by reference to the table, that on the 1st of January 1839 only 85,412, and on the 1st of January 1840 only 80,034, would be alive; so that in the first year 14,588, and in the second year 5378, must have died. Again, of 100,000 children born in sixty-three healthy districts of England on the 1st of January 1849, only 89,705 would be alive on the 1st of January 1850, and only 86,700 on the 1st of January 1851; so that in the first of these two years 10,295, and in the second year 3005, of the children had perished. In Manchester, matters are far worse. Of 100,000 born in that populous city on the 1st of January 1838, the table shows that, at the end

of that year, only 73,118 would be alive, and at the end
of the second year only 61,632 would be living. So,
throughout the five years, the rate of mortality may be
compared. The general result may be thus stated:—
Of all the children born alive in England, 14½ per cent.
die in the first year, and nearly 20 per cent., or one-
fifth, within the first two years; while in Manchester,
more than 26½ per cent. die within the first, and upwards of 38 per cent. within the first two years. Comparing the whole period of the first five years of age
in England and Manchester, it will be seen that of all
the children born alive throughout England, 26 per
cent., or more than one-fourth, and in Manchester
upwards of 48½ per cent., or nearly one-half, die
within the first five years; while in sixty-three healthy
districts of England not more than 17½ per cent. die
in the same period.

From these incontrovertible facts, corroborated by
returns derived from other countries, the reader may
conceive how many elements of destruction must still
be in activity, even in those parts of Europe where
science has made the greatest advances, and where
the treatment of the young is considered the most
rational, when *one in every seven* infants ushered into
the world perishes within the first year, and *one in
every five* within the first two years of existence!

Looking, then, at the fact that a great mortality
prevails in infancy, even under what are considered
the most favourable circumstances, the question naturally presents itself—Is this mortality a necessary part
of the arrangements of Divine Providence, which we
can do nothing to modify; or does it, on the con-

trary, proceed chiefly from secondary causes, purposely
left to a considerable extent under our own control,
and which we may partially obviate, or even render
innocuous, by making ourselves acquainted with the
nature of the infant constitution, and carefully adapting our conduct to the laws or conditions under which
its different functions are intended to act?   The following considerations may enable the reader to answer
this question.

If we consult the past history of mankind, there
will, I think, be little difficulty in determining that
the appalling waste of infant life is *not* a necessary
and intended result of the Divine arrangements, but is
occasioned *chiefly*, though not wholly, by our own
ignorance and mismanagement, and consequently may
be expected to diminish in proportion as our knowledge and treatment improve—in other words, in proportion as we shall discover and conform to the laws
which the Creator has established for our guidance and
preservation.   But, as the consequences flowing from
this conclusion are of great interest and importance
in a practical point of view, I shall venture into some
detail in its further elucidation.

If the prevalent destruction of life in early infancy
be a part of the established order of nature, and
merely such as may be expected to result from the
accidents and vicissitudes inseparable from human
existence, it is plain that we shall never be able to
diminish it by any exertions of our own, and need not,
therefore, take the trouble to inquire into its causes, or
attempt their removal.   If, on the other hand, it be
true that ignorance and disregard of the laws of God

imprinted on the infant organism, are the principal sources of the mortality, and we can succeed in impressing that truth on the minds of parents, as well as of medical men, our prospects will be far more encouraging.

Again, if the infant mortality be the result of an unalterable decree of Providence, without regard to good or bad management, we may expect to find it nearly the same in all ages and states of civilization, and bearing no relation whatever to the conduct of others; whereas, if it be chiefly owing to causes which we have generally the power to guard against, it will be found to vary in amount, and be in direct relation to the favourable or unfavourable circumstances in which the child is placed, and the good or bad treatment to which it is subjected. Although few of my readers will be at a loss to decide which of these two suppositions is the true one, still, in order that nothing may be left to uncertainty or conjecture, let us first contemplate the extent to which, in past times, infant life has fallen a sacrifice to ignorance and bad treatment, that we may afterwards contrast it with the comparatively favourable results of management of a more enlightened though still far from perfect kind.

We have already seen that, in England, the average mortality of infants among rich and poor is about one in every seven, before the end of the first year from birth. So directly, however, is infant life influenced by good or bad management, that, about a century ago, the workhouses of London presented the astounding result of TWENTY-THREE *deaths in every twenty-four* infants under the age of one year! For a long time this frightful devastation was allowed to go on, as beyond the reach of human remedy. But when at last, in consequence of a parliamentary inquiry having taken place, an improved system of management was adopted, the proportion of deaths was speedily reduced from 2600 to 450 a year! Here, then, was an annual loss, in a single institution, of 2150 lives, attributable, not to any unalterable decree of Providence, as some are disposed to contend, as an excuse for their own negligence, but to the ignorance, indifference, or cruelty of man! And what a lesson of vigilance and inquiry ought such occurrences to convey, when even now, with all our boasted improvements, *every tenth infant still perishes within a month of its birth!*

We do not require, indeed, to go so far back as a century ago, for such a deplorable example of the deadly results of ignorance : we may find an equally striking one in Mr Maclean's account of his visit to St Kilda in 1838.* After remarking that the population of St Kilda is diminishing rather than increasing, he states, that this unusual result is partly owing to the prevalence of epidemics, but chiefly to the excessive mortality which is at all times going on in infancy. "EIGHT OUT OF EVERY TEN CHILDREN," says he, "DIE BETWEEN THE EIGHTH AND TWELFTH DAY OF THEIR EXISTENCE!" Admitting even the approximative truth of this startling averment, the reader will naturally wonder what poisonous quality can so infect the air or

* Chambers's Edinburgh Journal, Nov. 1838.

soil of St Kilda as to cause such a frightful destruction
of life ; and will infer that here, at least, some powerfully deleterious influence must be at work, which no
amount of human skill can successfully cope with.
So far, however, is this, from being the case, that, as
Mr Maclean expressly states, " the air of the island is
good, and the water excellent ; " " there is *no visible
defect on the part of nature;*" but, on the contrary,
" the great if not the only cause is the filth amidst
which the people live, and the noxious effluvia which
pervade their houses." In proof of this, he adduces the
family of the clergyman, "who lives exactly as those
around him do in every respect, except as regards the
condition of his house, and who has a family of four
children, *the whole of whom are well and healthy;*"
whereas, according to the average mortality around
him, at least three out of the four would have
been dead within the first fortnight. When it is
added that the huts of the natives are small, low-
roofed, and without windows, and are used during the
winter as *stores for the collection of manure*, which is
carefully laid out upon the floor and trodden down till
it accumulates to the depth of several feet, the reader
will not hesitate to conclude with Mr Maclean, that had
the clergyman's children been subjected to the same
mismanagement with those of the other islanders, not
one of them, probably, would have survived ; and
that, on the other hand, had the children of the poor
islanders been as carefully and judiciously attended to
as the clergyman's, they also might have grown up in
perfect health and vigour.

To find ample confirmation of the principle which
these examples so forcibly illustrate, we have only to
contrast the rate of mortality in infancy among the
poor with that among the rich; the mortality in
densely-peopled manufacturing towns with what is
found in the open country; the proportion of deaths
which formerly occurred with that which now occurs
in public hospitals; and, above all, the enormous
waste of life in foundling hospitals—where the natural
food of the child and the watchful solicitude of the
mother are withdrawn—with the comparatively small
mortality in private families, where these advantages
are enjoyed. This comparison I shall now proceed
shortly to make.

It has already appeared (Chapter II.) how greatly
the condition of infants is affected by THE DEGREE OF
HEALTH AND COMFORT ENJOYED BY THE MOTHER DURING
PREGNANCY. Where this is the most favourable, there,
in ordinary circumstances, will the offspring be the
most healthy, and most capable of resisting the agency
of hurtful influences. On the contrary, where bad
health and misery predominate during pregnancy, the
greatest risk is run by the child, and the proportion
even of children *born dead* is much higher than usual.
In the case of illegitimate children, above all, the
mothers are exposed to privations of every kind; and
among such children, accordingly, the proportion of
the still-born is by far the greatest. At Berlin, for
example, it appears that "the still-born out of 100 illegitimate births were, during the half of the preceding century, *three times* more numerous than the still-

born out of 100 legitimate births, and this state of
matters is not yet improved."[*]   Here, then, is ample
proof of the direct influence of the state of the parent
on the fate of the child even prior to birth ; and we
have already traced the same influence on the constitution of the child subsequently to birth.   As things
stand at present, many of the comforts, and some
of even the necessaries of life, are beyond the reach
of the poorer classes—a circumstance diminishing the
chances of infant life amongst them.   Thus, while,
according to the foregoing returns, the average mortality under two years of age, in the healthy districts
of England, may be rated as one-seventh of the whole
number alive under the same age, the mortality among
the poor, especially in large cities, is above three times
that amount.

The same general truth is established by a " Table
showing the proportion out of 1000 registered deaths
which have occurred at various ages in the whole of
England and Wales, and in each of 25 divisions,"
given in the Registrar's First Report, already quoted.
From this table it appears that, " in the mining parts
of Staffordshire and Shropshire, in Leeds and its
suburbs, and in Cambridgeshire, Huntingdonshire,
and the lowland parts of Lincolnshire, the deaths of
infants *under one year* have been more than 270 out
of 1000 deaths at all ages ; while in the southern
counties of England, in Wiltshire, Dorsetshire, and
Devonshire, in Herefordshire and Monmouthshire,
and in Wales, the deaths at that age, out of 1000 of

* Quetelet sur l'Homme, &c., vol. i. p. 129.

o

all ages, scarcely exceed 180 ;" or, in other words,
the deaths under one year in the last-mentioned
counties, where the population is scattered and the
air pure, are *one-third fewer* than those in the first-
named places, where the population is living either
in the midst of crowded manufactories, or on a flat
and marshy soil. It is true that, to obtain a perfectly
accurate proportion, the amount of population, at the
different periods of life, in each of these two great
divisions, requires to be also taken into account; but
even without this, the difference is so great as to
establish the marked influence of external causes on
the rate of infant mortality.   In Manchester, of 1000
born alive, 384 die before they attain two years of
age; while in 63 healthy districts of England, only
133 of 1000 die in the same period ; thus again showing the destructive influence of bad air and want of
the comforts of life, in towns and in the manufacturing districts.   In like manner, the value of sanitary
measures in improving the health of those towns which
have availed themselves of the Public Health Act, is
shown in a striking manner by the following table : *—

| Name of Towns. | Death-rates per 1000 | | Number of Lives saved per 1000 per Annum. |
	Before application of Public Health Act.	After application of Public Health Act.	
Alnwick	35·2	28·3	6·9
Barnard Castle . .	33·3	25.9	7.4
Berwick	28·5	21·2	7·8
Bangor	35·1	80·9	4·2
Durham	26·0	22·7	3·8
Ely	25·6	19·3	6·3
Salisbury . . .	32·2	27.0	5·2
St Thomas's . .	26·9	23·0	3·9

* Practical Results of Sanitary Legislation in England ; in Com-

Here, however, it may be proper to remark, that the high rate of infant mortality in manufacturing towns and districts is not owing exclusively to bad air and want of the comforts of life. In part, at least, it arises from the baneful practice of administering laudanum in large and frequent doses to infants, in order to keep their quiet during their mothers' absence at the factory—a practice which annually destroys thousands, and at the same time perverts or uproots those natural feelings of tenderness and affection which are the best guardians of infant health.

An instructive example of the extent to which infant mortality may be diminished by rational treatment, will be found in an abstract given by the late Dr Joseph Clarke from the Register of the Lying-in-Hospital of Dublin; in which it is stated that, at the conclusion of 1782, out of 17,650 infants born alive, 2944, or nearly every SIXTH child, died within the first fortnight. This extraordinary fatality seemed to Dr Clarke to be caused chiefly by the great impurity of the air in the wards; and accordingly, by adopting means calculated to ensure better ventilation, the number of deaths was speedily reduced to only 419 out of 8033, or about one in 19¼, instead of one in 6 l To show still more clearly how much of the mortality was the effect of mismanagement, I may add, that, during the seven years when Dr Collins was master of the same institution, the cases of *trismus* were reduced, by still farther improvements in ventilation

and increased attention to cleanliness, to so low an
average as three or four yearly; whereas in 1782,
they caused nineteen-twentieths of the deaths.* Dr
M'Clintock, the present master of the Hospital, states
that a death from *trismus* now occurs only once
or twice a year, and that the sanitary condition of
the establishment is satisfactory.† A more striking
proof of the fatal effects of impure air and the contrary on infant life could scarcely be adduced.

The preservative effects of improved treatment are
nowhere more evident than in the city of London.
In M'Culloch's "Statistics of the British Empire,"‡
we find a table quoted from Mr Edmunds, "showing
the total births and the deaths under five years of age,
according to the 'London Bills of Mortality,' for 100
years, in five periods of twenty years each; also, showing the number dying under five years out of 100 born;"
the results of which, obtained, according to Dr Farr,
by an unexceptionable method, "demonstrate that,
for the last century, the mortality of children in
London has been constantly on the decline." The
table is as follows:—

	1730–49.	1750–69.	1770–89.	1790–1809.	1810–29.
Total births . . Total deaths un-} der 5 years . }	315,456 235,087	307,895 198,604	349,477 180,068	880,898 159,571	477,010 151,794
Dying per cent. } under 5 years }	74·5	68·0	51·6	41·8	31·9

Here it will be observed, that the deaths under five

* Collins's Practical Treatise on Midwifery. p. 513; London, 1860.
† Letter to the Editor, July 18, 1859.
‡ Fourth Edition, vol. II. p. 543.

years of age have fallen gradually from 74·5 to 31·8 per 100; and we find from the Registrar-General's returns, that a decrease is still going on, and that the deaths are now so few as 28·5 per 100. This will be seen by the following table for LONDON, within the Registrar-General's limits:—

Registered births and deaths under five years of age, and proportion dying under five years out of 100 born.*	1840-44	1845-49	1850-54	1855	1856	1857
Total births regist.	302,957	348,080	401,253	85,532	87,435	89,577
Total deaths under 5 years of age	98,422	111,387	118,329	25,025	24,128	25,512
Dying per cent. under 5 years .	32·5	32·0	29·5	29·3	27·6	28·6

Having thus shown, on a large scale, and through a long series of years, how much infant mortality may be reduced by good management, I might next refer to the experience of Foundling Hospitals for conclusive evidence of the fearfully destructive influence of bad treatment, where the unhappy outcasts are deprived of a mother's care, and subjected to many of the inconveniences by which health is most easily affected and life destroyed. But it will be sufficient to adduce the case of orphans, who, next to foundlings, are the most unfortunately situated for the preservation and enjoyment of life, and among whom, consequently, all other conditions being equal, the mortality is much greater than among children who are tended with a mother's care, and cherished with a mother's affection. Yet it is not less instruc-

* *Vide* the Registrar-General's Annual Reports.

tive than cheering to observe how much it is in our
power to do, by kind and rational treatment, even for
that unfortunate class. Of this we have a remarkable
example in the Orphan Asylum of Albany in the State
of New York, which was opened in the end of 1829
with about 70 children, but in which the average up
to August 1836 subsequently amounted to 80.   During the first three years, when an imperfect mode of
management was in operation, from four to six children, and sometimes more, were constantly on the sick-
list; one or two assistant-nurses were necessary; a
physician was in regular attendance twice or thrice
a week; and *the deaths amounted in all to between
thirty and forty*, or nearly one in every month. At
the end of this time an improved system of treatment
was adopted, and, notwithstanding the disadvantages
inseparable from the orphan state of the children, the
results were in the highest degree satisfactory.   "The
nursery was soon entirely vacated, and the services
of the nurse and physician no longer needed; and, FOR
MORE THAN TWO YEARS, NO CASE OF SICKNESS OR DEATH
TOOK PLACE.   In the succeeding twelve months there
were three deaths, but they were new inmates, and
diseased when they were received, and two of them
were idiots." The superintendents farther state, that
"since the new regimen has been fully adopted, there
has been a remarkable increase of health, strength,
activity, vivacity, cheerfulness, and contentment,
among the children. The change of temper is also
very great. They have become less turbulent,
irritable, peevish, and discontented, and far more

manageable, gentle, peaceable, and kind to each other."*

Here, then, is convincing evidence that it really is in the power of man to prevent and mitigate infant suffering by knowledge and the enlightened exercise of reason. When we contrast the health and comfort enjoyed by the poor orphans under one system of treatment, with the sickness, sorrow, and loss of life entailed on them by the other, we are forced to admit that parents themselves are in a great measure the arbitors of their children's fate, and that a heavy responsibility attaches to those among them who carelessly undertake such a trust, without any attempt to qualify themselves for the adequate discharge of the duties involved in it. I am anxious to impress this upon the reader, because it is only under a conviction that it *is* in our power to avert many of the evils which afflict the young, that an active interest can be felt in investigating the origin of these, and assiduously using the means required for their prevention and removal. If any of the diseases which commonly destroy life in infancy can be warded off by proper care and good treatment, as the above example strikingly shows, no parent can remain indifferent to the inquiry by what means so desirable an end may be accomplished: nothing can justify neglect where its consequences are so evidently serious.

It may be argued, that the examples which I have given are extreme cases, and that no such mismanagement or fatality occurs in strictly private life. Most

* Alcott on Vegetable Diet, p. 217. Boston, U.S., 1838.

of them, certainly, *are* extreme cases ; but on that very
account they have been selected, as showing the more
incontestably how extensive the sphere of our influence is, and how important it is to the young that
our management of them should be in strict accordance
with the nature of the infant constitution and with
the laws of health. But though it be in hospitals and
other institutions for children that the most fearful
results of bad treatment occur, we must not infer that
the records of family practice are altogether unstained
with similar errors, and that even among the wealthier
classes nothing more can be done for the preservation
of infant health and life. On the contrary, we have
too good reason to believe, that, among the best educated classes, many lives are cut short by mismanagement in infancy, which might be saved if the parents
possessed in time a portion of that knowledge and
practical sense which dire experience sometimes im-
presses upon them when too late.

    The grand principle, then, which both parents and
medical men ought to have ever before their eyes, is,
that human life was not intended to be extinguished
at its very dawn ; and that its early extinction, whenever this occurs, is from the operation of previously
existing causes, some of which might have been discovered and removed, while others might have been,
if not entirely, at least partially counteracted. This
being the case, the first duty of parents obviously is,
to make themselves acquainted with the general nature
and proper treatment of the infant constitution, that
they may not unnecessarily risk the welfare of their

child, and their own peace of mind, upon the mere
chance of finding a well-qualified substitute in a lower
and still more imperfectly educated class than their
own. To the right-minded mother, the management
and training of her children ought to appear in the
same light as the exercise of a profession. It is her
natural and special vocation ; and she is as much
bound to fit herself for the discharge of its active
duties, as the father and husband is to prepare himself for the exercise of the profession by which he is
to provide for their support.

Admitting, then, that every mother should possess
a general acquaintance with the nature and functions
of the infant constitution, and with the conditions
required for their healthy performance, it may be
asked, Where is the necessary information to be obtained, seeing that none such is taught to girls at
school or at home, and that very few treatises fitted
for their perusal are anywhere to be met with? This
difficulty is not without force. The desirableness of
including such instruction in the education of women,
and the possibility of giving it intelligibly, have as
yet been strongly perceived by only a few, and little
has been done to supply the want. Now, however,
the omission is becoming every day more apparent,
and several works, more or less suited to the purpose,
have accordingly made their appearance. But as none
of them embraces all that I conceive to be required, I
have ventured on the present attempt to supply the
necessary information in a plain and intelligible way,

not with the view of superseding other works, but of
adding to their acknowledged utility.

The following important remarks, the result of
Mr Simon's extensive experience, will form a fit conclusion to the present chapter:—

"The *death-rates* of young children," he remarks,
"are among the most important studies in sanitary
science, not only on their own account, but as affording
a very sensitive test of the sanitary circumstances of
the district. Where infants are most apt to die, the sur-
vivors are most apt to be sickly; and where the children
struggle through a scrofulous childhood to realize an
abortive puberty, they beget a still sicklier brood than
themselves—less capable of labour, and less susceptible
of education—feeble in body and mind. A high
local mortality of children almost necessarily denotes
a high local prevalence of those causes which determine a degeneration of the race." *

* Introductory Report on "Papers relating to the Sanitary State of
the People of England, by E. Headlam Greenhow, M.D." By John
Simon, Esq., the Medical Officer of the Privy Council.

CHAPTER IV.

In this chapter I shall endeavour to give the
reader such an intelligible account of the infant constitution, and of the chief conditions by which infant
health is influenced, as may be practically useful in
the hands of every parent of ordinary capacity. In
the choice of the subjects, and in the manner of
treating them, I shall endeavour at once to embrace
every important truth bearing upon infant health,
and to avoid offending even the most sensitive delicacy; and wherever I may fall short of attaining
my aim, I shall rely on the indulgent forbearance
of the reader, in the full assurance that allowance
will be made for the difficulties inseparable from the
subject.

From the evidence adduced (Chap. III.), the conclusion is irresistible, that the health and life of the
infant depend essentially on the kind of management
to which it is subjected, and the nature of the circumstances by which it is surrounded. Where both

these are favourable, the child will enjoy the highest degree of health of which its natural constitution is susceptible; and where the management is bad, or the child's situation unfavourable, its life and health will always be correspondingly precarious.

In practice, the principle implied in the foregoing propositions admits of many most useful applications; and on this account it is that I am so anxious to impress it on the mind of the reader. It alone explains the progress which has been already made in diminishing infant mortality, and encourages us to renewed exertion, in the belief that disease and death will be averted from infancy in proportion as we shall succeed in bringing our treatment into harmony with the laws of the human constitution, which are *laws of the Creator*. Much as the management of infancy has been improved of late years, a great deal yet remains to be done; and when we consider how little regard has been hitherto paid to the discovery or fulfilment of the conditions required for the healthy performance of the animal functions, and how much disease has thence arisen, we cannot but look forward with hope to the time when the principles of physiology shall be taught in every elementary school, and become a living guide to the parent as well as the physician, in directing the management of the young.

Let it never be forgotten, then, that disease and untimely death are the results, not of chance, or of any abstract necessity, but simply of the infringement of the *conditions* on which God has decreed the healthy action of the various organs of the body to depend, and which

have therefore been appropriately named the ORGANIC
LAWS. When these conditions are fulfilled, health is
preserved ; when they are neglected or infringed, the
action of the organ is impeded or disordered—in
other words, *disease* begins. Thus, when a fit of indigestion is occasioned by excessive eating or drinking, the disorder proceeds from infringement of that
law which requires, as a prerequisite of healthy
digestion, that the food and drink be adapted in
quantity and quality to the state of the constitution,
mode of life, and powers of the stomach. In like
manner, when inflammation of the eye is excited by
lengthened exposure to a very bright or concentrated
light, the disturbance arises from disregarding the
law, that light must bear a certain relation to the
natural constitution of the eye. If, in defiance of
this law, we exercise the eye with a light either too
intense or too feeble, or if we look continuously
through glasses calculated either to concentrate or
disperse the rays of light in a higher degree than that
to which the structure of the eye is adapted, disorder
of its organization, or, in other words, disease of the
eye, is sure to follow ; and so long as the deranging
cause is allowed to remain in operation, we shall use in
vain the best-devised treatment for the cure of the
disease. But, on the other hand, the moment we
adapt the light and the exercise to the altered state
of the organ, so as to give due scope to the preservative powers of nature, the very same treatment may
speedily succeed, because now the laws of the function are conformed to. Equally vain is the attempt

to cure indigestion by doses of medicine, without fulfilling the requisite conditions of health of the stomach,
by adapting the diet and mode of life to the deranged
state of the organ.

From these considerations it is evident, that in
every instance we must inquire what the *cause* of bad
health is, and upon what organs its chief effect is
produced. In infancy, for example, convulsions are
frequent and dangerous; and if, without attempting
to discover their exciting cause, we merely prescribe
for the convulsions themselves, we shall not only often
fail to arrest them, but probably leave their causes
in full operation, when it may be easy, by the removal
of these, to prevent the recurrence of the fits. Thus,
one cause of convulsions is breathing impure air,
another is the irritation of teething, and a third is
improper diet; so long, therefore, as fresh air is withheld, or the irritation of the gums unallayed, or the
diet ill adapted to the child, our attempts to remove
the disorder must terminate in disappointment.

In the same way, all the causes of disease are in-
fringements of the conditions of health of some organ
or organs of the body; and were it in our power to
discover the whole of these conditions in reference
to *all* the organs, as well as to fulfil them perfectly,
we might prevent disease altogether, and prolong our
lives till the natural period of decay. The grand aim,
therefore, in attempting to improve the treatment of
infancy, ought to be, THE DISCOVERY AND FULFILMENT
OF THE CONDITIONS ON WHICH THE HEALTHY ACTION OF
THE PRINCIPAL ORGANS AND FUNCTIONS DEPENDS.

By fixing our attention steadily upon this guiding principle, two excellent practical results will be gained. The FIRST is, that we shall never witness suffering or disease without being instantly stimulated to the discovery, removal, and future avoidance of its cause; and the SECOND, that we shall be kept constantly alive to the influence of surrounding agents, and thus led to the earliest detection of errors which might be fraught with destruction if left long unremedied.

To this view of the origin of disease it has been objected, that diseases are specially sent by a kind Providence for the spiritual benefit of the sufferer, and not with reference to any physical errors or omissions with which he may be chargeable. But this objection arises from a very narrow conception of the workings of God's providence, and is contradicted by daily and hourly experience, as well as by the habitual conduct of mankind. No man capable of observing and reasoning can fail to know that health is affected by his own conduct, and is under the influence of fixed laws; nor is there a living being that does not act habitually and instinctively on the faith of this being the case.

It is true that disease and recovery both proceed from the Divine will, and that, like every other dispensation, they ought to be made available to moral and religious improvement, as well as to a better observance of the laws of health. But it is not less true that, except in cases of miraculous interposition, the Divine will acts through secondary causes and according to an established plan, to which we, as created intelligent beings, are plainly required to conform. To know this plan is therefore of high importance to all, but chiefly to those whom God himself has entrusted with the guardianship of a whole family's health and happiness. A natural cause exists for every disease, whether we can see it or not; and, in general, we CAN discover it by careful examination. It therefore becomes a sacred duty to study the infant economy, and endeavour to discover the causes of the diseases by which infant life is endangered.

In inculcating these views, I am so far from disregarding the influence of Divine providence, that, on the contrary, my chief object is to enforce attention to its ever-present existence, and, by explaining the mode in which it operates, to point out the surest way of obtaining its aid in attempts to improve our condition. God acts according to an unchanging plan, established by Himself; and to disregard the rules of conduct which the study of that plan reveals to be His will, when it shows that their observance is indispensable to our happiness, is as truly to rebel against His authority as if we were to act at variance with His written commandments. To understand the operation of the external causes of disease, we must have some acquaintance with the nature and conditions of the bodily functions. Without this knowledge, we shall often fail to detect aberrations from their healthy action in time to prevent the mischief which is sure to ensue, and which, with it, might easily be obviated. Nothing is more common than for patients and parents to declare that no cause of any kind has been in operation, where the physician is able to trace one of a very influential kind. Nay, it occasionally happens that, from ignorance of the laws of the animal economy, the parents cannot comprehend the action of a cause when it is pointed out to them; and deliberately leave it in full play, in the belief that it is nowise injurious.*

For this and other reasons it is very desirable, not only that every parent should possess some knowledge of the structure and laws of the animal economy, but that, in laying down rules for the improvement of health and the prevention of disease, every opportunity should be embraced by the medical attendant to explain the laws and functions to which the rules have reference, and thus to inculcate the utility of a more accurate and timely observance of every circumstance likely to derange healthy action. Such shall be my aim in the following pages.

When, with the aid of the principle just laid down, that illness always results from the infringement of some law of the animal economy, we look around us and try to discover why the children of one family are almost always healthy, and those of another almost always ailing, we generally succeed in tracing the result either to the bodily constitution derived from the parents, or to a difference in the management or external circumstances of the respective families. Occasionally, indeed, we are entirely at a loss to assign

* See APPENDIX B, for some account of the most prevalent diseases of infancy.

any sufficient cause; but even in such cases, reason
and analogy entitle us to assume that causes do exist,
although we have not succeeded in discovering them.
Sometimes they are hidden from our view only because the medical attendant has not had sufficient
opportunity to discover them, and the parents are too
little acquainted with the animal economy to be able
to tell when and in what respects their management
is imperfect. I have in several instances experienced
this truth, and been unable, when first called in, to
fix upon any error of regimen or treatment to account
for the illness; and yet, upon more familiar acquaintance with the circumstances of the family, I have
found adequate causes in full operation. In no circumstances, then, ought the medical practitioner to
content himself with getting a few brief answers to
questions; nor should he receive the same statement
as always bearing precisely the same meaning in the
mouths of different persons. Much erroneous practice
arises from overlooking the latter source of error.
Let the physician interpret with caution the statements he receives, and verify them as much as possible by personal observation. Let him also make
sure that everything which he recommends is *understood in the sense in which he means it;* and from time
to time investigate personally the general management of the child, without waiting till some glaring
error has been committed, for the correcting of which
his assistance is urgently required. Every sensible
parent will duly appreciate such attention, and eagerly
afford facilities for the necessary observation.

CHAPTER V.

HAVING pointed out (Chap. I.) the conditions in the health of the parents which INDIRECTLY affect the health of the infant at birth, we have now to consider those causes which act DIRECTLY on the infant after it has entered on an independent existence.

Before birth, the child may be considered as virtually a portion of the mother's organism; for its life and growth are wholly dependent on her. But when once ushered into the world, what a vast revolution in its mode of existence takes place! In an instant it is transferred from unconscious repose, solitude, and darkness, to life and light and action. From being surrounded by a bland fluid of unvarying warmth, it passes at once to the rude contact of an ever-changing and colder air, and to a rougher touch, even from the softest clothing, than it ever before sustained. Previously nourished by the mother's blood, it must now take in and digest its own food, and throw out its own waste. The blood, till now purified and restored through means of the mother's system,

must henceforth be oxygenated by the lungs of the
child itself.   The animal heat, formerly derived from
the mother, must now be elaborated by the action of
its own organs.   Hitherto defended from injury by
the mother's sensations and watchfulness, it must now
receive external impressions through its own nerves :
through its smiles or its cries, it must now announce
to her the fact of its safety or danger.

Such is the revolution which occurs in the life of
the new-born infant, and such are the changes which
render the period of early infancy so full of danger
when their nature is misunderstood, and the treatment is not in harmony with the infant constitution.
Let us inquire, then, what the peculiarities of the infant organism are, and in what manner these changes
are brought about.

NERVOUS ACTION and MUSCULAR MOTION are unquestionably the functions first excited at the sudden entrance of the new-born creature into the outer world.
From the moment when it ceases to be a part of its
mother's system, the continuance of its life depends
on the commencement of *respiration* or breathing.
If that be delayed or suspended for a few minutes, it
perishes as if suffocated.   But before it can begin to
breathe, and to circulate its own blood, *the stimulus
must be felt* which renders breathing an imperative
act.   Accordingly, the infant is no sooner born than it
is roused into action by the sudden and disagreeable
contact of the colder air upon the sensitive nerves of
the skin, and immediately begins to breathe.   The
excited sensibility of the nervous system is thus the

primary source of the involuntary impulse which causes the lungs to play, though doubtless the peculiar stimulus arising from the presence of venous blood in the lungs has also some influence in making the respiratory motion begin. In order to give the infant this quick sensibility, and excite immediate reaction through the reflex system of nerves, the nervous filaments are well developed from the first, and are copiously distributed to the tender skin. The manner in which they are instrumental in making respiration begin, will be easily understood if we consider the suddenness of the infant's transition from a temperature of 98° or 100° to one of 60° or 65°, and recollect the panting and sighing, from irregular action of the respiratory muscles, which plunging into a cold bath produces in an adult, especially if delicate and excitable. So disagreeably vivid, indeed, is the impression made on the child by the cold air, that in most cases it immediately begins to *cry;* which act, as it consists in hurried and irregular breathing, has the advantage of more quickly and effectually expanding the lungs, and giving a wholesome stimulus to the circulation through their vessels. Hence crying is always considered a satisfactory sign of a child's vigour on coming into the world.

Another important purpose fulfilled by the quick sensibility of the skin in early infancy, is protection from external injury. The organism of the new-born child is so feeble and delicate, that a very slight cause is sufficient to disturb its health. A slight excess of cold or of heat, a little hardness or roughness in the

material of its clothing, any trifling neglect of cleanliness, or constraint of position, may suffice to induce
general or local disease. Hence, if such sources of
irritation were not immediately felt by the infant, and
felt so acutely as to force it to sound the alarm for
their removal, serious disease might be induced, or the
child might perish, without any previous indication
that mischief was going on. But let it never bo forgotten that, while this great susceptibility of the
nervous system is bestowed for the protection of the infant, it necessarily increases the danger where any mor-
bific cause is allowed to act. Hence the rapid course,
and frequently fatal termination, of many infantile
diseases; and hence also the much greater efficacy,
at that age, of preventive than of curative treatment.

Nervous sensibility and muscular motion being
thus begun, the functions next called into action for
the preservation of life are those performed by the
lungs and heart—namely, RESPIRATION and CIRCULA-
TION. Thus three important changes follow instanta-
neously on the birth of the infant: the excitement of
the nervous system to action; the expansion of the
lungs and establishment of respiration; and an alteration in the course of the venous blood, which is
now made to pass through the lungs, instead of, as
before, going directly from the right to the left side
of the heart. But there is yet another indispensable
condition of independent life, formerly provided for
by the parent, which must come into play at birth;
I refer to the supply of ANIMAL HEAT.

A certain degree of heat is essential to the well-

being of all warm-blooded animals. If it is either
too high or too low, all the functions suffer, and, in extreme cases, death soon follows. To obviate these
sources of danger, Nature has so constituted the
human organism, that, within certain limits, it pre-
serves an equality of temperature, whether the heat
of the surrounding air be above or below its natural
standard. This temperature, in the healthy adult,
is about 98°, or 50° above the average temperature in
Great Britain; hence it is plain that, without some
provision for producing heat, the body would quickly
be cooled down, even in summer, to a fatal extent.
What, then, is the provision actually made?

Food is the primary source of animal heat, and the
development and diffusion of this heat are effected by
means of *digestion, respiration,* and *circulation.* When
the supply of food is sufficient, and other circumstances are equal, the rapidity with which animal heat
is generated is in proportion to the size of the lungs,
and the freedom with which they play in a pure and
temperate air. Now we have only to look at the
small chest and feebly developed lungs of the infant,
and to consider the comparative inactivity to which
it is doomed in the early months of existence, to feel
assured that in it this source of heat must be scanty
indeed.

Nor is it more favourably situated in regard to
the other source—a full and nourishing diet; for in
early infancy the milk is watery and unstimulating,
and conduces but little to the chemical changes by
which heat is evolved.

It must be added, that the nervous system also
exercises a marked, though indirect, influence on the
generation of animal heat. Where a strong nervous
stimulus is at work, there heat is always more freely
evolved ; during inaction, as in sleep, its generation is
least rapid. Hence the fatal effect of yielding to
drowsiness when exposed to intense cold ; and hence
the need of warmer coverings during sleep than we
can bear while awake, and the frequency of colds
induced by falling asleep in the open air, unprotected
by additional clothing. Now, a much greater proportion of infantile than of adult life is spent in sleep.

If, then, ample nutrition, free respiration, and active
nervous influence, are the chief sources of animal heat,
we cannot expect its rapid evolution in infancy—the
very period at which these functions are most imperfect. Notwithstanding this, however, it was once, or
rather still is, a matter of popular belief, that infants
have a great power of resisting external cold. But
Dr Edwards has demonstrated, that, in accordance
with what might be expected *a priori*, the power of
generating heat is at its minimum in all animals
immediately after birth, and that it rises progressively
as their development, strength, and internal activity
increase. Accordingly, it appears that in prematurely
born children the heat of the body is several degrees
below the natural standard, and is very easily depressed still farther by exposure. In one instance
of a seven-months' child, the thermometer stood at
89° Fahr. instead of 98°, being nine degrees below the
usual temperature in the adult.

The extreme care with which the lower animals protect their young from cold might have led sooner to a perception of the truth.   Dr Edwards observed a very great and rapid diminution of temperature in the new-born offspring of most carnivorous animals when removed from the mother, but a loss of only 2° or 3° of heat when lying close to her body.   Young sparrows, in like manner, have a temperature of 95° or 96° in the nest, a week after being hatched ; but when removed from it, their temperature falls in a single hour to 66½°, that of the atmosphere at the time being as high as 62°.*   Man forms no exception to this general rule ; and as the power of generating heat is comparatively feeble in infancy, while a regular high temperature of the body is necessary for existence, it follows, that whatever withdraws heat faster than it is generated must be injurious in exact proportion to the natural weakness of the constitution, and to the extent and rapidity with which the cause acts.

The practical conclusions deducible from these facts are, as we shall afterwards see, of great importance, and of very general application ; but for the present it will be sufficient to bear in mind, that, so far are infants from possessing a power of successfully resisting cold, they, in common with the young of all other warm-blooded animals, cannot even sustain their own temperature, and soon perish unless duly protected ; and that the degree of animal heat which is indispensable to the continuance of life cannot be kept

* Müller's Elements of Physiology, translated by Dr William Baly, p. 76.

up until the three great processes of *respiration, circulation*, and *digestion*, are fully established. To the last of these it is requisite now to direct the attention of the reader.

After a short period of repose, sufficient to allow it to recover from the turmoil of birth, the infant awakes to demand, in obedience to a powerful instinct, the gratification of *appetite*. For the first time, it receives food into its own stomach, and commences the process of digestion for its own sustenance. This function is necessary, not because life cannot exist without it, as in the case of respiration and circulation, but because growth and waste are the concomitants of life, and materials must be supplied for building up, and for the replacement of what is lost. Hence, the taking of food is not an immediate and pressing want like that of breathing, but may be delayed for several hours with perfect safety and propriety. At the end of this time, however, it must be begun, and continued at short intervals till life draws to a close.

The new-born infant, being thus dependent on supplies of nourishment from without, which its own system must *digest* and *assimilate*, its organs of digestion are sufficiently developed to assume at once their now necessary office. From the simplicity of its natural food, and the small quantity taken in at a time, digestion goes on very actively, and the nutritive *chyle* is soon ready to be taken up by the absorbent vessels, the use of which is to imbibe it from the inner surface of the small intestines as fast as it is formed, and convoy it to the right side of the heart to be mixed with the venous blood, and, by exposure to the air in the air-cells of the lungs, converted along with it into arterial or nutritive blood. But the lungs and chest being still small, and respiration feeble, if the child is encouraged to suck too much or too frequently, and chyle is brought to the lungs in larger quantity or faster than it can be easily converted into good blood, disturbance of health from the circulation of *imperfect* blood necessarily follows. Or, if stronger food, such as chicken-tea or beef-tea, be given too soon, with the view of strengthening a weak child, the chyle formed may be imperfectly sanguified in the lungs, and feverish irritation result. This is a frequent occurrence, and the consequences are often very serious.

Nutrition and growth being thus provided for, it is clear that, without some regular outlet for the effete matter which has already served its purpose in the system, and some means of removing the indigestible part of the food, repletion and oppression would ensue, and soon lead even to the destruction of life. This danger is, however, effectually obviated by the *organs of excretion*, through which the old and effete particles, and the refuse of the food, are removed from the system.

The principal excretory organs are the Bowels, the Kidneys, the Skin, and the Lungs; and as we proceed, we shall find that a proper balance between the organs of *nutrition* and those of *excretion*—between the supply and the waste—is an essential condition

of health, not only in infancy, but at every period
of life. If the nutritive functions preponderate, disease arising from repletion will be the consequence;
whereas, if the excreting organs exceed in activity,
the body will soon waste away and perish, unless a
timely remedy be provided.

The function of excretion being thus a necessary
accompaniment or consequence of nutrition, we find
the various organs by which it is carried on ready to
start into activity soon after birth. The Bowels and
the Kidneys are already in full working order, and require only the presence of their natural stimuli to
excite them to action. Accordingly, the infant has
not been many hours in the world before the then
watery milk of the mother has the effect of relieving
its bowels from the dark and slimy secretion, called
meconium, which had accumulated in them. They
are thus prepared for the assimilation of the richer
milk which speedily takes the place of the early watery
secretion. The supplies of milk required by the infant being very frequent, and the quantity of bile and
other fluid secretions being very considerable, the
bowels act frequently, and yield a more liquid discharge than in maturer life. The kidneys, stimulated
in like manner by the watery nature of the food, become active for the first time, and secrete urine in small
quantities, which also is frequently discharged, the
bladder, like the bowels, being still of small capacity.

In addition to these channels of excretion, two
more remain to be noticed. These are the *Skin* and
the *Lungs.* In certain states of the body and weather,

the exhalation by the skin alone exceeds in weight
the whole amount thrown out by the bowels and
kidneys together;—a fact which may convey some
notion of its importance to health. In the ordinary
state the exhalation is invisible, and is thence named
insensible perspiration. After active exercise, or in
hot weather, it appears in the form of sweat, or
sensible perspiration.

The lungs constitute another important channel
of excretion. In humid still weather, perspiration
and pulmonary exhalation go on very imperfectly;
and hence the dulness and discomfort so often experienced under a "leaden" atmosphere. When the
air is very hot and dry, these processes go on too
rapidly, and produce a feverish irritability and thirst,
which, if continued for some time, are sure to be succeeded by disease. On every account, then, constant
attention should be given to the temperature, the moisture, and the purity of the air by which the young are
surrounded. If we allow perspiration, for example,
to be checked by prolonged exposure to cold and
moist air, an effort will be made by some of the other
excreting organs to get rid of the hurtful particles retained in the blood, and which ought to have been
thrown out by the skin; but even when the effort
proves successful, it is always at the risk of the over-
activity thus induced terminating in disease. Hence
the necessity of avoiding every cause likely to disturb
the natural balance between the different excreting
organs, and to throw the labour of one upon another
which is not intended for it.

To understand more fully, however, the importance
of a healthy state of the *functions of excretion*, it, is
necessary to be aware of the highly noxious influence
exercised by animal matter which has already served
its purpose, and is retained in the system contrary to
the intentions of Nature. When respiration, for example, is seriously impeded, the venous blood ceases
to be oxygenated, and can no longer get rid of the
carbon and other materials which are usually thrown
out in its passage through the lungs. The result is,
that for a short time it passes onwards unchanged;
but, as it is unfit in that state for the support of life,
dissolution speedily ensues. In like manner, when
the effluvia which ought to escape from the surface by
perspiration are prevented from passing off, they tend
to produce fever of a malignant character. When,
again, the urine is not duly secreted, the corrupt
animal matter which ought to have been eliminated
by the kidneys remains in the blood, acts upon it as
a poison, alters its natural composition, destroys the
health, and, in extreme cases, proves speedily fatal.
The same thing holds good with the bowels. If
they are not duly relieved, the excretion of the fæcal
matter by the mucous membrane is impeded, and the
blood is contaminated by its retention. At the same
time the more fluid portion of their contents is absorbed
into the system, whereby the residue acquires an unnatural hardness, and thus proves a direct source of
irritation to the bowels, and increases their liability to
disease.

The grand object to which all the various functions

which we have just passed in review directly contribute, is evidently the *preservation and continuance
of life.* Without them, the body would speedily become a mass of inanimate matter, and, as such, fall
into decay. Beyond this, however, they provide for
nothing; and were man limited to the possession of
these functions, he would have a merely vegetative
existence. They are called ORGANIC FUNCTIONS. They
are essential to the maintenance of life, but serve no
other end. Their action being independent of the
will, and unattended with consciousness, they go on
whether we are awake or asleep, and whether we
bestow a thought upon them or not. They are common to the whole animal, and, generally speaking,
vegetable kingdom also—in short, to every substance
possessed of *organization.* Hence their distinctive
appellation of *organic* functions.

We now come to speak of another class of functions
—the higher, or ANIMAL FUNCTIONS. These have relation, not to the mere *life* of man, but to *the purposes
for which conscious life was given;* they, as well as
those styled organic, require the aid of organs for their
performance. The brain, the organs of sense, and the
organs of voluntary motion—the muscles, and bones,
and their respective nerves—are the great organs of the
animal functions. It is through their instrumentality
that all the operations of intelligence and of emotion
—acts *peculiar to animals*—are performed. By means
of the brain and the organs of sense, the infant becomes *conscious* of his own existence, and perceives
that of the beings who minister to his comfort and

safety. By the same means he sees and smells, hears
and touches, and gradually learns to distinguish one
object from another : impressed agreeably by one object, he stretches his hand towards it by means of his
muscles and bones—towards the light, for example, or
towards his mother's breast ; impressed disagreeably
by another, he shrinks, by the same means, from its
contact, and seeks for safety from injury. As he
grows up, and his brain is developed and consolidated,
his feelings acquire strength and permanency : he
manifests kindness, and reciprocates affection ; he re-
sents and repels aggression, acquires a sense of pro-
perty, seeks the love of those around him, imitates
their actions, distinguishes what is just from what is
unjust, and learns to clothe his feelings and ideas in
words ; and, as his years increase, becoming gradually
acquainted with his position in the great family of
mankind, he at length comes to recognise the duties
which society imposes on him, and the consequent
necessity under which he lies to seek that knowledge,
and exercise that judgment, which shall best enable
him to make his own way in the world as an independent being. By the nobler of these powers and emotions, all of which act through the medium of the
brain, is man distinguished from the beasts that perish;
and to them he is indebted for the privilege of knowing and worshipping the one true God, the Author
and Preserver of his being.

Some of the animal functions are possessed by the
lower animals even in higher perfection than by man,
in consequence of a superiority of special organization.

Thus, there are creatures distinguished by greater acuteness of smell and hearing, by greater reach of vision and vivacity of passion, than man; but in strength and comprehensiveness of intellect, in moral energy, and, above all, in that profound devotional feeling which, more than any other, reveals to him the existence of, and connects him with, the Deity, man stands alone—at once the most privileged and only responsible of all the creatures that God has called into existence. These high gifts are uniformly accompanied by a peculiar and ample development of brain, which none of the lower animals is ever found to possess.

From this short review of the higher or *animal* functions, it will be evident that *they* constitute the really characteristic qualities of man, and that the *organic* functions are required merely to sustain the machinery through which the others operate. A man is not a man because he eats, and digests, and breathes, and circulates blood, and grows, and decays; if he were, a sparrow or a fly might take rank along with him. He is a man because he *thinks*, and *feels*, and *acts* in a certain way, and is the subject of moral responsibility; and he eats and digests *merely because he must possess organs by which to feel, and think, and act, and these organs must be sustained in life and vigour.* He must have eyes; because, without a structure arranged in due relation to the properties of light, no luminous impression could be received. To hear, he must have ears, placing him in due relation to the vibrations of the air; and to act, he must have nerves,

D 2

muscles, and bones. Pursuing the principle a little further, it is plain that the *mind* itself, to which impressions are conveyed, and from which the will emanates, must also be connected with organization during life; and the organ with which it is more immediately connected is ascertained, beyond all doubt, to be the Brain. It is thus, strictly speaking, the *mind*, and its instrument the *brain*, which constitute the distinguishing features of man; and eyes, and ears, and legs, and arms, are required only because, placed as we are in a material world, the mind could not act upon material objects, nor be acted on by them, unless it were associated with, and assisted by, material instruments.

Accordingly, there is nothing in the whole range of creation more wonderful, or more indicative of the omniscience and omnipotence of God, than the exquisite adaptation which everywhere subsists between the character of the individual organisms, and the instincts and powers by which animal life, in its various gradations, is characterized. Not only, indeed, is the organism of all kinds of animals peculiarly adapted to their wants and modes of life, but the modifications which it undergoes in the same individual, at different ages, are in admirable harmony with the position and circumstances of each. In the human being at birth, for example, how tender the organism, how soft the bones, how frail the muscles, how feeble the senses, how defective the mind; but, on the other hand, how active the nutrition, and how admirably in harmony with the constitution and wants of the infant! In beautiful accordance with its mental state, Nature has, by the softness of its bones, and the feebleness of its muscles, denied the infant all power of self-regulation, and consigned its safety to the watchful care of maternal feeling; and only in proportion as it grows, and becomes acquainted with the external world, does it acquire the powers of motion and self-regulation, because then only can it enjoy them in safety, or apply them to use. Arranged as is the order of the development of the functions by the Omniscient Creator, how admirably does each harmonize with the others, and how perfectly do all contribute to one common end — the preservation and welfare of the creature!

Ushered into a world where everything is absolutely new to it, and where its safety depends at every instant on its proper treatment, the infant is thrown at first entirely on its mother for support and protection; and these are secured to it by the strongest feeling which woman can experience—that devoted love of offspring which seldom fails even amid the agonies of death. Ignorant of its own nature, and of everything around it, the infant is wisely denied such power of motion as it could use only to its own detriment. And, unable as it is to act for itself, ripened consciousness has wisely been withheld from it; for this would have added misery to its lot, without a single compensating advantage. It passes its earlier days in sleep and dozing, and wakes up only for a moment to satisfy the predominating instinct—the appetite for food—on which its future development depends.

Such is an outline of the peculiarities of the infant organism and functions. It is far from being complete, because a full description of them would be out of place in a work like the present. But it will suffice to give the reader a general idea of the constitutional characteristics of the young; and, in laying down practical rules for their management, I shall take occasion to explain further, wherever it may seem necessary, the physiological principles on which their application rests.

CHAPTER VI.

HAVING pointed out the peculiarities of the infant
constitution, I now come to lay down practical rules
for its management at birth, and shall explain, as we
proceed, the Physiological Principles on which their
application rests.

The new-born infant is so susceptible of cold as to
be painfully roused by the sudden transition from the
unvarying high temperature of the womb to the comparative coldness of even our summer atmosphere.
On this account, our first care, immediately on the
birth of the infant, ought to be, to envelope it in soft
warm flannel, and in cold weather carry it to the
neighbourhood of a good fire, but out of the line of
its direct rays. If the infant is active, and breathes
freely, it may forthwith be washed, to free it from
the tenacious coating of unctuous mucus which
served for its protection during its sojourn in the
womb, but which now becomes a source of irritation,
and a direct impediment to the healthy action of the

skin. The removal of this coating is most con-
veniently effected by immersing the child in a small
warm bath, while the head is supported by the left
hand of the nurse. By this plan every part of the
body is effectually protected from cold, while the
position of the infant is the one best suited to the
feebleness of its frame, and admitting most easily of
the head and face being thoroughly washed, without
any risk of the impure water running into its eyes.
After being carefully washed, it ought to be rubbed
gently all over with a soft sponge, great care being
taken not to chafe or injure the skin by too much
friction. Treated in this way, the mucus separates
easily, and the use of soap or any oily substance in
addition is rarely required. Part of the mucus is apt
to adhere to the folds of the skin and joints, to the
ears, eyelids, and other irregular surfaces, unless it be
cleared away by very careful washing. But as the
eyes are extremely delicate and easily injured at
birth, great caution should be exercised not to touch
them with the sponge which has been used to cleanse
the rest of the skin, or to allow any of the water, now
loaded with impurities, to drop upon the eye or eyelids.
Neglect of this precaution is one cause of a severe
form of inflammation of the eyes, which is apt to
come on within two or three days after birth, and
often ends in blindness. To avoid all risk from this
cause, perfectly clean water, and a clean sponge,
should be used for washing the eyelids.

The temperature of the water used for washing the
infant ought to be the same as that of the body—

namely, from · 96° to 98° Fahrenheit. *Momentary immersion* in water two or three degrees warmer is sometimes very useful in rousing the vital energies of a feeble or languid infant.

Immediately on being taken out of the bath, the infant should be received on a large pillow covered with several soft warm napkins, laid across the nurse's knees. By this means it may be dried easily and quickly, and *gentle* rubbing be continued with the hand over the whole surface till a genial glow is excited. To prevent any risk of cold, everything used should be comfortably warm. The room also ought to be warm, and free from draughts; but too near an approach to a large fire should be avoided.

If any part of the skin, after being gently but carefully dried, is observed to be ruffled, it should be dusted with a little hair-powder.

The infant being now washed and dried, a thin and fine flannel bandage, five or six inches broad, and long enough to go once or twice round the body, should be applied, partly for warmth, and partly to protect the navel-string, and prevent the bowels from being forced outward at the opening of the navel during crying or other sudden effort. In winter and cold weather, flannel is undoubtedly the best material for such a bandage; but when the skin is unusually tender, or the weather hot, a fine cotton or linen roller may be substituted. Occasionally, flannel lined with thin cotton or linen is used, but in this climate flannel itself is rarely found to be oppressive. Whichever substance is used, care must be taken not to make the bandage too tight, otherwise the breathing will be impeded.

Arrived at this stage of the proceedings, it is the custom of some merely to wrap up the child loosely in a flannel shawl or blanket, and put it to sleep, the rest of the dressing being delayed till it awakes refreshed at the end of several hours., Others, again, complete the dressing before laying the child in its cradle. In determining which of those courses to follow, we may safely be guided by the state of the infant. If it is very feeble, or fatigued by the washing and drying, the first plan will be preferable. In either case, it will drop asleep almost immediately on being laid down, and will not awake, probably, for some hours. In the mean time, we shall, for the sake of the connection, continue our remarks on the subject of the dress.

DRESS.—The leading qualities required in the clothing of infants are lightness, softness, and warmth; and it must therefore vary according to the climate and season. In construction, it ought to admit of being easily put on and taken off; and while it affords ample protection to the body, it ought to admit of the fullest expansion of the chest and abdomen, and perfect freedom of motion in the limbs. Provided it fulfil these ends, there will be no occasion for interfering with the mother's taste, or the fashion of the day. But whatever tends either to compress the body, or to restrain the arms or legs, ought to be unrelentingly forbidden; and particularly every approach to the practice, still prevalent in some parts of the Continent, of swaddling the infant in rollers like a mummy.

If the child is born prematurely, or in winter, or has a weak constitution, flannel ought generally to be preferred for the whole of the dress in contact with the skin. From the protection which it affords, and also the slight stimulus which it gives to the skin, it is extremely useful in warding off the internal congestions, and inflammatory and bowel complaints, to which weakly children are liable. But when, as sometimes happens, from unusual sensibility or other causes, flannel irritates the skin or induces perspiration, cotton or fine linen should be preferred—care being taken never to put them on till they are made comfortably warm.

As to the other parts of dress, it is impossible to lay down rules applicable to every case. The chief things to keep in mind are, that perfect freedom of motion in the limbs, and the absence of all pressure on the chest or bowels from undue tightness of the dress, are indispensable to health ; that the generation of animal heat is less active in infancy than at a later period of life, and that the dress ought to be such as to ensure due warmth at all seasons. But, however prejudicial exposure to cold may be in infancy, *excessive wrapping up*, or keeping the child in too hot rooms, is no less hurtful, and ought to be as scrupulously avoided. For obvious reasons, tapes and buttons should be used, instead of pins, for fastening the dress.

The common practice of dressing infants in long

flowing clothes during the first few months is advantageous, by protecting the body and lower extremities against cold air and draughts ; and in cold weather the feet should be further protected by soft woollen socks or knitted worsted shoes, which retain their warmth without compressing them.

The head is very commonly kept too warm in infancy; which, considering the natural tendency to nervous excitement in early life, is an improper practice. In warm weather, the thinnest possible covering will be sufficient for its protection ; and even in cold weather, a warmer cap will be required only when going into the open air.   Within doors, the temperature is generally kept high enough by fires to render much wrapping up neither necessary nor safe.   When colds are induced by wearing thin caps, it is generally in consequence of the infant being laid to sleep with the head immersed in a very soft warm pillow, whereby an unusual flow of blood towards the head takes place, accompanied by considerable perspiration on its surface.   In such circumstances, the rational remedy is, not to put on a thicker covering by day, but, by the use of a proper pillow, to guard against overheating by night.   When the head is kept very warm, the nervous excitability is greatly increased, so that the infant is easily affected by slight changes of temperature, and any accidental irritation is more likely to be followed by spasmodic or convulsive fits.

When, after the lapse of a few months, strength and activity, and that desire for motion which naturally accompanies them, become developed, the dress requires to be so arranged as to leave the feet free and unencumbered. Soft warm stockings, and easy comfortable shoes, are then advisable, but no compression in any form ought to be permitted. Corns, and derangement of the natural positions of the toes, are almost invariably the consequence of too tight and ill-made shoes, which press unequally, and do not admit the full expansion of the anterior part of the foot. In making the change to short clothes, regard must be had to the weather, and due care be taken to keep the legs and feet warm when the child is carried out into the open air.

Nearly akin to dress by day is the provision of proper bed-clothing during the night. If an infant is buried under a mass of bed-clothes when asleep, and dressed in the ordinary way when awake, the very transition will be hurtful.

In arranging night-coverings, the soft feather-bed is very often estimated as nothing; that is to say, the same provision of blankets is considered equally indispensable whether the child is laid upon a firm mattress or immersed in down. The mother, looking only to the coverings laid *over* the child, is apt to forget those on which it lies, although, in reality, the latter may be the warmer of the two.

But, as already mentioned, the infant possesses a low power of generating heat, and therefore it requires to be rather warmly clothed during sleep, as well as during its waking hours.* Yet here, as in

* From overlooking the necessity of having the under surface of the body kept warm in bed, a great error was committed in one of the

everything, extremes ought to be carefully avoided,
and while due warmth in bed is provided for, reason
and consistency should be adhered to, and excessive
heat as scrupulously guarded against as debilitating
cold.

Edinburgh workhouses a few years ago. During a severe winter, a
number of children slept in beds unprovided with mattresses, and
with nothing but the canvas bottom and a single fold of blanket to
lie on. The consequence was, that they lay shivering and sleepless,
and most of them became seriously diseased.

CHAPTER VII.

For some weeks after birth, the whole time of the infant is occupied in sleeping and feeding, and the predominant functions are those of digestion, nutrition, and excretion. Hence, the first and most imperative want, after the functions more immediately essential to life are fully in operation, is a regular supply of materials out of which the nutrition and development of the body may be effected, and the continual waste of the system repaired.

Accordingly, no sooner does the infant awake out of its first sleep, than it manifests the activity of a powerful instinct, impelling it to supply the want just mentioned. This instinct is the *appetite for food.* As soon, therefore, as the mother has sufficiently recovered from her fatigue — generally within eight or ten hours—the infant, in compliance with its own earnest desire, should be put to the breast. At first, the milk is secreted in small quantity, and, from its watery consistence, resembles whey more than milk; but during the next few days it gradually

becomes more copious, rich, and nutritious. This
arrangement is in admirable harmony with the state
and wants of the infant. At birth, the bowels are
loaded with the dark and slimy *meconium* already
mentioned, and the first step towards the preparation
of the digestive organs for their functions is the expulsion of this now useless, and, if longer retained,
probably hurtful matter. For this purpose, nothing is
so suitable as the watery milk first secreted. It affords
to the bowels the precise stimulus required to excite
them to act, without the risk of undue irritation: consequently, when the infant is freely admitted to the
mother's breast, the meconium is usually cleared out
within a day or two; and, in proportion as the milk
becomes richer and more nutritious, the stomach and
bowels become fit for its reception and digestion.

From ignorance of the general sufficiency of the
means thus provided by Nature for the expulsion
of the meconium, it is still the practice with many
nurses to refuse the breast till a purgative has been
administered to the child, by way of preparing its
stomach and bowels for the reception of the mother's
milk.   But in most instances this proceeding is
wholly unnecessary, and in many it is injurious.
Occasionally, no doubt, the aid of a mild laxative
is required to avert a greater evil; but the medical
attendant is the only judge of such a necessity, and
unless by his special direction none ought ever to be
given. In the first milk of the mother, Nature has
provided a laxative adapted to the delicate organism
of the infant; and therefore, when we *unnecessarily*

act in opposition to this arrangement, it is at the double risk of irritating the bowels of the child by the needless purgative, and of giving the mother pain from the unrelieved distention of her breasts—a state which often terminates in acute inflammation and the formation of an abscess.

When no action of the bowels is obtained within several hours after birth, and the child obviously suffers from the delay, a few tea-spoonfuls of tepid sugar and water, or half a tea-spoonful of fresh drawn castor-oil, may be given, which will answer every purpose; all more active medicines should be forbidden.

Sometimes, from the imperfect health or constitution of the mother, the secretion of milk is delayed so long that it becomes necessary to administer nourishment to support the strength of the child. Such retardation arises chiefly from previous inattention on her own part to the laws of health; and, when it does occur, the child should be put to the breast from time to time, to solicit and aid the effort of Nature.

When, from the state of the mother, it becomes necessary to administer food to the new-born infant, we should adhere as close as we can to the intentions of Nature, and give in preference that kind of nutriment which approaches most nearly to the mother's milk. Were it possible to put the child to the breast of another woman also just delivered, it would be desirable to do so; but such an opportunity rarely occurs, unless in consequence of a previous arrangement. The next best thing consists in substituting ass's milk, or cow's milk diluted with a half or more

of water and slightly sweetened. A few tea-spoonfuls may be given at a time, and repeated at proper
intervals, till the mother is able to nourish the infant
herself; or, still better, it may be given from a bottle
properly fitted with an artificial nipple. Cow's milk
given in this way is decidedly preferable to gruel,
panada, arrowroot, chicken-tea, or any other preparation less analogous to the natural food of the
child. At this early period, the digestive organs are
unprepared for the reception of vegetable matter in
any form, and, when given, it rarely fails to irritate the
stomach and bowels. Cow's milk, properly diluted
and sweetened, is, on the other hand, nearly the same
in composition as the mother's milk, and is therefore
the best temporary substitute for it.* The greatest
caution should be used not to exceed in quantity, and
not to repeat the allowance oftener than about once
in two or three hours. A single ounce of milk, well
digested, will yield more nourishment than double the
quantity when it oppresses the still feeble stomach.

In an ordinary state of health, and under ordinary
circumstances, the flow of the mother's milk will be
fully established within from one to three days after
delivery; and, in exact proportion to the wants of
the child, its nature will be changed from a watery
to a more nourishing consistence. When this has
taken place, and the mother continues in health,
there is no reason whatever for giving the child any
other food, at least for several months.

The mother's milk being thus the natural and best

* For the qualities of the milk of different animals, see APPENDIX C.

food of the infant, the next point is to determine at
what intervals it may be admitted to the breast.
Here, again, it is indispensable to warn the parent
against hurtful excess; for if the stomach is too frequently replenished, or too much distended, the digestion necessarily becomes deranged, and gripes and
flatulence torment the child. The usual practice
with inexperienced and ignorant mothers is to offer
the breast whenever the child cries or shows the least
indication of uneasiness, no matter from what cause,
as if hunger were the only sensation which the young
being could experience. From earliest infancy, *regular periods* should, as far as possible, be observed in
giving nourishment; and it is surprising how very
soon the infant accommodates itself to the practice.
The quiet repose enjoyed during the intervals is beneficial alike to parent and child, and is an ample reward for the very small trouble required to establish
the habit at first.

It is a great mistake to treat crying as an infallible
sign of an empty stomach. New as the infant is to
the surrounding world, it shrinks instinctively from
every strong sensation, whether of heat or of cold, of
pressure or of hardness, of hunger or of replotion, and
its only way of expressing *all* disagreeable feelings is
by crying. If it is hungry, it cries; if it is over-fed, it
cries ; if it suffers from the prick of a pin, it cries ; if
it lies too long in the same position, so as to receive
undue pressure on any one part, it cries; if it is exposed
to cold, or any part of its dress is too tight, or it is
held in an awkward position, or is exposed to too

E

bright a light or too loud a sound, it can indicate its
discomfort only by its cries ; and yet the one remedy
of ignorant nurses for so many different evils is, not
to find out and remove the true cause of offence—but
to offer the child the breast !

It is a mistake to be over-anxious always to put an
immediate stop to crying. To a considerable extent,
crying is an intentional provision of Nature, and is
called into play by every unpleasant sensation. It
is only when often repeated, long-continued, and
really caused by suffering, that it is detrimental. In
general, the two kinds of crying are easily distin-
guishable, and very few mothers will long confound
them and treat them as identical. As the infant has
no other means of expressing any disagreeable sensation plainly enough to enforce immediate attention,
crying ought to be considered simply as a signal of
distress ; and instead of constantly ascribing it to
hunger alone, and perhaps filling to repletion a stomach
already overburdened with food, we should endeavour
to discover the real exciting cause, and seek the surest
means of its immediate removal. But this kind of
crying must never be confounded with the plaintive
wail which characterizes infantile disease, and which
betokens suffering and sometimes danger.

The great principle (explained in my work on *Digestion and Diet*) of proportioning the supply of food to
the quantity of material expended in growth and that
carried away as waste, is equally applicable to infancy
as to more advanced life. During the first weeks of
existence, the infant does nothing but sleep, digest,

and grow, and it therefore requires to be fed more
frequently than at a later period. On an average,
from two to three hours may be allowed to elapse between its repasts; and as it becomes older, the interval
should be gradually extended. If the breast be not
habitually offered as the readiest means of silencing
the child, there will rarely be any active desire for it
at a shorter interval than two and a half or three hours.
But if it be demanded *in an unequivocal manner*, the
mother will be quite safe in yielding to the child's entreaties, only taking care that it does not overload its
stomach. At all times, indeed, the indications of
appetite may be implicitly followed as a guide in infancy; but the greatest care is requisite not to confound healthy appetite with the craving arising from
listlessness or uneasiness.

During the night, as well as during the day, the
infant requires to be fed, but not so frequently. At
first it may demand the breast perhaps thrice in
the course of one night, but afterwards twice or only
once. Delicate mothers who are desirous to suckle
their infants should have undisturbed rest during the
night, the child being fed once or twice by the nurse
with a little cow's milk and water. This arrangement
will tend to preserve the mother's health, and enable
her to suckle her infant when she might otherwise
fail, and perhaps injure both her own health and that
of the child in the attempt to nurse. There are great
differences of constitution in children; some require
and digest double the quantity of milk which suffices
for others. The quality of the milk also varies with

the health of the mother; and according as it is more or less nutritious, the demand for quantity will vary. Hence it is truly important for the mother to be able to read aright the significant language of the infant, and, while she avoids too frequent feeding, never to refuse it the breast *when its call is clearly expressed* and its health is benefited by gratifying it. But if she mistakes the mere expression of uneasiness for appetite, and gives suck when only freedom from pain is required, the consequences will be an increase of uneasiness and indigestion in the infant, and probably irritation of the breast in the mother. When the infant rouses himself and seems rejoiced at the sight of his nurse, it is almost a sure sign that he is hungry. But if he continues unmoved and careless, or vomits frequently, or is plagued by colicky pains or a tendency to bowel-complaint, and especially if the evacuations are green and unhealthy, and the skin is hot, it is clear that he is getting the breast too often, and that his diet should immediately be regulated accordingly. The nurse's diet should be inquired into at the same time, as it may require to be modified.

Jaundice is often induced in infancy by neglect of these indications, and it will be in vain to attempt its cure by medicines unless the diet be speedily altered. Opiates, carminatives, and the other remedies usually resorted to, may lull or hide the expression of pain, but they will never effect a cure without the removal of the cause.

Fatigue, vivid mental emotion, and all other causes of violent agitation of the mother's system, produce

an immediate and injurious effect on the quality of
the milk. Hence the propriety, which every rational
mother will perceive, of preserving habitual equanimity
of temper, and of refraining from offering the breast
for some time after fatiguing bodily exertion, or, still
more, after much excitement of mind. From neglect
of this rule even fatal results have ensued, of which a
striking instance will be found at page 138.

It is now generally agreed that, during the first
six months, no kind of food is so congenial to the infant as its mother's milk. Between parent and child
there is a natural relationship of blood and constitution, which, during health, adapts them to each other
with a harmony and completeness that can scarcely
exist between the infant and any other woman. The
mother, therefore, is peculiarly bound, by every tie
of duty and affection, to become the nurse of her
child; and nothing but ill health and positive inability
can excuse her for devolving this duty on another.
Formerly, it was common in fashionable life to consign
the tender infant, without any cause, to the breast of
a stranger, to the injury alike of the mother and the
child; but now, reason and the better feelings of our
nature have so far obtained the ascendency, that,
except when interdicted by professional authority, an
attempt is made by most mothers to suckle their offspring, and generally with complete success.

It is quite true that, from feebleness of constitution or infirm health, some mothers are incapable of
nursing, and must resign the duty to others, however ardently they may long to fulfil it. But it is no

less true that, in many instances, the inability arises
entirely from the mode of life they choose to lead,
and from the want of ordinary self-denial in their
diet and general regimen. The secretion of milk
is a purely bodily function, and, consequently, is
affected by every change in the health. It is
copious and nourishing when the health is good, and
becomes defective or altered when that is impaired,
or the habits are improper. In the abstract, this is
admitted by every one; but when, in conformity
with the principle implied in it, we point out to an
uninformed mother the necessity of regular attention
to air, exercise, cheerful occupation, evenness of temper, early hours, and moderation of living, as the
means whereby she may enjoy sound health, and so
become a good nurse, we often find it very difficult to
make more than a momentary impression upon her.
Uninstructed in the laws of the animal economy, she
cannot perceive the importance of any observances
the good effects of which do not become palpable
within a few hours; and when perseverance in a right
course is recommended as an indispensable condition
of future benefit, she too often assents for the moment,
only to give way to the first fancy that flits across
her mind, or the first random advice that is offered
to her. Having no fixed principles by which to guide
her judgment, she cannot discriminate between what
is in accordance with, and what is in opposition to,
the laws of Nature; and hence her conduct becomes
capricious, inconsistent, and frequently injurious to the
infant whose welfare she is anxious to promote.

Next to irregularities in diet, one of the most frequent causes of deranged health, affecting the qualities of the milk, is the neglect of daily exercise in the open air. In the case of wet-nurses, this should be carefully attended to. The mother, unaware of the importance of regular exercise in sustaining the general tone of the system, is often guided by mere fancy or convenience in going out, and does not consider either the selection of the best time of day, or the length, kind, and regularity of exercise, as of the least consequence. Proper exercise in the open air is, however, an essential condition of health, and none of the bodily functions suffer sooner from the neglect of it than digestion and the various secretions. But as the special object of the present volume is the management of *infancy*, I must refer the mother to my other works for an exposition of the laws of exercise and digestion.

Except in the instance of either such delicacy of body or such excitability of mind in the parent as ought, in fact, to have prevented her from entering into the married state, or the accidental attack of some serious disease, it very seldom happens that the mother who pays due attention to the laws of health is unable to suckle her child. This truth might indeed have been inferred beforehand from the experience of the working-classes, among whom it is rare to meet with a mother possessed of the ordinary comforts of life who cannot nurse her infant. But then such a mother is generally placed in circumstances favourable to health. She is employed all day in active exertion,

is much in the open air, has a sufficiency of plain
nourishing food, without any temptation to excess in
quantity or to the use of stimulants, observes early
hours, and is free from the anxieties and restraints
of fashion. Were the rich compelled to be equally
observant of the laws of health, both during gestation and after delivery, we are entitled to infer that
they also would be excellent nurses.

The circumstances which, among the middle and
higher classes, are most influential in impairing the
fitness of the parent for the duties of a nurse, are precisely those which deteriorate the general health—
namely, neglect of exercise; living in over-heated,
ill ventilated rooms during the day, and worse ventilated rooms, often made still closer by drawn bed-
curtains, during the night; the use of soft, relaxing
feather-beds; dissipation of mind, or the absence of any
serious or healthful interest or occupation; indulgence
in late hours night and morning, and giving way to
passion and caprice of temper; eating more than the
system requires, or the stomach can digest; drinking
unseasonably or too largely of strong tea, malt liquors,
or other beverages; living in an unhealthy situation;
inattention to the state of the skin, and to proper and
sufficient clothing; excessive novel-reading; and, in
short, all the circumstances which I have elsewhere
commented on as destructive of health.* While such
causes as these are left in operation, the mother has
herself to blame, and not Nature, if she finds her bodily

* See the Author's works on "Physiology applied to Health and
Education," and on "Digestion and Diet."

functions disordered to such an extent as to deprive her of the power of nursing her offspring.

A sound state of the general health being the chief condition required to constitute a good nurse, every mother who wishes to suckle her own child ought to adhere scrupulously to that mode of life which experience has proved to be most suitable to her constitution.

If any mother who may read these pages should still remain unconvinced of the propriety of adhering to a simple and unstimulating diet while acting as a nurse, I would earnestly direct her attention to the unquestionable fact, that the best and healthiest nurses are to be found among women belonging to the agricultural population, who, although actively employed, and much in the open air, scarcely ever taste solid animal food, or fermented liquors of any kind, but live principally on vegetable and farinaceous diet. Mothers so circumstanced rarely find any difficulty in nursing their children, provided they have a sufficient supply of their simple food, and are not over-worked.* This result is of itself sufficient to prove that the best supply of healthy milk is to be derived, not from a concentrated and highly nutritious diet, but rather from one consisting of a due proportion of mild vegetable, farinaceous, and liquid food, with a moderate allowance of meat, and without either wine or malt liquor. Even as regards the quality of

* I do not allude to the miserably-fed and over-worked wives of the agricultural labourers in some districts of England, where the mothers have scarcely milk enough to suckle their children for three months.

E 2

the milk, there can be no doubt that a mild diet is of great advantage. The milk derived from the use of concentrated food is too rich and stimulating for most infants.

Supposing the health of both mother and child to continue good, and the supply of milk abundant, no reason whatever can exist for giving any other food till the child is six or seven months old, when the teeth usually begin to appear. Both medical men and mothers used to advise the addition of gruel, arrow-root, or some other farinaceous food, almost from the first month; and the common results were, impaired digestion and a greater liability to convulsions and other diseases of irritation, especially during the time of teething. But now a better acquaintance with the laws of the animal economy, joined with a more implicit reliance on the wisdom and benevolence of the Creator, has at last made us see that the more closely we adhere to the path which He has marked out for us, the more successful shall we be in rearing the young.

Unfortunately, however, mothers are sometimes unable to supply a sufficiency of milk for the adequate nourishment of their infants; and it then becomes a question how the deficiency is to be supplied. Where the mother is healthy and the milk good, but too scanty to be the sole sustenance of the child, the balance is decidedly in favour of her continuing to suckle, and giving some mild supplementary food. But if the deficiency proceeds from impaired health in the mother, from her milk disagreeing with the

child, or from any other cause likely to injure the
nursling, the substitution of another breast is clearly
indicated; and the sooner the change is made, the
better for both mother and child.

Where additional nourishment is required, the
principle for its right selection is, that the kind be
procured which is most nearly allied in its nature to the
mother's milk. Ass's milk, or cow's milk diluted with
water according to the age of the child, and slightly
sweetened, comes very near to the qualities of the
mother's milk, and therefore forms the best addition
to it, when such is required.* If it is found to agree,
nothing else should be given till the appearance of the
front teeth indicates the propriety of a change. But
when, as occasionally happens, milk proves too heavy,
and gives rise to frequent vomiting, acidity, flatulence,
and gripes, advantage may be derived from diluting
it with well-made barley-gruel, or arrow-root, instead of water. Sometimes, also, when diluted milk
disagrees, the addition of a small quantity of rusk,
or well-baked bread cut into slices and toasted almost
to dryness, then boiled in a small quantity of water,
to which milk is afterwards added, obviates every
inconvenience, and restores the evacuations to their
healthy state. But, as already remarked, these additions are seldom proper in the first months of infancy; and when the diluted milk is found to disagree, it behoves the physician to satisfy himself,
by careful examination, that no error is committed in
the mode of feeding, or in the frequency and quantity

* See above, p. 96, and APPENDIX C.

of tho meals, before having recourse to a change which
may itself become the source of new evils.

When supplementary food of any kind is found
necessary, we must bo careful to imitate Nature by
giving it very slowly. The milk drawn from the
breast does not flow rapidly, and therefore, when ass's
or cow's milk is given, a sucking-bottle should be
employed, through which tho supply should be equally
slow. The milk, if possible, should be used fresh from
the cow, and be made tepid, or as near as may be to
the temperature of tho mother's milk. This is best
done by placing the sucking-bottle in warm water for
a short time before feeding the child. To facilitate
swallowing, the infant ought to be supported in a reclining position while feeding, as the improper custom
of laying it on its back exposes it to the risk of
choking. The moment it indicates indifference to its
food, not a particle more should be offered.

In healthy infants the first teeth appear about the
sixth or seventh month, but in delicate children often
not till the twelfth or fifteenth month. In some
families the late appearance of the teeth appears
hereditary. The ordinary rule is to continue the
nursing till after the appearance of the teeth, provided
the mother retains her health, and the milk is good
and abundant, and agrees well with the child. It
is the state of the health of both mother and child,
and not the number of months since birth, which
ought to regulate tho diet. One child is as far advanced at four months as another is at six; and some
additional food is usually given about the sixth or

seventh month, not because it is the sixth or seventh month, but because at that age the incisor teeth are generally cut—a clear indication that the digestive organs are now prepared for other food. And, in like manner, children are usually weaned at the end of the ninth or tenth month, not because a certain period of time has elapsed, but because about that age certain changes in the system, indicating the propriety of an alteration of food, generally occur. When, therefore, those changes are delayed, the change of diet ought also to be delayed, even for months beyond the ordinary time, if the state of the child should render this necessary. It is, I repeat, the condition of the organism, and not the mere lapse of a certain number of months, which ought to determine the change of diet and the period of weaning.

About the time, then, when the front teeth appear, milk, sweetened, and thickened with a small proportion of arrow-root or barley-gruel, may be given twice a day, and the intervals between suckling be gradually lengthened. Where milk disagrees even when combined with farinaceous substances, barley-gruel, or weak chicken or veal broth, thickened with some kind of farinaceous food, may be substituted; care being taken to regulate the quantity according to the powers of the digestive organs of the child, and to give the food slowly by means of a proper feeding-bottle. If the child is lively and excitable, the gruel will suit best; whereas, if he is soft, lymphatic, and inactive, the chicken or even beef tea will prove more congenial to the system. One kind of food, however, will sometimes agree for a week or two, and subsequently produce indigestion; a change must therefore be made as occasion requires, and no obstinate adherence to routine be allowed to interfere with the welfare of the infant. When the bowels are confined, barley-gruel will suit better than anything else. When they are too open, boiled milk with arrow-root will be preferable.

The utmost care is necessary to keep the bottle with which the child is fed perfectly clean and free from all odour. The farinaceous food should never be added to the milk till the moment the infant is to be fed; and the bottle, immediately after it has been used, should be thoroughly washed and laid in a basin of cold water. The best artificial nipples are made of prepared India-rubber.

WEANING.

The next subject to be considered is the time and manner of *weaning*—a process which used formerly to be much more formidable than it is now.

The time of weaning ought to be determined chiefly by two circumstances,—the health and state of the mother, and the development and health of the child. When the health of the mother continues perfect, and the supply of milk abundant, weaning ought, as a general rule, to take place about the ninth or tenth month, when the development of the teeth usually shows that a change of food is proper. But in delicate children teething is often delayed several months later, and in such a case weaning ought also to be delayed, that the organism may be fully prepared for the change before it is carried into effect. Cases, however, occasionally happen, where the first teeth do not appear for a year, or sometimes two years, even when the children are not particularly delicate. This occurs as a peculiarity in some families. In most cases, the general development of the child must be more considered than the condition of the teeth.*

In weak scrofulous children the teeth are often very late in appearing, and this may generally be taken as a sure sign that the breast ought still to constitute the chief source of their nourishment, whatever their age may be. At the same time, if the child is not thriving, chicken-broth may be given once or twice a day, and its improvement under this treatment will be an indication that it may be gradually weaned.

If, before the expiration of the usual time of nursing, the supply of milk proves insufficient for the nourishment of the child, and the health of the mother begins to suffer, it may become necessary, for the sake of both, to wean it gradually before any indications of teething are seen. But in this case, weaning is recommended not as proper in itself, but merely as the smaller evil. To continue nursing under such circumstances would lead to more mischief than giving it up.

Weaning either too soon or too late is attended

* For the indications afforded by the progress of teething, see APPENDIX D.

with almost equal disadvantages; and unless under
peculiar circumstances, of which the physician is the
best judge, the development of the teeth, together
with the general condition of the child, ought to determine the time of weaning. It is fortunate when
weaning can be effected in fine weather, when the
child can be much in the open air; as nothing
tends more than such exposure to soothe the nervous
irritability by which the process is so frequently accompanied.

The important rule in weaning is, to accustom the
child gradually to the use of other nourishment, and
to withdraw the breast from it by equally slow degrees. Formerly the transition used to be made suddenly, to the direct injury of both mother and child.
Now, however, it is accomplished in such a gradual
manner that many sustain no inconvenience from it.
If, when the front teeth begin to appear (about the
sixth or seventh month, for example), some light food
be given once or twice a-day, and the quantity be
afterwards gradually increased and repeated so as to
lessen the desire for the breast in an equally gradual
manner, weaning will be found comparatively easy
and safe for both mother and child. It ought never
to be effected while the infant suffers under the irritation of teething or any active disease, as the risk of
convulsions or serious intestinal disorder would thus
be greatly increased.

After the child has been weaned, its principal
nourishment ought still to consist of the liquid or
semi-fluid substances which have for some time con-

stituted its supplementary food ; and no considerable change in this respect should be permitted until after the appearance of the eye-teeth. As growth advances, however, some addition may be made to the diet previously in use. But whatever modification of it is allowed, the utmost care should be taken to guard against too full and nourishing a diet soon after the weaning has been accomplished.

One of the chief sources of danger at the time of weaning is the tendency of the mother or nurse to consider every cry of the child as a sign of hunger, which she must immediately hasten to satisfy. By yielding to this impulse, she often unwittingly increases the natural irritability of the infant constitution, till, by the indigestion arising from too frequent feeding, more irritability passes at last into actual disease. It is, no doubt, painful to a mother's feelings to witness apparent suffering in her child; but it is still more painful to her to discover that she herself has been the instrument of converting a temporary evil into a source of serious danger to life. Rightly managed, the child soon becomes reconciled to the change in its diet, and resumes its natural placidity.

When a striking increase of appetite, amounting to craving, shows itself soon after weaning, and especially when it is accompanied by evident fulness in the abdominal region, it ought at once to arrest attention. Generally speaking, these symptoms are the result of over-feeding or of too rich a diet ; and if the errors be persevered in, the child's health will infallibly suffer from intestinal irritation and its usual consequence, glandular enlargement.*

Before concluding this branch of the subject, I must caution mothers and nurses very earnestly against having immediate recourse to medicine in order to remedy every little ailment which may appear during the time of nursing or weaning. Unfortunately, there is a common tendency to consider disease as an extraneous something thrust into the system, which must be expelled by force before health can be restored, and with which the mode of management has little or nothing to do: whereas disease is merely an aberration from the regular mode of action of the organism, generally caused by errors in regimen, and often to be put an end to by returning to a right course. The consequence of the above error is, that, on the first symptom of disease, medicine is resorted to for its expulsion, while the cause is left in undisturbed operation. The evil is consequently aggravated instead of being removed, and many children are thus destroyed by medicine who might have been restored to health by patient and well-directed care without the aid of the apothecary. It is the commonest of all declarations in the nursery, that " the child was uneasy, or griped,

* Some of the best remarks on artificial nursing and weaning are taken from a work by Dr Von Ammon, physician to the King of Saxony. Rearing by the hand is much more common in some parts of Germany than in this country; and as his opportunities of superintending it seem to have been numerous, his opinions are entitled to more than usual consideration. (" Die ersten Mutterpflichten und die erste Kindespflege." 3d edit. Leipzig, 1839.)

or feverish, and *I gave it so and so,*" without the most distant allusion being made to *why* it was uneasy or feverish, or whether anything was done to remove the cause. There is no more pernicious habit than that of having recourse to medicine in every ailment of the child; and the mother or nurse who makes frequent use of it without advice, is unfit for the duties imposed on her.

CHAPTER VIII.

To complete our sketch of the treatment of early
infancy, we have next to speak of the requisite
arrangements for cleanliness, exercise, and sleep.

In infancy, CLEANLINESS is of the first importance to
health. Not only is the skin extremely delicate, sensitive, and easily injured, but it is, as already described,
the seat of a continual *excretion* or *exhalation* of waste
matter, in the form of perspiration. The perspired
fluid holds in solution some animal matter and various
saline substances; besides which, there is a secretion
of an oily matter from the cutaneous surface, to keep
the skin soft and pliable, and also, in some degree, to
protect it from injury. This secretion is most abundant on the scalp, in the arm-pits and folds of the joints,
and also on the forehead and nose. It is this oily
matter which prevents the hair from becoming dry,
and causes water applied to the skin to gather into
globules. In the folds of the skin it prevents the
contiguous surfaces from irritating each other, as, by

their mutual friction, they would otherwise be apt to do.

In infancy, this oily secretion rarely exceeds in quantity what is absolutely required to preserve the softness and pliability of the skin; and during health, unless allowed ·improperly to accumulate, it never gives rise to any unpleasant odour.

When the impurities thrown out by perspiration are allowed to remain long in contact with the skin, they become a source of irritation, and, by obstructing its pores, impede farther exhalation. The consequence is, that the waste matter either is partially and hurtfully retained in the system, or escapes through some other channel, such as the bowels, kidneys, or lungs, at the risk of deranging these organs by over-tasking their powers. At other times the skin itself suffers, and becomes the seat of troublesome and obstinate eruptions.

Keeping in view the composition of the perspired matter, wo must provide, in the first place, for the ready escape of the invisible vapour which forms so large a portion of it; and, secondly, for the frequent removal of the solid saline residue left in contact with the skin. The former purpose will be completely effected by using a light and porous dress not too tightly fitted to the body, and by frequently changing it. The latter will be best accomplished by frequent and regular ablution with tepid water. Some recommend also the use of soap; but as the saline particles are soluble, and easily removed by water alone, and as the soap serves only to combine with and remove the oily secretion, I consider such an addition as in general unnecessary, and frequently hurtful, in early infancy. For removing any *external* or accidental impurity from the hands, face, or arms, soap is useful, and even necessary. But applied habitually to the whole body, it is injurious; for the removal which it effects of the protecting oily secretion leaves the yet tender skin dry, harsh, and subject to cracking and painful excoriations, and in every way more susceptible of injury than before. I have noticed this result even in adults, who were in the habit of washing the body with soap when in the warm bath. For a time I could not discover why many of them took cold after it, and it was only after continued experience that I found reason to ascribe it to the above-mentioned cause. On all ordinary occasions, then, ablution with pure soft water is to be preferred.

The safest and most convenient way of washing the infant in warm water is unquestionably by immersion in a bath comfortably arranged for the purpose, as recommended in Chapter VI. By this means its wet body is exposed to the air but for a moment, when about to be dried; whereas, when the child is placed in a small tub, with the greater part of the body out of the water, and is washed by laving the water over it with the hand or a sponge, the continued and repeated exposure of its delicate skin to the warm water and cold air alternately is very apt to be followed by chills or other bad consequences. The bath, therefore, ought always to be preferred;

and, while the child remains in it, the whole surface of the body, and especially the folds of the skin and joints, should be carefully rubbed with a soft sponge, so that every vestige of impurity may be removed. The infant should then be quickly but gently rubbed dry with soft napkins, and afterwards with the hand, and be carefully dressed.

The best time for washing it is in the morning as soon as it is taken out of bed; and for bathing, the evening, after its last meal, and before being put to sleep. If, from the delicacy of the child, or any other cause, it becomes necessary to give it the breast immediately on awaking in the morning, it is better to delay the washing and dressing for an hour or more, till digestion be advanced. This precaution is of importance, especially in the earlier weeks of existence, when the exertion would be likely to prove injurious if the washing or bath were used with a full stomach.

On account of the great susceptibility to cold which exists in infancy, and the difficulty with which the system resists the influence of any sudden change, the temperature of the water ought, at first, to be nearly the same as that of the body—namely, from 96° to 98° Fahrenheit, and always to be regulated by a thermometer as the only sure test. If the nurse judge by the hand alone, she will often commit an error of several degrees, according to the varying state of her own sensations. The younger the infant, the more rigidly should this standard be adhered to, as it is not till after growth and strength have made some progress that it becomes safe to reduce the temperature by a few degrees. The reason of this has already been sufficiently explained.

In addition to the regular morning ablution, the tepid bath should be repeated every evening for a few minutes. Properly managed, and of the proper temperature, it has the double advantage of soothing the nervous system and promoting an equable circulation of the blood towards the surface. To restless and irritable children, also, the evening bath is often of the greatest advantage, from the quiet and refreshing sleep which it rarely fails to induce. It ought not, however, to be either too long continued or used in a cold room, or immediately after nursing or feeding. With these precautions, the most unequivocal advantage often results from its use, especially in scrofulous and delicate subjects. But when used too warm, or continued too long, it is apt to excite undue perspiration, and to increase the liability to cold.

We occasionally, though rarely, meet with children who, from mismanagement or some other cause, are frightened by immersion in water, and others with whom the bath decidedly disagrees. In such instances, of course, it ought to be given up, and simple washing or sponging with tepid water should be substituted. But in all circumstances, the greatest care must be taken never to allow an infant to be exposed to the air with the skin even partially wet; for imprudent exposure may be productive of some serious inflammatory affection. Many of the complaints made

against the use of the bath arise entirely from injudicious management, and the neglect of the most
obvious precautions.

Some physicians and parents prefer the cold to the
tepid bath, even from birth; but reason and experience
concur in condemning it, and it is only when the infant is strongly constituted that it escapes unhurt
from the use of the cold bath. After the lapse of a
few months, however, the temperature of the water
used for the morning ablution should be gradually
reduced, provided the child continue healthy and the
season of the year be warm. I need scarcely add,
that when sufficient reaction and warmth do not
speedily ensue after the use of cold bathing, it ought
to be immediately abandoned, and the tepid bath substituted in its stead.*

At whatever temperature ablution and the bath are
used, gentle friction of the whole body afterwards,
with a soft dry towel or flannel, will be both useful
and agreeable. In warm weather the child may, before being bathed, be allowed to play about for a few
minutes undressed, and to enjoy the luxury of what
Franklin calls an air-bath. In this respect its own
pleasure may be consulted. If it is strong enough to
bear the exposure with advantage, it will seek it. If
not, it will shun the contact of the air, and of its
own accord seek for shelter. In the country, the children of the peasantry may often be seen, of a summer

* For farther information on this subject, see the author's work on
" Physiology applied to Health and Education," chap. v.

F

morning, disporting themselves with infinite glee *in puris naturalibus* at the cottage door.

Another important element of cleanliness in infancy is the immediate removal of every soiled or damp portion of the dress, and the careful washing from the skin of every vestige of impurity arising from either of the natural evacuations. In early infancy, the discharges from the bowels and bladder are frequent and involuntary; but after a short time, an attentive nurse can generally discover some indications of what is about to happen, and take measures accordingly. It is surprising how early regularity in this respect may be introduced, by a little care and attention on the part of the nurse.

EXERCISE.—In infancy, motion of the body is as essential to health, and the desire for it is as unequivocally manifested, as at any period of life. To regulate it properly, we have only to keep in view the state of the infant organism, and the laws under which the principal functions are performed; so that neither the bones nor the muscles, while in their soft and feeble condition, shall be required to do duty beyond their strength. In the beginning of life the exercise of the infant ought to consist simply in being carried about the nursery or in the open air, in a horizontal or slightly reclining position on the nurse's arm,—and in gentle friction with the hand over the whole surface of the body and limbs after the bath, an operation which is no less agreeable to the infant than beneficial in promoting a free and equable circu-

2

3

for their own amusement, excite their infants to
muscular exertion long before the organism is fit for
its beneficial performance. But while active exercise
is incompatible with the condition of the infant, the
passive exercise implied in being carried in the nurse's
arms and exposed to the wholesome and invigorating influence of the open air, is eminently favourable to its health, and should be adopted to a much
greater extent than it generally is. In a climate like
that of Britain, prudence is of course required to protect the infant with clothing suitable to the season,
and never to expose it needlessly in harsh damp
weather. When the child is born in summer or late
in spring, its exercise should be confined to the limits
of the nursery and adjoining room, well ventilated for
the purpose, for about ten or fourteen days; after
which it may be cautiously carried into the open air
for fifteen or twenty minutes at a time. But when
it is born in winter or late in autumn, it ought not to
be taken out till after the lapse of four or six weeks,
and then only in fine mild weather, and for a short time
till it becomes habituated to the air. The length of
time ought then to be gradually and greatly extended.

Whatever the season of the year may be, much
caution is required to avoid injury from thoughtless
exposure to the strong light of day, and more especially to bright sunshine. For several weeks the eye is
extremely delicate and susceptible of injury, and
vision very imperfect. If, therefore, the infant be
suddenly or rashly exposed to the rays of the summer

sun, or even to strong day-light, the structure of
the eye may be injured, and the sight weakened or
destroyed.

In fine summer weather, a child can scarcely be
too much in the open air, if the morning and evening
dews and chill be avoided; and therefore the daily
exercise out of doors should be gradually and cautiously extended, from fifteen or twenty minutes at
first, to an hour or two, and at last to several hours a
day, in proportion as it can be borne. Most infants
naturally delight in the open air, when they are sufficiently protected; but in winter and spring much
caution is required on account of the great and dangerous susceptibility of cold at that age, when the power
of generating heat is, as we have seen, so low. This
beneficial influence of moderate heat and injurious
effect of cold are exhibited on a large scale in the
relative mortality in infancy in temperate and cold
climates. Children thrive remarkably well in warm
countries up to a certain age; whereas in cold countries, and even during the winter in temperate regions,
they die in considerable numbers. In an inquiry
which was instituted by Dr Milne Edwards to discover the cause of the greater mortality of infants in
France during winter than during summer, and in the
northern than in the southern departments of that
country, this was proved to be owing chiefly to premature exposure to cold, in carrying the infants to the
office of the *Maire* within a few days after birth, for
the purpose of being registered in legal form. Ordinary medical experience confirms the inferences de-

ducible from these facts; for careful investigations
have shown that many children perish annually from
inflammation of the lungs, and other inflammatory
diseases, caused by imprudent exposure to cold, especially when the clothing is inadequate.

Influenced, then, both by experience and by knowledge of the infant constitution, we ought to beware
of exposing very young or delicate children to the
full force of the cold in winter or spring. After the
first month, healthy infants, if properly protected
from the weather, may be advantageously taken out
in fine days even in winter; but the early part of the
day, and the most sheltered situations and purest air,
should be chosen for the purpose. If, notwithstanding every precaution, the child give indications of
suffering, or of being depressed by the cold, we should
abstain for a time from sending it out, and give it the
necessary exercise in a large well-aired room.

When an infant is taken out for exercise, the nurse
should be careful never to carry it *in a sitting posture*,
during, at least, the first four or five months.   If this
precaution be neglected, its large and heavy head will
be observed to hang over on one side, in such a way
as to impede the breathing.   Hufeland mentions a
case in which even death was caused by a sudden
jerk of the head to one side in a very young infant.
The mother ought, therefore, to have a watchful eye
over the nurse while exercising the child, unless she
feels assured, from knowledge of her character, that
implicit confidence can be placed in her.   When the
child is carried out in the nurse's arms, the arm on

which it rests should from time to time be changed. This alternation will be equally advantageous to nurse and infant. After the fourth or fifth month, the sitting posture may be allowed for a few minutes at a time, if the child seems to like it.

In *lifting* young children, the nurse should be very careful always to place the hands, one on each side of the chest, immediately below the arm-pits, and never to lay hold of the child by the arms, as is sometimes thoughtlessly done. In infancy, the sockets of the joints are so shallow, and the bones so feebly connected with each other, that dislocation of the arms, and even fracture of the collar-bone, may easily be produced by neglecting this rule.

The common custom of dandling, swinging, and jolting very young infants, is highly improper. In a very moderate degree such exercises seem to be agreeable to them, and need not be prohibited ; but in the rough way in which they are sometimes administered, they cannot but be prejudicial.

When an infant is strong enough to be placed in a sitting posture, exercise in a child's carriage is preferable to being carried in the nurse's arms; but in cold weather, great care must be taken to protect the child by proper clothing from being chilled. That these little carriages are often so improperly used, is no reason against their proper and judicious use.

When a certain degree of strength has been acquired, a desire for more extended and independent motion gradually shows itself, which many nurses are in the habit of gratifying by fostering premature attempts at walking. The best way, however, of indulging this new craving, is to place the child on the carpet, and allow it to move and extend its limbs, crawl on all-fours, or tumble about at its own pleasure; putting, at the same time, a few playthings within its reach. To facilitate this, the ordinary long dress ought to be curtailed about the fifth or sixth month, or as soon as the power of self-exercise shows itself. If the weather be cold, a longer and warmer dress can easily be put on when the child is carried into the open air.

By exercise thus adapted to the state of the system, the infant will be strengthened, and learn to walk much sooner, and with a more firm and erect carriage, than if prematurely set on its feet and supported either by the arm or by leading-strings. The chest also will be more fully developed, and the whole system consequently benefited. With moderate caution on the part of the attendant, there is nothing to fear in thus indulging the infant; for it is even amusing to see how careful it generally is about its own safety when left to itself. When a mother takes entire charge of the exercise of an infant, and judges of its risks by her own anxious feelings, she is sure to err. But remove all external means of injury, and leave the child to its own direction, and it will very rarely hurt itself. It will crawl till its bones become firm enough to bear the weight of the body, and its muscles powerful enough to move them.

The next stage of exercise is WALKING; and here,

again, provided we do not stimulate the infant to premature efforts, we may safely trust to itself. After a
child has acquired a certain degree of vigour and command over its muscles by crawling about, it will begin
of its own accord to try to stand and walk, by laying
hold of chairs, or seeking a little support from the
nurse. But we should be careful not to accustom it
to rely too much on the guidance and assistance of
others. If we entice it to walk before the bones and
muscles are adequate to the exertion, the consequences
cannot fail to be bad. When support is given by
leading-strings, it is at the risk of compressing and
deforming the chest; when, on the other hand, the
child is upheld by one arm, the immediate effect is to
twist the spine and trunk of the body; while, in both
cases, the lower limbs are apt to bend, and the child,
by constantly trusting to its conductor's guidance and
protection, acquires a heedlessness in its exertions
which is prejudicial alike to body and mind. The
strong effort of the will required to execute every
movement gracefully and successfully is withdrawn,
and gives place to an indifference which is fatal to
unity of action in the delicate muscles. A child
trained to walk independently may no doubt get a few
falls; but, on the supposition that all hard bodies have
been removed out of its way, and that it is practising
on a carpet or a lawn, under the superintendence of a
watchful nurse, it runs far less risk of sustaining injury from falls than it is certain to do if leading-
strings and other artificial supports be substituted,
which tempt it into fallacious estimates of its strength,

and expose it to worse dangers from the carelessness
of its attendant. It is a great error to be so anxious
about an infant's safety as to watch its every movement, and be ready to sound the alarm at every trifling
risk. The personal experience of a fall teaches the
child much more effectually how to avoid future accidents than a thousand exclamations of caution from
its nurse, which are calculated to foster timidity and
irresolution far more than reasonable prudence and
presence of mind. In infancy, as in later life, the
grand principle of education ought to be to promote
SELF-REGULATED ACTION, whether of body or of mind,
and to guide inexperience to the mode in which
Nature intended the action to be performed. So long
as we continue to be machines moved by the will
and defended by the prudence of others, we cannot
acquire that strength of body or that degree of mental
endowment of which our constitution is naturally
susceptible:—even from early infancy, this principle
holds good. In our own country, we sometimes see
poor children but two or three years old acting as
guardians to infants little younger than themselves,
and displaying in that capacity a degree of intelligence,
steadiness, and presence of mind, hardly to be expected at so early an age.

SLEEP.—The management of sleep is the next subject for consideration in the treatment of infancy.

During the first month or two of life, the powers of
the system are wholly occupied in carrying on digestion, nutrition, and growth, and the time of the infant

is divided between sleep and feeding. Indeed, it can
scarcely be said ever to be awake ; and only after the
lapse of several weeks do sensation and consciousness
become sufficiently active and distinct to constitute
intervals of real wakefulness. At this period, then,
it is not so much the length of sleep, or best time for
it, that requires our attention, as the situations and
conditions under which sleep ought to be allowed.

From the first the infant should sleep in its own
bed or cot, care being taken to have it sufficiently
covered, particularly in cold weather. An excellent addition to the usual coverings of a child's
cot will be found in a small *duvet;* it is at once
the lightest and warmest of coverings, and may
be used or omitted according to the temperature of
the room.

After the first month, the bed should be without
curtains. These exclude air as well as light ; and
therefore, when the child goes to sleep, it is far better
to darken the room by means of window-shutters,
than to attach curtains to the cradle. When, again,
a nursery is so badly constructed that the cradle must
be exposed to a draught wherever it is placed, a screen
will afford the necessary protection. The modern suspended cot is an improvement on the old-fashioned
cradle, and its additional height from the floor is
useful in allowing greater accessibility to the mother's
bed.

As to the length of time to be allowed for sleep in
infancy, it has been already remarked that, for three
months after birth, nutrition and sleep constitute

nearly the whole sum of existence. The infant
awakes to feed, and presently goes to sleep again.
In proportion as the organism develops, the desire
for activity will increase, and that for frequent sleep
diminish ; and it is our business to follow in the footsteps of Nature, and merely remove any impediments
which accident may throw in her way.

Regularity also ought, as far as possible, to be observed in the hours of wakefulness and sleep. In the
animal economy, there is a periodicity adapted to
that of the physical world, which tends to the return
of the same state of the system at regular intervals,
and which it is very important to cultivate. Unless
regularity of sleep be established and adhered to,
neither mother nor child can enjoy that undisturbed
repose during the night which is so essential to health.
If the infant be encouraged to start up at any moment
of the day or night and demand the breast, or if this
be constantly offered to it as a means of soothing its
cries, whether it be hungry or not, perpetual restlessness and discontent must ensue ; and, these once
established as a habit, the mother's peace and enjoyment, along with the child's health and welfare, are
sure to be sacrificed. The infant may be quieted for
the moment in this way, but at the expense of ten-
fold trouble and disappointment afterwards.

While endeavouring to accustom the child to regular hours for eating, sleeping, and all other natural
operations, we should, especially as he grows older
and stronger, bear in mind that night is peculiarly
the season for sleep, and that no arrangement should

be permitted to interfere with the natural tendency to
it at that time. Guided by this principle, we should
endeavour to regulate the habits of the child in such
a manner as to appropriate an hour or two in the
middle of the day to that sleep which, more or less,
all children then require, till after two or three years
of age. Their activity may not be entirely expended,
but under a judicious system of management they
will be perfectly ready at this time for an interval
of rest; whereas, if they be excited to activity, and
sleep be deferred to a later part of the day, it will
always be at the risk of producing restlessness in the
early part of the night. To nervous, excitable children, the mid-day sleep is very beneficial; and it may,
in their case, often be continued with great advantage
for the first three or four years, and even longer.

When a child is put to sleep, whether by night or
by day, *light and noise ought to be carefully excluded.*
Even when these do not prevent sleep, they tend to
render it troubled and unrefreshing, and, by rousing
nervous sensibility, render the infant liable to spasmodic and convulsive attacks from any accidental
irritation. · Many persons act in direct opposition to
this rule, and think it of no consequence what talking
or noise goes on in the nursery, provided the infant
be not roused up broad awake. This is a great and
pernicious mistake.

When the stomach is distended, and digestion just
beginning, sleep is apt to be uneasy and disturbed.
The infant, therefore, ought not, as a general rule, to
be put to rest immediately after a full meal. During

the first month, no doubt, it goes to sleep directly
after having the breast; but at that early age it takes
little at a time. It is at a later period that the precaution requires attention.

So much must always depend on individual constitution, health, and management, that no fixed hours
can be named at which the infant should be put to
rest. If it sleeps tranquilly, and when awake is active
and cheerful, and if its various bodily functions are
executed with regularity, we may rest assured that no
great error is committed, and need not concern ourselves whether it sleeps an hour more or an hour less
than another child of the same age. Where, on the
contrary, it sleeps heavily or uneasily, and when
awake is either dull or fretful, and the other functions
are perverted, we may be certain that some error is
committed, and that the child is either rocked to
sleep immediately after a full meal, or otherwise mismanaged by the attendant.

There are few things which distress an anxious
mother, or annoy an impatient nurse, more than sleep-
lessness in her infant charge, and there is nothing
which both are so desirous to remove by the readiest
means that present themselves. A healthy child
properly treated, and not unduly excited, will always
be ready for sleep at the usual time; and when it
appears excited or restless, we may infer with certainty
that some active cause has made it so, and should try
to find this out and remove it. If no adequate external cause can be discovered, we may infer with
equal certainty that its health has in some way suffered,

and that it is sleepless because it is ill. In this case,
the proper course is to seek professional advice, and to
employ the means best adapted to restore the health ;
after which, sleep will return as before. From not
attending to the true origin of the restlessness, however, and regarding it merely as a state troublesome
to all concerned, many mothers and nurses are in the
habit of resorting immediately to laudanum, sedative
drops, poppy syrup, spirits, and other means of forcing
sleep, without regard to their effects on the disease
and on the system ; and are quite satisfied if they
succeed in bringing on the appearance of slumber, no
matter whether the reality be sleep, stupor, or apo-
plectic oppression. The mischief done in this way
is inconceivably great ; and in the Reports on the
Health of Towns which have been laid before Parliament, as well as in the Registrar-General's Returns of
Births, Marriages, and Deaths in England, we find
ample evidence that enormous quantities of quack
" cordials," " anodynes," and even spirits, are recklessly given to produce quiet and sleep, and are the
cause of many deaths. Flowers and strong-smelling
perfumes ought to be excluded from the sleeping
apartments of infants, as they act injuriously on their
delicate nervous system.

In infancy, as in adult age, it is highly conducive
to health and sound sleep that the night and bed-
clothes should be thoroughly purified by several hours'
exposure to the air every day, immediately after the
child is taken up. The effect of perfectly fresh coverings is soothing and healthful in a high degree.

CHAPTER IX.

It sometimes happens that, notwithstanding every attention, the inability of the mother to nurse her child becomes so decided as to compel her to desist from the attempt, and to procure a substitute. I shall now, therefore, consider the qualities by which the choice of a nurse ought to be determined.

From the exposition already given of the intimate relation which subsists between the constitution of the mother and that of her infant, the reflecting reader will readily infer that, in the healthy state, her own milk is that which is best adapted for the support and nourishment of the child; and that, when a nurse is required, care should be taken to select one resembling the mother as closely as possible in all essential points. As a general principle, this is unquestionably true. But in practice it often happens, that the very circumstances which force us to employ a nurse are those which also oblige us to depart from this principle, and prefer a woman of an entirely different constitution. Before entering on the consideration

of these exceptions, however, we shall first briefly
direct attention to several conditions, in regard to
which it is important to the infant that the nurse
should approximate more or less closely to the
mother.

In all ordinary cases it is an advantage that the
mother and nurse should be nearly of the same age.
By this I do not mean that, when a delicate young
woman becomes a mother at the premature age of
seventeen or eighteen, we should take pains to procure
a nurse equally immature in constitution; or that,
when a woman at the extreme verge of the child-
bearing period gives birth to an infant, we ought to
consign it to the charge of one equally advanced in
years. Neither of these extravagances is required;
all that is wanted is, that the offspring of a young
mother should be suckled by a young in preference to
an old nurse, and that the child of a woman in middle
life should be suckled by a nurse arrived at least at
maturity. This reasonable degree of adaptation between the nurse and child is required simply because
the quality of the milk is influenced by the time
of life, and the milk of a woman of forty years
of age is found not to be suitable for the infant
of a woman of twenty. In like manner, it is desirable that both mother and nurse should have been
delivered nearly about the same period, because the
quality of the milk alters with the lapse of time.
Some resemblance, moreover, between mother and
nurse in the general form and proportions of the
body is advantageous, as experience has shown that

the children of thin, tall mothers rarely thrive on the
milk of short, thick-set nurses. In selecting a nurse,
special regard ought also to be had to the general
constitution of the mother, whether our object be to
counteract or to develope the peculiarities which the
infant has derived from her.

The causes which disqualify a mother for nursing
may be divided into two kinds. Under the first head
may be included the comparatively rare cases in which
a well-constituted and previously healthy mother is
rendered incapable of nursing, either by a sudden
attack of illness, or by some unforeseen accident, not
admitting of an immediate remedy. In such cases,
the general principle applies almost without modification ; and if it were possible to procure what wo may
term a duplicate of the mother (that is to say, a nurse
resembling her in all respects), there cannot be a doubt
that she would be the fittest person to supply the
mother's place. Where, however, as most frequently
happens, a nurse becomes indispensable from the
mother's constitutional delicacy,—instead of seeking
points of resemblance to the parent, our chief object
is to find a nurse free from the constitutional debility,
and liberally endowed with all the properties in which
the mother is held to be defective. It is only by this
means that the infant can be preserved from the injurious influence of the impaired constitution of the
parent. Experience has amply proved that the
greatest benefit may result from transferring the
feeble child of a delicate mother to the breast of a
healthy and vigorous nurse,—to one, in short, whose

superiority lies in the very qualities in which the
parental constitution is most defective. At the same
time, the *general character* of the nurse's constitution,
however healthy, must not deviate too far from that
of the mother, otherwise her milk will not suit the
child.

I have already observed that, in all cases, regard
should be had to the relative dates of delivery of the
mother and nurse. This caution is required, because
the milk secreted immediately after the birth of the
infant is very different in its properties from that
which is secreted a month or six weeks later. This
can be remedied in a great degree by putting the
nurse upon a light, cooling, and rather fluid diet for
the first few weeks; and this should always be done
when her milk is older than that of the mother.
During the whole period of suckling, the diet of the
nurse should be strictly regulated. A tranquil mind
and even temper are particularly desirable in a
nurse, and care should be taken to inquire into this
point.

The pernicious influence of passion in the nurse
on the system of the child is strikingly illustrated
by a case mentioned in the excellent little work
of Dr Von Ammon, already referred to.* "A carpenter fell into a quarrel with a soldier billeted in
his house, and was set upon by him with his drawn
sword. The wife of the carpenter at first trembled
with fear and terror, and then suddenly threw herself
furiously between the combatants, wrested the sword

* Die ersten Mutterpflichten und die erste Kinderpflege, p. 102.

from the soldier's hand, broke it in pieces, and threw
it away. During the tumult some neighbours came
in and separated the men. While in this state of
strong excitement, the mother took up her child from
the cradle, where it lay playing, and in the most perfect health, never having had a moment's illness;
she gave it the breast, and by so doing sealed its fate.
In a few minutes the infant left off sucking, became
restless, panted, and *sank dead on its mother's bosom.*
The physician, who was instantly called in, found the
child lying in the cradle as if asleep, and with its features undisturbed: but all his resources were fruitless; it was irrecoverably gone." Cases so remarkable seldom occur in private life; but, unhappily,
there are many instances in which perpetually recurring fits of bad temper, especially near or during the
time of suckling, produce similar effects in a more
slow and gradual manner, but with almost equal certainty—and if anything can exert a salutary influence
on mothers who are prone to the indulgence of passion,
it must be the contemplation of such a case as that of
the carpenter's wife.

Another strong reason for rejecting a nurse characterized by a bad temper or other moral disqualifica-
tions, is the general system of mismanagement and
concealment which cannot fail to ensue, and which
it is sometimes so difficult for the mother to detect,
that the health of the child may be ruined without
any one being able to discover why it is suffering
at all. The natural character of the nurse, indeed,
makes such a difference in the manner of doing a

thing, and consequently exercises so direct an influence on the welfare of her charge, that the infant
will sometimes be observed to pine under treatment which appears, to a superficial observer, the
same as that under which it formerly throve. We
may be unable to point out a single omission in the
treatment required, yet, *in the manner* of conducting
it, enlightened maternal affection may, on careful
inquiry, discover a difference amply sufficient to account for the difference of effect. No watching or
exhortation by the parent can remedy a deficiency
like this; the only security against it lies in. a right
choice at the first.

When a mother suckles her own child, she takes
the alarm at once, and seeks an immediate remedy
when she finds the supply of milk insufficient for its
support. But it is otherwise with an ill-chosen nurse.
Not feeling the same strong interest in the well-being
of the infant, and afraid of losing her situation by
confessing that her milk is deficient, such a nurse is
often tempted to conceal the fact, and give the child
in secret some unsuitable food, in the hope that tho
deficiency will not be discovered. From the very
concealment which is practised, it is in the highest
degree improbable that the food so provided will be
either proper for the child, or given at proper times
and in a proper manner; and hence may arise indigestion and bowel-complaints, the true sources of
which, if entire confidence is placed in the nurse, may
never be suspected. We cannot, therefore, attach too
great importance to moral character in the selection

of a nurse, for every change is attended with serious inconvenience.

The choice of a nurse ought never to be finally decided upon without the sanction of a well-informed physician, whose duty it is to inquire and examine carefully into the state of her health. We have reason, however, to know that this very important and responsible duty is often performed in a very careless manner. External appearances are sometimes deceitful, and a healthy-looking nurse may in reality be very unfit for the purpose. At the same time, there are certain requisites which afford a strong presumption of fitness, and which ought therefore to influence our decision. Among these may be mentioned sound health, a good constitution, and freedom from any hereditary taint; moderate plumpness, a fresh and clear complexion, clear cheerful eyes, with well-conditioned eyelids, deep red-coloured lips without crack or scurf, sound white teeth, and well-formed, moderately firm breasts, with nipples free from soreness or eruption. But even with such indications, we should still inquire into the state of the principal bodily functions, and make sure that there is a sufficiently copious secretion of good milk. Of both the quantity and the quality of the milk we may form an opinion by examining the condition of the nurse's own child—whether it is plump and healthy, or the reverse. Of the good quality of the milk we may judge also by its bluish-white colour, somewhat watery consistence, slightly sweetish taste, and the absence of smell. Dropped into water it

should have a light cloudy appearance, and not sink
at once to the bottom in thick drops. But, upon the
whole, the surest test is that afforded by the state
of the nurse's child. If we find it healthy, active,
good-natured, and neatly kept, we have one of the
surest tests of the qualities of the nurse.

When a nurse is first installed, it is advisable that
the mother should for a time watchfully superintend
all her proceedings, and assure herself, by frequent
and unexpected visits to the nursery, that everything
is attended to with due regularity, and in a right
spirit. If it be found that the nurse is, of her own
accord, regular in suckling the child, scrupulously
attentive to cleanliness, gentle, patient, kind, and
never put out of humour by fretfulness, or by being
roused in the night, and that she is habitually contented, cheerful, and active, the mother may then lay
aside anxiety, and be thankful for her good fortune.
But if, on looking into the nursery unexpectedly, she
find the child hungry, fretful, or dirty, the room damp,
badly-aired, or over-heated, and the nurse sullen, indifferent, or slothful, she may at once decide that the
woman is unfit for her charge. When a good nurse
is once secured, the mother can scarcely overrate her
value, or be too careful to attach her to herself and
the infant, by treating her habitually with considerate
kindness and regard. But no excellence in the nurse
can absolve the mother from the duty of watching
over the health of her child in all essential points.
By doing this carefully in the case of her first
child, the intelligent young mother will understand

the management of her future children (we speak
from observation) much better than most nurses who
may have had the charge of numerous children, and
consider themselves experienced. Nurses are not
sufficiently educated to profit by their experience,
and, for the same reason, they are generally presump-
tuous and full of prejudices.

Of all the vices to which nurses are liable, one of
the most injurious is intemperance, whether open or
clandestine, and the analogous practice of taking
opiates or other stimulants, by way of procuring rest
and supporting the strength. Even the too liberal use
of porter or ale, so common with mothers and nurses,
is not unattended with permanent danger, and ought
to be scrupulously guarded against. Many women,
acting on the notion that extraordinary support is
required during the time of suckling, have sunk by
degrees into the lowest state of degradation, from imprudent, and what they considered necessary, indulgence in fermented liquors. We have already seen
that, when necessary, Nature provides for the demand
by a moderate increase of appetite and digestive
power, which ought to be gratified by ordinary wholesome food, but not excited still farther by the use of
fermented liquors of any kind. Occasionally, no
doubt, wine or malt liquor is plainly required to keep
up the health and strength; but in such cases its use
ought to be cautiously regulated according to the
necessities of the system. The custom, which prevails
too much in England, of allowing nurses large
quantities of strong malt liquor, is injurious to the

health and temper of the nurse, and still more so to
the infant whom she is suckling. The best nurses
require none; and the quantity allowed should in all
cases be moderate, and sanctioned by the medical
attendant.

But perhaps the worst of all the bad practices of
which a nurse can be guilty, and certainly the one
most directly destructive of infant life, is the habit in
which many mothers, as well as nurses, indulge, of
administering, of their own accord, strong and dangerous medicines to children. Not to mention the
thousands of cases in which health is injured by the
injudicious use of medicines in infancy, it appears
from a Return printed by order of the House of Com-
mons, of all inquests held in England and Wales in
1837 and 1838, in cases of death from poison, that 72,
or nearly one-seventh of the whole number, resulted
from the carelessness of mothers and nurses in administering medicines, with the properties of which
they were unacquainted, in doses far beyond those in
which they are ever prescribed by medical men. The
return shows, for example, that the deaths of very
young children (MOST OF THEM AT THE BREAST) from
opium or its preparations, were 52 ; and from opium
or laudanum, given by mistake for other medicine,
20 more.

In addition to such cases of absolute poisoning, and
to those so prevalent of late years among the manufacturing population, from the habitual drugging of
infants with laudanum, to keep them quiet or asleep
during their mothers' absence at the mill, it is well

known to practitioners that much havoc is made
among young children by the abuse of calomel and
other medicines, which may procure momentary relief,
but often cause incurable disease in the end; and I have
been astonished to see how recklessly remedies of this
kind are had recourse to, on the most trifling occasions,
by mothers and nurses, who would be horrified if they
knew the nature of the power they were wielding,
and the extent of injury they were inflicting. Whenever a child shows any symptoms of uneasiness, instead of inquiring whether it may not have been
caused by some error of regimen, which only requires
to be avoided to remove the suffering, many mothers
and nurses act as if it were indispensably necessary
to interfere immediately and forcibly with the operations of Nature, by giving some powerful medicine to remove the uneasiness, and if relief does not
soon ensue, by repeating the dose. In this way it
is not uncommon for a medical man to be sent for in
alarm, and told that the child began to complain at
such a time,—that, *notwithstanding* that a large dose
of calomel, or laudanum, or tincture of rhubarb, was
immediately given, and repeated several times, it is
still very ill, and becoming hourly worse,—and that,
if he cannot *do something* instantly, it will soon be beyond recovery. Whereas it may appear, on examination, that there was at first only a slight indisposition
which required no active treatment at all, and that
the urgent symptoms were caused solely by the intended remedies.

That there are cases of disease in which active

G

means must be promptly used to save the child, is
perfectly true; but these are cases of which no
mother or nurse ought to attempt the treatment.
As a general rule, indeed, where the child is well
managed, medicine of any kind is very rarely required;
and if disease were more generally regarded in its
true light, simply as an aberration, produced by some
external cause, from a natural mode of action, we
should be in less haste to attack it by medicine, and
more watchful, and therefore more successful, in preventing and removing it.   Where a constant demand
for medicine exists in the nursery, the mother may
be sure that there is something essentially wrong in
the management of her children.

It sometimes happens that the quality of the milk
becomes deteriorated by the unexpected renewal of
the monthly period in the nurse; and if the fact be
concealed, the child may suffer, without any suspicion
of the true cause being excited.   Occasionally it becomes necessary, in such circumstances, to change the
nurse.   At other times, if the nurse be really healthy,
the child will continue to thrive as well as before,
especially if assisted at intervals by a little suitable food.   The possibility of such a change taking
place ought therefore to be kept in mind, and a
remedy provided when it does occur, and is attended
with bad effects.   It is in the earlier months of infancy that serious mischief is most likely to arise
from this cause.   When the change occurs after the
sixth or seventh month, it is usually of less consequence.

CHAPTER X.

ARTIFICIAL NURSING.

ALTHOUGH the infant ought, if possible, to be brought up at the breast as already described, it sometimes happens that the mother is utterly unable for the duty, and that a suitable nurse is not to be had. In such circumstances no resource is left but to rear the child by the hand, as it is called, or artificial nursing.

This, of course, ought never to be resorted to where it can be avoided. Strong healthy children may thrive under careful management although denied the breast; but very few delicate children, and still fewer of those prematurely born, survive when brought up by the hand. Where the stomach and bowels are very irritable, as they almost always are in feeble children, the difficulty is greatly increased. The character of the climate, and the season of the year, also affect the result in a marked degree. But at all times, and under all circumstances, artificial nursing requires the most watchful attention and the greatest sacrifice of time on the part of the mother, as it is only by the most unremitting management

and judicious care that the disadvantages inseparable from it can be successfully overcome.   Under
favourable circumstances, however, many children
grow up in health and strength although reared
entirely by the hand.   In the south of Germany,
according to Von Ammon, this plan is followed to a
great extent where the mother is unable or unwilling
to suckle the child—and with a considerable degree
of success ; but in the north of Germany a nurse is
almost always preferred.

When a child is to be reared by the hand, we have
to determine, first, the kind of nourishment best
fitted to supply the place of the mother's milk ; and
secondly, the manner in which that nourishment
ought to be given.

Taking into consideration the imperfectly developed
state of the digestive organs at birth, and the simple
and harmless nature of the milk then secreted by the
maternal breast, we may safely infer that the most
suitable nourishment for the new-born infant will be
that which makes the nearest approach to its natural
food.   For this reason ass's milk deserves the preference over every other kind of food ; but when this
cannot be obtained, cow's or goat's milk, properly
diluted and sweetened, may be substituted.   At first,
about one-third of water should be added to cow's
milk, and a still larger proportion to goat's milk ; but
after a week or two the proportion may be gradually
diminished.   Much, however, depends on the food
which the animal is taking.   As a general rule, it is
safer to dilute rather freely, provided the supply to

the infant is abundant, as the superfluous water
readily passes off by the kidneys.[*]

The food of the infant ought to be given at the
same temperature as that of the mother's milk (96° or
98° Fahr.), because that is the heat most suited to
the organism of the child. In general, this condition
is little attended to by nurses; and yet the temperature might easily be determined, and all possibility of
mistake be prevented, by means of a thermometer.
In preparing the milk and water, it is better to heat
the water and pour it upon the milk, than the reverse. Both ingredients should be perfectly fresh and
sweet, and on no account should any remaining portion be set aside and heated again for a subsequent
meal. The infringement of this rule is a frequent
cause of severe and troublesome indigestion.

The manner in which food is given is also of importance, and accordingly we should follow Nature
and supply it very slowly. For this purpose, a sucking-bottle, fitted with an artificial nipple pierced
with very small holes, is generally used, and answers
much better than feeding by the spoon. The best
artificial nipples are made of caoutchouc; but, whatever material is used, great care must be taken not
to have the holes too large, else the milk will
flow too fast. The utmost cleanliness, too, is indispensable; and neither the bottle nor the nipple
should ever be laid aside after use without being
thoroughly washed with hot water, and afterwards

* For a full account of the composition of the milk of different
animals compared with that of woman, see APPENDIX C.

laid in cold water, to prevent any sour smell arising from the fermentation of the milk adhering to it. Neglect of this precaution, and especially allowing the milk to remain in the bottle for hours, cannot fail to do harm, as the want of perfect cleanliness and sweetness in the food, or in the vessels used in giving it, tends strongly to derange digestion. When an artificial nipple is employed, care must be taken not to have it of too great length ; otherwise the child may compress its sides in the act of sucking, and effectually prevent the milk from flowing at all.

The indispensable necessity of cleanliness, and the propriety of always using fresh milk and never reserving any portion of it for a subsequent meal, will be readily understood by those who have observed the rapidity with which milk becomes acid, and imparts to the bottle a sour, disagreeable smell, which it is extremely difficult to destroy.

The next points for consideration are the intervals at which a child brought up by the hand should be fed, and the quantity that should be given at a time ; and here, again, we cannot do better than take Nature for our guide.

We have already seen that, for two or three weeks after birth, the infant sleeps almost continually ; it wakes up for a moment at intervals to suck a little, and again goes to sleep. The stomach, being small and unaccustomed to its functions, can bear only a small quantity of nourishment at a time. In accordance with this natural arrangement, similar intervals should be observed in artificial feeding as in ordinary nursing; and the first sign of indifference may be safely relied upon as an indication that the child has had enough. As a general rule, six or eight table-spoonfuls will be sufficient at one time for the first two or three weeks; and it should be remembered, that rearing by the hand frequently fails solely from in-judicious and too frequent feeding. Many nurses, acting under the erroneous notion that liquid food contains little nourishment, think it necessary to administer it often, and thus oppress the stomach and excite vomiting. Observing, again, that immediate re-lief follows the emptying of the stomach, they farther adopt the notion that vomiting is a sign of health, and by this false reasoning are led to persevere in a course of positive mischief to the child. If the child is observed to thrive well and sleep quietly, and its bowels continue in a regular state, the proportion of water added to the milk may be gradually diminished after the first three or four weeks; and about the fourth or fifth month the milk may be given almost undiluted, provided the child is lively and active, and no contra-indication appears. Care should be taken to select the milk of a healthy cow, as it is well known that a large proportion of the cows confined in cities become the subjects of tubercular disease.

In general, the mode of artificial nursing above described will be found to answer better than any other which can be followed. When successful, it ought to be persevered in, as in natural nursing, till after the appearance of the front teeth, when the same change in diet will be required as if the child

had been brought up at the breast. But in both instances we should be careful not to anticipate Nature
by making the change before the advance in the
organism indicates its propriety.

In some constitutions, cow's milk does not agree
when merely diluted and sweetened, but answers perfectly well when a large proportion of water and a small
quantity of any well-prepared farinaceous substance
is added. When, therefore, after the first month or
two, diluted milk does not agree, a small proportion
of farinaceous food, such as arrow-root, sago, barley-
gruel, and, after these, rusks well boiled, may be added
to the milk—the water being first strained off. The
bouillie in common use in France as the first food of
infants is made by gently roasting the best wheat-
flour in an oven, then boiling it for a considerable
time, either in water or in milk and water, and adding
sugar to it. When carefully made, not too thick, and
free from knots, it is considered an excellent food,
especially when the use of milk excites a tendency
to diarrhœa or colicky pains. On changing to the
bouillie, digestion often improves, and the evacuations become healthy and painless.

In some instances, especially when the bowels
are sluggish, thin barley-gruel, with or without the
addition of weak chicken-tea or beef-tea, answers
well. The grand rule ought to be, to follow what
seems best suited to the individual constitution.
In soft, flabby children, the chicken or beef tea is
often most useful ; while in thin, active, and irritable infants, the milk and farinaceous diet answers

best. But in trying the effect of any alteration, we must not be too rash, and, because no advantage is apparent within a day or two, conclude that therefore it will not agree. Often the effects of a partial change of diet show themselves so gradually, that it is sometimes only after a week or two, or even longer, that we can decide whether benefit will result from it or not.

In some children of a lymphatic constitution and low vitality, it is necessary to begin the use of chicken-tea, mutton-broth, or beef-tea, earlier than usual, as any less animalized food does not agree with them. In general, however, it will be soon enough to have recourse to animal broths some time after the incisor teeth have appeared. But if the milk and farinaceous diet already recommended shall be found to disagree, chicken-tea or weak mutton-broth, to which a little arrow-root, or ground rice, or rusk, is added, ought immediately to be tried, provided we make sure beforehand that the indigestion proceeds from the nature, and not from the quantity, of the food previously in use. In general, EXCESS IN QUANTITY, OR TOO FREQUENT FEEDING, IS THE REAL CAUSE, although the blame is always laid upon the *quality* of the food.

The great difference between farinaceous food and animal broths is, that the former nourishes without exciting, while the latter are always more or less stimulating. As in infancy the natural tendency is to excitement, milk and farinaceous substances are in ordinary cases most suitable ; but occasionally we meet with infants so defective in constitution as to

require some stimulus. In such cases, chicken-tea,
or even beef-tea, may be used with advantage, provided due caution be exercised to avoid making it too
strong or giving too much of it, and to leave it off the
moment any indication of its doing harm is perceived.
It is in foundling hospitals, and other receptacles for
poor and weakly children, that the greatest benefit is
obtained from the temporary use of animal broths;
just because it is such infants who require and bear
the stimulus which attends their use. But it would
be a great mistake to infer that the healthy, well-
constituted infants of the middle and higher classes
require, or will not suffer by, the premature use of
animal food, even in its mildest form.

In whatever way the infant is brought up, ITS
TREATMENT AFTER BEING NURSED OR FED is far from
being a matter of indifference. During the first weeks
after birth, it will fall asleep immediately after having the breast; and this, as being the order of Nature,
ought rather to be encouraged. If, from thoughtless
gaiety or activity in the nurse, it be dandled or carried
to the window, or otherwise excited, indigestion will
be apt to follow; accompanied, probably, by nervous
irritation and colicky pains or bowel-complaint. Even
when so much sleep is no longer required, quietude
for some time after feeding should be encouraged, as
much bodily action immediately after meals is unfavourable to easy digestion, particularly in a delicate
constitution.

CHAPTER XI.

Having obtained a general acquaintance with the peculiarities of the infant constitution, and its immediate management, at birth, during the period of nursing, and at that of weaning, we have now to consider the external conditions and mode of management which experience has shown to be most conducive to the full and regular development of the infant organism, and the preservation of infant health. Of these, some, such as the locality in which we live, and the purity of the air we breathe, are so invariable and so decided in their action on the infant constitution, as to leave no difficulty in laying down rules with regard to them, which shall admit of universal application. Others, again, such as food, clothing, and exercise, vary so much in their effects, according to the age and constitution, &c., that we require to exercise much discrimination in modifying them to suit the circumstances of the individual case ; and it is here that the counsel of the medical attendant comes in with marked advantage. As most of what

may be called the general conditions of infant health
are more or less directly connected with the NURSERY,
it will be convenient to treat of them all under that
head.

A well-situated, well-arranged, and well-managed
nursery is more important to the health of the infant
than most parents are aware of, because it combines
within its range various agents which are in constant
although silent action on the constitution, and exerts
an influence for good or for evil on the whole animal
economy. When it is borne in mind that, from the
nature of the climate of this country, infants of the
middle and higher classes spend, during great part of
the year, twenty of the twenty-four hours of their exist-
tence within doors, the importance of attending to the
purity of the air of the nursery will appear evident.
Where, from an unsuitable situation, or imperfect
house-accommodation, the local influences are of an
unfavourable kind, the infant too often falls a sacrifice.
Where they are favourable, on the other hand, even
children of a delicate constitution will sometimes grow
up strong and healthy. Of this general truth the Government inquiries into the sanitary condition of
towns and villages furnish manifold and most instructive proofs.

It may however be objected, that among the poor,
and even among the less wealthy of the middle ranks,
necessity and not suitableness often determines the
choice of a residence, and the appropriation of the
rooms. But admitting this to be the case, it is still
an advantage to be acquainted with the local con-

ditions and domestic arrangements most conducive to infant health. Even among the working classes, there are few indeed who, when once convinced of the existence of an evil, will not or cannot do something to mitigate the disadvantages under which they suffer, and at least choose between a greater and a smaller evil. If they *must* reside within a certain distance of the scene of their daily labour, they may nevertheless have it in their power to prefer a better to a worse locality, and a better to a worse constructed house within that limit. But before they can attach any importance to such a choice, they must be made aware of the influence of surrounding circumstances upon their own and their children's health; and hence it is nearly as much for their advantage as for that of the rich, that they should be made acquainted with the facts required for the guidance of their judgment.

SITE OF THE HOUSE.—The first and most essential requisite in a nursery is the constant supply of pure air. To obtain this, a residence should be selected in a dry and rather elevated situation, removed from humidity and all sources of contamination, and, at the same time, sheltered from the violence of the wind. When a choice can be made, the country should be preferred to the town; as one of the clearest results for which we are indebted to the late statistical returns and sanitary reports is the fact of the superior healthiness of the country, especially for the young. The close vicinity to the house of trees or thick

shrubbery, of ponds, undrained meadows, or sluggish
water-courses, ought to be scrupulously avoided; for,
however ornamental they may be, they are invariably
prejudicial to health, not only from the humidity and
in many cases the impurities which they diffuse
through the air, especially at night, but also from the
obstruction which they present to free ventilation.
For the same reason, narrow valleys, and localities
shut up by thick woods or overhung by hills or
mountains, ought never to be chosen as the sites of
houses or villages. From overlooking the unfavourable influence of a stagnant humid air, families going
to the country in pursuit of health often sustain
serious injury, by settling in situations which a better
acquaintance with the laws of the animal economy
would have taught them to be very ill suited to the
infant constitution.

For those who are obliged to reside in towns, it is
of great importance to secure the best situation within
their reach. Even in point of economy, not to mention the suffering and anxiety attendant on illness, it
will be cheaper to pay more for a suitable house in a
dry, well-aired quarter, than a smaller sum for one in
a low-lying or crowded part of a town.

In addition to a dry and airy situation, a good
exposure and cheerful prospect are well worthy of
attention in the selection of a residence for the young.
In a cloudy and uncertain climate, like that of Britain,
a southern aspect is extremely desirable, not only
because it is warmer and more cheerful, and allows
of a more free admission of air, but because the

agency of sun-light, as a gentle and wholesome stimulus, is scarcely less necessary for animal than for vegetable life.   Deprived of its beneficial and enlivening stimulus, the child becomes pale and sickly in appearance, its blood is imperfectly oxygenated, and a proneness to diseases of debility arises.

A situation with a gay and cheerful aspect is also particularly desirable, because it is one of those silent but constantly operating agents which imperceptibly but certainly influence both the health and character of a child.   And it ought never to be forgotten, that in exact proportion to the susceptibility of the infant organism is the importance of attending to all these apparently minute points.   A dull and confined prospect is a source of dulness and ennui to the naturally active mind of a child, which cannot feel dispirited or gloomy without suffering in its health and its development; so that, whether we regard its bodily strength or its mental character, we should be equally solicitous to provide for it a cheerful and enlivening prospect.

The NATURE OF THE SOIL on which a house stands, and the existence or non-existence of efficient drainage, also exert no small influence on its salubrity. A dry, gravelly soil, or at least one thoroughly drained to some depth, ought always to be preferred. A damp soil necessarily imparts humidity to the lower part of a dwelling, and seriously affects its salubrity.   An elevated site is no guarantee of dryness of soil: on some hills moisture abounds as much as in a level

marsh; and from overlooking this fact, great errors are
often committed in selecting sites for country-houses.

POSITION OF NURSERY.—In selecting rooms for a
nursery, those which have a southern exposure should
be preferred, for the reasons already mentioned when
treating of the locality. That a nursery ought also
to be LARGE, AIRY, EASILY WARMED and EASILY VENTI-
LATED, will, I think, be readily admitted; for, without
such conditions, it is evidently impossible to surround
the infant with that pure and renovating atmosphere
which is indispensable to health. In one respect,
indeed, pure air is even more essential to the formation of good blood than supplies of proper food.
The influence of the air we breathe NEVER CEASES FOR
A SINGLE MOMENT OF OUR LIVES. By night and by day
respiration goes on without a pause; and every time
we breathe we take in an influence *necessarily* good
or bad, according to the quality of the air which sur-
rounds us. No wonder, then, that a cause thus permanently in operation should, after a lapse of time, produce great changes on the health; and no wonder that
attention to the purity of the air we breathe should
amply and surely reward the trouble we bestow in
procuring it. Accordingly, of all the injurious influences by which childhood is surrounded, none operates more certainly or extensively than the constant
breathing of a vitiated air; and, on the contrary, few
things have such an immediate and decided effect
in renovating the health of a feeble child as change
from an impure to a pure atmosphere.

Vitiated air and bad food are the two grand sources of that hydra-headed scourge of infancy and youth in this country—*scrofula;* and either of them, in a concentrated state, is sufficient to produce it without the co-operation of the other. But when both are combined, as they often are among the poor living in the lanes and cellars of our larger towns, then scrofula in its worst form is the result. Accordingly, we can produce scrofula in the lower animals at will, simply by confining them in a vitiated atmosphere, and restricting them to an impoverished diet. Of the latter cause I shall have occasion to treat afterwards.

VENTILATION OF THE NURSERY.—Scrofula, in one or other of its numerous forms or complications, is acknowledged to be in this country perhaps the most prevalent and fatal disease which afflicts the earlier years of life. It is estimated that tubercular disease, in all its forms, including pulmonary phthisis, destroys on an average 65,000 persons annually in England. So powerful is the continued breathing of a cold, damp, and vitiated atmosphere in producing it, that where such a cause is allowed to operate, the most promising combination of other conditions will often prove insufficient to ward off the evil. Baudelocque even goes so far as to insist that impure air is " the true cause, the only cause perhaps, of scrofulous disease: . . . . wherever we find scrofula, that cause exists; where it exists, we find scrofula; and where it is absent, scrofula is not known." I agree with Sir James Clark, by whom this passage is quoted, in thinking that Baudelocque's conclusion is rather overstrained; but the opinion which it embodies is nevertheless instructive, as an additional testimony to the highly deteriorating influence of a vitiated atmosphere. Sir James himself, indeed, remarks, that were he to select the two circumstances which more than any others influence health during the growth of the body, " they would be, the proper adaptation of food to difference of age and constitution, and the constant supply of pure air for respiration."* In another place he expresses the conviction, that living in an impure atmosphere is even more influential than defective food in deteriorating health, and that the immense mortality among children reared in workhouses is ascribable even more to the former than to the latter cause.

In an excellent little treatise on scrofula, published so long ago as 1810, the late Mr Richard Carmichael of Dublin, who afterwards did so much to elevate the character of the medical profession, and to stamp his authority with weight, drew attention to this cause, and, on the strongest evidence, denounced the great impurity of the air in the Dublin House of Industry as tho grand cause of the excessive prevalence of scrofula among the children at the time he wrote.

I have already noticed the very great mortality which occurred year after year among the infants in the Dublin Lying-in Hospital, till its cause, vitiated air, was at last discovered and obviated, and the mortality

* On Consumption and Scrofula, p. 233.

consequently reduced from one in every *six* to only *one
in every twenty* children, within the first nine days, on
an average of five years. Now, the mortality is only
one in *forty*. That, notwithstanding all our boasted improvements, impure air is still a very frequent source
of disease in infancy, may be safely inferred from the
great mortality in early life which takes place in most
of the larger towns as compared with that in country
districts.

Dr Farr, who draws up and analyzes the returns of
the Registrar-General, distinctly attributes the excess
of mortality in towns to the impurity of the air as the
chief cause. "The occupations in cities," he says,
"are not more laborious than agriculture, and the
great mass of the town population have constant
exercise and employment; their wages are higher;
their dwellings as good, their clothing as warm, and
their food certainly as substantial, as that of the agricultural labourer. The Poor-Law Inquiry and successive Parliamentary Committees have shown that
the families of agricultural labourers subsist upon a
minimum of animal food, and an inadequate supply
of bread and potatoes. *The source of the higher mortality in cities is therefore the insalubrity of the atmosphere.*" In accordance with this conclusion, Dr Farr,
after a careful investigation of the returns from a great
variety of localities, affirms that "it will be found,
cæteris paribus, that the mortality increases as the
density of the population increases; and *when the
density and the affluence are the same, that the rate of*

* Registrar-General's First Report, p. 79.

*mortality depends upon the efficiency of ventilation, and of the means which are employed for the removal of impurities."** If these inferences be correct (and all subsequent investigations tend to confirm them), the reader will feel no surprise at the earnestness with which I insist upon purity of air as essential to the preservation of infant health.

It may be said that, to prove the effects of habitually breathing a vitiated atmosphere, I have referred only to extreme cases. This is quite true ; for it is by well-marked cases that the nature and extent of the evil can be most clearly demonstrated. But the same principle applies to every degree of impurity. The only difference is in the intensity of the result, and this is a point that parents should ponder well. If breathing a very vitiated air so deteriorates the blood as to cut short life by convulsions within nine days, as was the case in every *sixth* infant in the Dublin Hospital, the less vitiated atmosphere of an ill-ventilated nursery will impair the quality of the blood in precisely the same way, and with equal certainty, but only less rapidly. The chief difference is, that in the one case the fatal consequences follow in a very short time, whereas in the other the health is only more slowly undermined, and a foundation is laid for diseases which may not prove fatal till after the lapse of years.

It is obvious, then, that rooms appropriated for nurseries should be in the higher part of the house, large, cheerful, not overcrowded with furniture, and provided

* Registrar-General's First Report, p. 79.

with the means of ample ventilation without exposing their inmates to currents of cold or damp air. No mother ought to be satisfied with herself until, in obedience to the demands of the infant constitution, she has provided for her children the most suitable and best-aired nursery within her power, and strictly prohibited every kind of operation by which its atmosphere can be vitiated, or its cleanliness impaired. If the size of the house will admit of it, the day-nursery should be entirely separate from the sleeping-room. The advantages of this are too evident to be dwelt upon. If there is only one room, it is almost impossible to secure adequate ventilation, because, even in summer, the draught from open windows is attended with risk, and, during at least two-thirds of the year in this country, the cold and damp atmosphere of our climate renders it impracticable to keep them open safely for a sufficient length of time, and sufficiently often. But the case is altogether different when there is a day-room in addition. Closely-drawn curtains, and other appliances by which a free supply of air is systematically cut off from the young, are highly prejudicial.

In the exposition of the peculiarities of the infant constitution given in a preceding chapter, it was shown that nervous sensibility predominates in early life, and modifies every infantile disease ; whatever tends, therefore, to moderate its excess is, to a certain extent, a promotor of health. Pure air, considered in this point of view—in its wholesome action on the nervous system—cannot be over-estimated. It is one

of the safest and most powerful nervous sedatives and
tonics ; and hence, among country children who are
constantly in the open air, we very seldom find that
morbid nervous excitability which afflicts so many of
the children of populous towns, and those of the
higher ranks who are brought up in close rooms.
In infancy, accordingly, pure air is an invaluable
means of diminishing the irritability attendant on
teething.

However suitable in size and situation the nursery
may be, adequate VENTILATION—*i.e.*, a *frequent*, and still
better a *continuous*, *renewal* of the air contained in it—
is indispensable to health. Caution must however be
exercised in effecting this, especially in winter. Before
the windows and doors are thrown open for a thorough
purification in the morning, the children should be removed into another room, and at all times they should
be kept out of the way of draughts from open windows
or doors, dust from sweeping, and damp from washing
the floors. It is for this reason that two rooms are so
desirable for the nursery.

When the weather is cold and the air moist, the
windows ought never to be thrown open till the children are removed and the sun has been for some time
above the horizon. The bed-clothes should be turned
down as soon as the child is taken up, and should be
exposed to the air for several hours, that they may be
entirely freed from the effluvia accumulated during
the night. This point is in general too little attended to.

Temperature of the Nursery.—Pure air being provided for, the next point which calls for consideration is the due regulation of the temperature of the nursery, a circumstance which is also of much importance, because, like the quality of the air, it is in almost continual operation. The atmosphere of the nursery ought, during the first few weeks, to be kept comfortably and equably warm, and never allowed to fall below 65°. For the first few days the temperature may be raised with propriety to 70°, if ventilation is duly attended to; but excessive heat and closeness must be rigorously guarded against.

In this country, open fire-places are in general use in nurseries, and they have the advantage of ensuring a certain degree of ventilation; but they are also the causes of many and serious inconveniences. By the constant rush of air to the fire, cold draughts from the doors and windows are necessarily produced, and it is often almost impossible to prevent mischief from the chills to which they give rise. A large screen placed behind the door to intercept the current of cold air, and diffuse it through the room, affords some protection. In winter this is especially necessary, as every time the door is opened a blast of cold air enters, quite sufficient to cause illness in a delicate child exposed to its direct influence. Cross draughts of air also ought to be guarded against by some similar contrivance.

In nurseries, the fire-place should be fenced with an iron or wire grating, as the surest protection against accidents; and care should be taken at all times to avoid exposing the infant to the glare and heat of a bright fire, and to prevent the older children from habitually placing themselves too near it.   Inflammation of the eyes, and even convulsions, are sometimes induced in infants by neglect of this precaution—the great delicacy of the infant organism rendering it peculiarly susceptible of injury, even from causes which exercise very little influence upon adults.

But, while due care is taken to protect the infant from cold, every approach to overheating must be scrupulously avoided.   When the temperature of the nursery is habitually too high, a degree of general relaxation, and of excitability of the nervous system, is induced, which greatly favours the development of the irritative and convulsive diseases to which infants are naturally liable, and which are so often the causes of premature death.   Another important consideration is the additional risk incurred by the transition to the cold external air, when the child is taken out for exercise.   The frequency of pneumonia, or inflammation of the lungs, in infancy, arises chiefly from this cause.*

As the system always endeavours to accomodate itself to the circumstances in which the person lives, it is clear that, if a child spends twenty-three hours out of every twenty-four in a heated atmosphere, its own power of generating heat will become propor-

* For some details on this very fatal disease in infancy, see AP-PENDIX D.

· tionally reduced ; so that when it is suddenly exposed, during the twenty-fourth hour, to the colder
open air, it is more liable to suffer from the transition than if it had been previously habituated to a
mild temperature.

CHAPTER XII.

DURING the earlier months of infancy, the child is intended to draw its whole nourishment from its mother's breast; the power of suction alone is required, and for this the action of the tongue, lips, and cheeks is amply sufficient. Accordingly, for some time after birth, the jaws are short, shallow, and unprovided with teeth; and the muscles which put them in motion are small, feeble, and delicate in structure.

But in the course of a few months, as the infant slowly advances towards a state of development in which a more consistent and nutritive food becomes necessary for its support, a corresponding change is observed to take place in the organism. The bones of the face gradually expand in their dimensions; the jaws increase in length, depth, and firmness of structure; the gums become more elevated and resisting on their upper edge; the cavity of the mouth enlarges; the muscles which move the jaw increase in size and power; and, in proportion to these changes, the infant manifests an increased tendency to carry to its mouth every object it can lay hold of, thus evidently contributing to develop still farther the bones and muscles concerned in mastication.

About the seventh month, however, a still more remarkable change begins, which does not terminate till after the end of the second year. I allude to the successive cutting of the first set of teeth, a process on the right management of which the immediate safety and future welfare of the infant very closely depend.

Teething, being a natural process, is not necessarily attended with danger, and under proper management a healthy child generally passes through it without much actual suffering. But in delicate or mismanaged children, teething is often the cause of much danger, and consequently of much anxiety to the parents. The possession of sound views in regard to it is therefore important.

The condition of the bodily organs will, as a general rule, be found exactly adapted, at every period of life, to the wants of the individual. From the infant at the breast, for example, teeth are withheld, because they would be not only useless, but an encumbrance, by interfering with its sucking. At a later period, however, when the infant's natural food is no longer fluid, but firm and consistent, teeth are given; because without them such food could not be broken down, or formed into a soft mass with the saliva, to fit it for being easily swallowed and perfectly digested. So also, when, from weakness of constitution or the effects of disease, the development of the system goes on with

unusual slowness, and solid food is not so soon required, the appearance of the teeth is also delayed;
thus affording another proof that weaning, and the
change of diet connected with it, ought to be regulated
by the progress of the organism, and not merely by
the number of months which have elapsed since the
child was born.

The TEMPORARY or MILK TEETH—twenty in number
—consist of eight *front, incisor,* or *cutting* teeth, four
canine or *eye* teeth, and eight *molar* teeth or *grinders.*
They begin to appear about the sixth or seventh
month, and are generally all developed at the age of
from two to two and a half years. About the seventh
year these temporary teeth begin to fall out, and are
by degrees succeeded by the permanent teeth, the last
four of which sometimes do not appear before twenty
or twenty-five years of age, and hence are called the
wisdom-teeth.

The PERMANENT TEETH—thirty-two in number, sixteen in each jaw—are divided into eight *front* or *cutting* teeth, four *canine* or *eye* teeth, and twenty *molar*
teeth or *grinders.*

Although even the first teeth are not cut earlier
than the sixth or seventh month, the rudiments of
both sets exist in the jaw long before birth. As it
would be out of place to trace their progress in a work
like this, I shall content myself with stating that the
ossification of many of the milk teeth is far advanced
even at birth, and that a certain degree of regularity
is observed in the order of their appearance.

The middle two incisors of the lower jaw are

generally the first cut, and are commonly soon followed by those of the upper jaw. After an uncertain interval, these are succeeded by the *lateral* incisors in both jaws.   After another interval, which brings the child to about the fifteenth or sixteenth month, sometimes the anterior molar, and sometimes the canine teeth, come next in order; and between the twentieth and thirtieth months the posterior molar generally also appear, and thus complete the whole of the milk teeth.

Generally speaking, teething has two distinct stages. In the first, the capsule of the tooth seems to swell and press upon the neighbouring parts; while, in the second stage, the tooth rises upwards, presses against, and then passes through the gum. The second process does not always follow the other immediately. On the contrary, a considerable interval may elapse between them, during which all goes on quietly.   Active symptoms of teething are thus often experienced without any teeth making their appearance; but, perhaps a few days, or a week or two later, the work is resumed, or, as now and then happens, the tooth has appeared without the system having undergone any additional disturbance.

" The first stage of teething is indicated by symptoms of general irritation in the mouth, and of some constitutional disturbance. The child becomes restless, and the saliva begins to flow in quantities from the mouth, and on the least uneasiness the infant cries, but in a little while smiles again with its wonted placidity.   Tears and smiles thus succeed each

other at intervals. The eyes and cheeks become red,
the appetite capricious, and thirst frequently considerable. Sleep is disturbed or interrupted by dreams,
and a general expression of uneasiness pervades the
frame. The gums, which were at first unaltered, begin to swell, and become inflamed and painful. The
child now carries everything to the mouth, and is
evidently relieved by rubbing the gums. The bowels
at this time are generally unusually open; and as a
certain degree of bowel-complaint is beneficial during
teething, its occurrence need not excite any uneasiness. After going on for a longer or shorter time,
these symptoms gradually abate, and are followed by
an interval of comfort and repose."

"The second stage of teething soon follows. Instead of regularly carrying everything to the mouth,
the child now often shows a fear of allowing anything
to touch it, and often cries when he happens to bite
unwarily. The gums and mouth become hot; a pale
or bright-red elevated spot appears on the gums,
which become very painful when pressed upon. The
child changes colour, the cheeks being frequently
flushed; he is restless, wishes to be laid down, and is
no sooner down than he is as anxious to be again in the
nurse's arms. Nothing pleases him. At one moment
he will demand the breast, and at the next abruptly
turn away from it. He snatches at everything, and
retains nothing. In short, he appears to be driven
about by successive and sudden impulses, without
being able to find rest in any position; and with these
appearances slight fever and bowel-complaint are often

combined. When once the teeth are fairly cut, however, all these symptoms vanish."* But many children, and especially those who are well constituted and judiciously managed, pass through the period of teething with scarcely any detriment.

The incisor are generally more easily cut than the eye teeth. The appearance of the latter, indeed, is often preceded by much constitutional disturbance, though their pointed form seems to indicate a facility in making their way.

Dentition being, as already stated, a natural process, it is not necessarily a period of danger. But a slighter cause is apt to give rise to disease during the period of teething than at any other time; and when disease does occur, it is aggravated and rendered more dangerous. The increased irritability is indeed the real source of the constitutional disturbance so often attendant on teething; and, consequently, the best method of carrying the child in safety through that troublesome and sometimes perilous process, is the adoption, from the day of its birth onwards, of *a proper system of general management.* Daily experience confirms the accuracy of this proposition, and shows that, while the symptoms of teething are generally severe in children much confined to the house and subjected to irregularities of diet, they are almost always mild in well-constituted children who have never been overfed, and whose exercise in the open air and general management have been conducted in accordance with the dictates of physiology.

* Von Ammon, *op. citat.* p. 182.

Having already explained the general principles of
infant management, I need not recapitulate them
here. But much as I have, on several occasions, insisted on the importance of pure air as a condition
of health, I cannot refrain from again urging it on
mothers as one of the surest preservatives against the
dangers of dentition. Nothing tends so directly as
the constant breathing of a pure air to counteract and
subdue that nervous irritability which is the characteristic of infancy, and the source of so many of its
diseases. If a child spends some hours daily in the
open air, occupies a large and thoroughly ventilated
apartment within doors, and is not overfed, it rarely
suffers much from teething. Whereas, when it is
taken out to exercise only at distant and irregular
intervals, and is cooped up in a warm or ill-ventilated
nursery, it is placed in the situation of all others the
most likely to render dentition a process of difficulty
and danger, because such are precisely the circumstances most calculated to increase the child's already
predominant irritability.

But while the child can scarcely be too much in
the open air in temperate or fine weather, and when
properly protected, the unusual susceptibility of the
system during teething renders great caution necessary in exposing it in harsh, cold weather. Thus, if,
from an ill-directed desire to strengthen the child, it
be rashly exposed, during teething, to cold or damp,
or to partial currents of air, inflammatory disease in
the windpipe or chest may easily be excited.* The

* See Appendix B.

same result may ensue if the clothing be insufficient to keep up the natural warmth of the surface and extremities.

The TEPID BATH is the only other part of the *general* or preservative treatment which it is necessary to notice here. From its power of allaying nervous excitement and promoting sleep, it is often a valuable resource before and during the irritation of teething; and it may then be safely continued for a longer time than when used merely for the purposes of cleanliness. Gentle and repeated friction over the surface of the body, also exerts a salutary and sedative influence on the nervous system, and should not be neglected.

A light cooling diet should be strictly observed during the acute stage of dentition, and even the ordinary food be considerably diluted. For the same reason, if teething commences before weaning takes place, the mother or nurse should adopt a mild and cooling diet, and carefully avoid all heavy and indigestible articles. The quality of the milk will thus become better adapted to the condition of the child, and tend to moderate the excitement to which the child is at this time peculiarly liable. The mother, also, should be doubly careful to avoid every source of disturbance to her own health, such as vivid emotional excitement, fatigue, and anxiety, as these directly affect the state of the child.

During the active stage of teething, there is a considerable tendency to congestion of the brain,

R 2

which often becomes a source of danger from the facility with which convulsions may then be induced,
or mere irritation be converted into inflammation of
the brain.   Hence the propriety of keeping the
head cool, and avoiding every kind of excitement.
Even too much anxiety to divert the child may become a cause of morbid irritation.   A quiet, soothing,
and cheerful manner is by far the most suitable, and
tends much to comfort the child.   The unusual flow
of saliva from the mouth acts beneficially in preventing and allaying undue excitement in the head, and
ought on no account to be checked.   The bowel-
complaint, also, so frequently attendant on teething,
is so useful in withdrawing the blood from the head
and lungs that it ought not to excite anxiety, unless
it is in excess and threatens danger as a distinct
disease.   When, from rash exposure or improper interference, the flow of saliva or the bowel-complaint is
arrested, convulsions and other serious forms of disease are of frequent occurrence.

It is very judiciously remarked by Dr Evanson,
that, while we abstain from exciting alarm about the
general disorder attendant on teething, we must, however, be watchful not to allow dangerous disease to
advance unchecked, in the belief that the symptoms
arise merely from dentition, and will cease with the
cutting of the teeth.   Both errors are sometimes
committed; and the only way to avoid them is, never
to allow our judgment to be carried away by undue
reliance on the universal truth of a general proposition.   We ought strictly to consider each case on

its own merits, and endeavour to distinguish between the symptoms produced solely by teething, and
those arising from co-existing and probably more
serious disease. On this subject it would be out
of place to enlarge here; but, for some excellent
practical remarks connected with it, I refer the
medical reader to a chapter on dentition in the able
work of Drs Maunsell and Evanson *On the Management and Diseases of Children,*—a work which embodies the most accurate information on this as on
most of the other important topics of which it
treats.

When the child suffers much from the swelled and
inflamed state of the gums, or when any uncertainty
or complication of unusual symptoms arises, the duty
of the parent is very obviously not to trust to her
own judgment or to chance, but at once to call in
professional aid, without waiting till active mischief
has gone so far as to endanger life. This is the only
way to assist the child effectually, and perhaps to
save the mother from the bitterness of lasting regret
and the torment of self-reproach. When, however,
the infant is uneasy merely, and no serious pain is
complained of, the mother may often administer relief
in the earlier stage by rubbing the gum gently with
the finger. When the gum is much inflamed, as it
is in the later stage, pressure will be hurtful; but the
time at which rubbing becomes agreeable can always
be detected by observing the behaviour of the child.
If there is not much tenderness, the use of a piece of
smooth coral promotes the passage of the tooth; but

a crust of bread answers better when the gum is inflamed, and at the same time it relieves the irritation
by increasing the flow of saliva.

When there is much pain and redness of the gum,
and the constitutional disturbance is considerable,
relief may be speedily obtained by dividing the gum
over the tooth with a lancet, and allowing it to bleed
freely.   Even in the first stage of dentition this
may be done with propriety, although there is no
expectation of the tooth immediately following.   In
the second stage, when the tooth is about to appear,
it is often imperatively called for, as the only means
of putting an end to severe suffering and averting
danger.   Even then, however, the tooth may not
appear for several days.   But as this part of the treatment is purely professional, I need not pursue the
subject.*

The SECOND DENTITION is seldom attended with
constitutional disturbance ; but the progress of the
teeth should be carefully watched, to see that they
come in their proper places and advance in the right
direction, and also that they are not so crowded
as to press injuriously on each other, or endanger
their permanent regularity.   Not only the form and
expression of the mouth, but the beauty and preservation of the teeth themselves, depend greatly on the

* For some interesting physiological observations on the process of
dentition, considered as an indication of the constitution and future
development of the infant, by Dr Whitehead of Manchester, see
APPENDIX D.

watchful attention paid to them, and on their being
judiciously managed during the progress of the second
dentition.

The importance of preserving their teeth should be
impressed on children from au early age; they should
be taught to clean them carefully with a proper brush
night and morning, and if after every meal, still
better. The formation of tartar on the teeth not only
taints the breath, but separates the gums from the
teeth, to the injury of both.

CHAPTER XIII.

THE period of infancy, to which this work more
especially refers, may be divided into two distinct
portions,—the first extending from birth to the time
of weaning, and the second from weaning to the full
development of the temporary teeth. In the great
majority of cases, weaning takes place between the
ninth and twelfth months, and the cutting of the
first set of teeth is completed about, or soon after,
the twenty-fourth month. In a general way, therefore,
the two periods may be accurately enough spoken of
as *the first and second years of infancy.* In using
these terms, however, I mean to express not the mere
lapse of time, but the constitutional or physiological
states which usually characterize the infant at these
different periods of its life.

The subjects discussed in the preceding chapters
refer chiefly to the first of these divisions; but the
second also demands no small share of our attention.
During the latter, the rate of mortality is indeed

greatly reduced from what it was during the first
year; but it still so far exceeds the average of any
other period of life, as to force the conviction upon
every reflecting mind, that there must be, in the constitution or external situation of the child, during the
evolution of the milk-teeth, some peculiarity which
renders it unusually susceptible of disease, and which
we must therefore carefully take into account in
regulating its mode of treatment. In the third and
subsequent years, the mortality declines so rapidly as
to prove that some of its causes must have been
peculiar to the infant state, while others which continue in operation must at least have lost a portion
of their power. The object of the present chapter is
to inquire what those causes are, and how they may
be most successfully controlled or counteracted.

CAUSES OF INFANT MORTALITY DURING THE SECOND
YEAR.—Many of the perils attending the first twelve
months of existence have already been shown to arise
partly from the very delicate state of the infant organism, and partly from defects of management. The
dangers incidental to the second year admit of a similar classification. The organism continues to be in a
state of rapid development, and the constitution is
still characterized by the same predominance of the
nervous and circulating systems which marks the beginning of life. The functions principally concerned
in nutrition and growth are consequently kept in that
state of high activity which any accidental irritation
suffices to convert into disease. The important pro-

cess of teething also goes on during the whole of the
second year, and, from the excitability which accompanies it, considerably increases the risk arising from
exposure to cold, errors of diet, &c.   To the infant,
moreover, everything is new and exciting.   At the
commencement of the second year, the senses are
scarcely more than beginning to convey distinct and
durable impressions to the mind.   The mind itself is
becoming conscious of new feelings and desires, and
takes pleasure in the examination of surrounding
objects.   The will now assumes a more definite expression, and with more vigour and precision directs
the bodily movements in the fulfilment of its wishes.
By and by the power of speech and social intercourse
becomes an additional source of interest and constantly recurring excitement.   The whole system, in
short, is not only excitable, but continually under the
influence of new stimuli; and, in the now very delicate state of the organism, it is not wonderful that
disease, often terminating fatally, should result from
mismanagement and other causes, which might be
successfully withstood at a maturer age.   Under such
circumstances, a few remarks, applicable more especially to the treatment required during the second
year, will not be without use.

During the second year, the state of the constitution differs only in degree from what it was
towards the end of the first; and the same principles by which our treatment was regulated at the
commencement of dentition continue applicable, with
only such slight and obvious modifications as the

change of circumstances may require. I shall therefore content myself at present with again urging the important practical fact, that the adoption, from the very first, of a mode of management in accordance with the nature and wants of the infant constitution, is by far the most effectual way to diminish the dangers of teething, and of all other infantile diseases. Hence it is that some feebly-constituted children are carried in safety through every obstacle, while, from mismanagement or neglect, the strong and healthy are cut down.

A large proportion of the diseases which destroy life in early infancy are more or less directly connected with the state of the digestive organs, and one of their principal sources is unquestionably *errors in diet.* On this point, perhaps more than on any other, parents are apt to be misled,—partly by their feelings, and partly by their ignorance; and hence a word or two of caution may be required.

DIET.—From a natural wish to strengthen the child, mothers are prone to give too much or too strong food, and to give it too frequently. If an infant is allowed to eat too fast, it is almost certain to eat too much; and, on the other hand, if it is not duly exercised or amused, it will desire food too often, not because it really stands in need of nourishment, but because it dislikes to be idle, and must be doing something. The common practice of soothing children by the offer of cake or sweetmeats is not less pernicious to health than injurious to their moral welfare; and

the child cannot be too early accustomed to abstain
entirely from eating during the intervals between
meals. The stomach, like other organs, requires a
period of repose to regain its tone after being engaged
in digestion; and if this be denied, and the child be
allowed to eat at its own will and pleasure, indigestion
will assuredly follow, and give rise to general disorder
of health.

Mischief is often done, during the second year of
life, through over-anxiety to strengthen the child by
strong food and the use of stimulants. This is a great
error. It is true that a healthy child who has been
weakened by accidental starvation may be rapidly
strengthened in this way: but in debility arising
from imperfect digestion or assimilation, or from an
irritable nervous constitution, the milder the food, the
more nourishment will it afford; and the stronger
and more stimulating it is, the less likely will it be to
restore the system to a healthy state.

It is certain that, as a general fact, much more
injury is done by giving animal food too soon than
by delaying it too long. After the incisor and the
anterior molar teeth have appeared, the child may
be gradually accustomed to more solid food. At
first, chicken-broth, or weak mutton-broth, freed from
fat, may be given in small quantity along with farinaceous food, and afterwards a little soft-boiled egg, or
light pudding, as an intermediate step towards solid
meat. When the teeth are somewhat grown and
able to masticate the food, a small bit of tender
chicken may be tried,—at first once in two or three

days, and by and by repeated oftener, when found to be relished and easily digested.

A small quantity of any light and well-cooked vegetable will also be allowable after the appearance of the teeth. Cauliflower, carrot, or stewed fruit will be highly relished and easily digested, provided the quantity be not too large.

When too rich food is given at an early age, with the view of strengthening a delicate constitution, the child generally becomes thin, excitable, and feverish ; and its health improves only when a change is made to milder nourishment. It is not the quality or quantity of food taken into the stomach which indicates the amount of support which it will afford. *Only that portion of it which is digested and assimilated* proves useful ; and hence, the surest way to impart strength is to give the kind of food that abounds most in the elements in which the system is deficient, and to administer it in such quantity as is best suited to the state of the constitution.

In childhood, the nervous and vascular systems predominate so much as to render the common use of fermented liquors, tea, coffee, and other stimulants, decidedly injurious, and it is only in cases of low vitality or disease (of which none but a medical man can judge) that any advantage is to be derived from their use.

To give a connected idea of the kind of diet required towards the end of the second year, I cannot do better than subjoin an extract from the very judicious work of Drs Maunsell and Evanson already referred to. "A healthy child of two or three years old, commonly awakes hungry and thirsty at five or six o'clock in the morning, sometimes even earlier. Immediately after waking, a little bread and sweet milk should be given to it, or (when the child is too young to eat bread) a little bread-pap. The latter should be warm; but in the former case the bread may be eaten from the hand, and the milk allowed to be drunk cold, as it is as well, at this meal, to furnish no inducement for eating beyond that of hunger. After eating, the child will generally sleep again for an hour or two; and about nine o'clock it should get its second meal of bread softened in hot water, which latter is to be drained off, and fresh milk and a little sugar added to the bread. Between one and two the child may have dinner, consisting, at the younger ages, of beef, mutton, or chicken broth (deprived of all fat), and bread. When a sufficient number of teeth are developed to admit of chewing being performed, a little animal food, as chicken, roast or boiled mutton or beef, not too much dressed, should be allowed, with a potato or bread, and some fresh well-dressed vegetables, as turnips or cauliflower. After dinner, some drink will be requisite; and a healthy child requires, or indeed wishes for, nothing but water. . . . Between six and seven o'clock, the child may have its last meal of bread steeped in water, &c., as at nine o'clock in the morning. A healthy child who has been in the open air during the greater part of the day, will be ready for bed shortly after this last-mentioned supply, and will re-

quire nothing further till morning. Similar regimen
and hours may be adopted throughout the whole
period of childhood; only, as the fourth or fifth year
approaches, giving, for breakfast and supper, broad
and milk without water, and either warm or cold,
according to the weather or the child's inclination.
The supply of food upon first waking in the morning
may also bo gradually discontinued, and breakfast
given somewhat earlier."

Before taking leave of the subject of infant diet, I
would again urge the necessity of paying much attention to REGULARITY in the time of meals. There
is a natural tendency to the observance of fixed
periods in all the operations of the animal economy,
which greatly facilitates the formation of habits of
order and regularity, more especially in early life,
and which, under the guidance of good sense, may bo
turned to excellent account even in the first months
of infancy.[*] When regularity and method havo been
once introduced, it is difficult to say whether the child
or the parent derives the greatest advantage from
them. If they promote in a high degree the health
and comfort of the child, they also relieve the parent
from a thraldom which is as sovere as it is incessant;
for nothing can exceed the slavish subjection in
which a mother is held when her child is once assured that by crying lustily it may procure any indulgence or amount of attention it pleases. Whereas,
when an infant has discovered that it is not to be the

* See the author's work on "Digestion and Diet," p. 69.

dictator; that its appetite is to be indulged only
at the right time; and that, while every kind and
proper concession will be cheerfully made, nothing
that is really wrong will be conceded to mere impor-
tunity, it instinctively yields the point, and enjoys in
consequence a far happier life than if it were allowed
to gratify, hurtfully, its every whim, and reign the
sole despot of the nursery.

The proper regulation of the QUANTITY of the food
is also of much practical importance. From ill-judged
kindliness, it is far from unusual to coax a child to
eat more than it actually desires. This is, I believe,
a frequent source of the indigestion and bowel-complaints so prevalent and fatal in early infancy. While
avoiding excess, however, we must be careful not
to go to the other extreme, and give an insufficient
allowance of nourishing food—an error sometimes
fallen into from a wish to render the child abstemious
and hardy in after-life. The true way to fortify the
constitution against future hardships and unavoidable
privations, is to secure in infancy and youth every
advantage which can be obtained by a well-conducted
general regimen, and A REGULAR AND AMPLE, BUT NOT
EXCESSIVE, SUPPLY of wholesome and nourishing food.
The mistake of administering inadequately to the
wants of childhood is not unknown even in the middle
and intelligent ranks of life, although much less frequent than the contrary error.*

* The reader is referred to a Memoir of the late James Hope, M.D.,
Physician to St George's Hospital, p. 4 (London, 1843), for an example
of the injurious effects of inadequate nourishment and exposure to
cold in his father's family.

But while regularity and quantity are thus attended
to in arranging the meals of the young, it ought also
to be kept in mind that some VARIETY is as advantageous in early as in later life ; and that to continue
day after day the same food, prepared in the very
same way, tends to weaken the stomach. With a little
ingenuity, some slight variation either in the substance or the mode of preparation of a meal may easily
be made, which will give a wholesome stimulus to
digestion. If, for instance, farinaceous food and milk
are at the time the proper kind of diet, it is easy
to make a little variety by occasionally substituting
arrow-root, soft-boiled rice, sago, bread-crumb, &c., for
each other. Or, when soup is allowed, by alternating
chicken-broth, mutton-broth, beef-tea, &c. A similar
plan may be followed with eggs, meat, and vegetables.
A change managed in this way, from one article to
another of a similar nature, is both agreeable and
healthful.

Many parents are in the habit of having their
children brought to table at the end of their own
dinner, and of giving them wine, fruit, and confec-
tions, when nothing but mischief can follow from
the indulgence. This practice ought to be scrupulously avoided, and we ought never to bring a child
into a place where we are partaking of any delicacy,
unless we intend also to gratify its desires. The
mere sight of food or drink is an infallible stimulus
to the infant appetite, just as light is to the eye,
or a suffering object to the feeling of compassion.
Even the principle of imitation comes into play with

peculiar force, and the child can see no good reason why he should be debarred from doing as others do, and becomes fretful and discontented when denied the gratification.

CLEANLINESS.—For many reasons, most of which will occur to the reader who has carefully perused the preceding pages, cleanliness should hold the same prominent place in the treatment of the second as it did in that of the first year of infancy. But, in accordance with the increased development and greater powers of reaction of the organism, the temperature of the water used for washing the child in the morning should, during summer, be gradually reduced from 80° to 75°, or even lower, in proportion as the increasing energies of the child render it safe and advantageous to do so. When the weather is warm, and the child vigorous and active, water at the temperature of the room may be safely used. During winter, however, or when the child is delicate and seems not to rally easily from the shock, we must be careful not to lower the temperature too much. As a general rule, the water used for the morning ablution, after the first year or fifteen months, should impart a feeling of coolness rather than of warmth to the skin.

When, as is generally the case, the morning ablution is intended merely for the purposes of cleanliness, the immersion should be continued only sufficiently long to have the child thoroughly washed, and well but gently rubbed while in the water with the hand or a soft sponge, and then quickly and thoroughly dried.

It is to the influence of the bath in equalising the circulation through all parts of the body, that the experienced Hufeland ascribes the great advantages derived from its judicious and systematic use in infancy, in preventing undue congestion or irritation in any one organ, or set of organs, such as the lungs, the heart, the brain, the stomach, or the bowels. For the same reason, he considers it as a most valuable auxiliary in the treatment of disease. At present, almost all our remedial agents, whatever the organs upon which they are specially intended to act, are applied directly to the stomach and bowels, so that *any internal irritation already existing, is often increased by the very remedy administered for its removal.* From this inconvenience the bath is entirely free. Properly managed, it soothes but never increases internal irritation, and often enables us to dispense with the use of drugs.

Dress is another subject for serious consideration in the management of infancy, as it acts directly upon the skin and general health either for good or for evil, according to the judgment with which it is regulated. In early life the skin is the seat of free and often copious perspiration, which always soils it more or less, so that a frequent change of the dress is as essential to cleanliness and health as the use of ablution and bathing. As the functions of the skin are easily repressed by anything approaching to a chill, the dress ought to be such as to afford adequate protec-

I

tion. In winter, soft flannel should be worn next the
skin, if the child be at all delicate or show any difficulty in maintaining its own warmth. In summer,
and in the case of robust children, it is less necessary, and sometimes even oppressive. The rule to
be followed is, to use the material which ensures
sufficient warmth without oppressing. This quality
may easily be determined by a little attention to the
feeling and comfort of the child. In many constitutions, soft warm cotton is preferable to flannel; but
when the skin appears dry, rough, and of a bluish-
white colour, this is a clear indication of its insufficient action, and flannel should at once be adopted.
The covering during the night also, as well as in the
day, requires to be carefully adapted to the season.

Except in the first months of infancy and in winter,
when ample protection against cold is certainly required, feather-beds and very soft pillows ought to
give place to well-made hair or cotton-wool mattresses, sufficiently firm to afford a certain amount of
resistance without allowing the body to sink into
them; or if feather-beds are used, they should be so
well stuffed as to have a moderate degree of hardness. A soft feather-bed is exactly equivalent to
an excess of warm clothing on the side of the body
immersed in it, and its bad effects are of the same
nature, only increased by the application being partial
instead of general. People imagine the warmth to
come only from the coverings above them, and in
consequence are apt to over-heat one side of the body,
while the other is left to suffer from cold.

The employment of insufficient clothing during the day, combined with that of soft, warm feather-beds, pillows, and blankets during the night, is one of the most hurtful forms in which the inconsistency of parents is displayed. Many of the unhappy children whose cold blue legs and anxious physiognomies used, a few years ago, to excite public compassion during winter, in our streets and squares, lay during the night pillowed on down, sunk in feather-beds, and covered with the warmest and softest blankets, as if on purpose to contrast with the nakedness of their exposure during the day; and the consequences were often very deplorable. In health, the sleep of childhood is too prompt, sound, and refreshing, to require such appliances to solicit its approach; and their use serves only to relax the skin, and increase its susceptibility to cold and disease.

In this country, a considerable improvement in the dress of children has taken place. Long warm worsted gaiters now envelope knees and limbs formerly blue and pinched from exposure to the wintry blast.

At all times, the dress of the young should be sufficient to protect them from every *abiding* sensation of cold or chill however slight, but not sufficient to overheat them or render exercise unpleasant. It should be light in material, and fit easily, so as to admit of the utmost freedom of motion and attitude. It should cover completely, but not tightly, the upper part of the chest and arms, especially in winter. Many delicate children suffer severely from the common custom of leaving the chest and shoulders almost

uncovered when within doors, and heaping on warm
clothing when going out. The risks of both extremes
are thus encountered, and great susceptibility of cold
is established where it might easily be prevented.

But while recommending adequate protection by
clothing against an *abiding feeling of cold*, I am very
far from advising that children should be brought up
under a regulated uniformity of temperature. On the
contrary, I believe too great uniformity to be almost
as injurious to healthy children, and, indeed, to adults
too, as sudden exposure to extremes of heat and cold.
Under constant uniformity, whether of temperature,
diet, employment, or exercise, the system loses the
cheerful spring which is the surest sign and best
blessing of sound health, and becomes a prey to slight
influences which would otherwise have been resisted,
not only with ease, but with delight.

EXERCISE AND PURE AIR.—Sufficient exercise and
pure air are indispensable conditions of health, and,
as already mentioned, both greatly conduce to the
safety of the child during the irritation of teething.
In fine weather, the child cannot be too much in the
open air, exercising his muscles in his own way, and
at his own pleasure. During the summer, in perfectly
dry weather, he may be allowed to crawl on the grass,
or on a cloth spread over it. By self-exercise of this
description, he will not only amuse himself better,
but develop his muscular strength, and acquire the
power of standing and walking sooner and more
securely than if attempted to be taught exclusively

by another. Premature endeavours to walk by the
aid of an attendant ought to be strictly forbidden.
When the child feels himself able for it, he will lose
no time in exercising his powers; and it is better
that he should gain strength by crawling for a week
or two longer on all fours, than that his limbs or spine
should become bent by premature exertion. Parents
and nurses often act very injudiciously by 'exciting
children to walk before their limbs are sufficiently
strong. It should be borne in mind that the bones of
the infant contain a much larger proportion of animal
matter than those of adults, and are consequently
soft and yielding. As age advances, the proportion of
earthy matter in the bones gradually increases, bearing a certain relation to the progress of teething, the
quick or slow progress of which may, as a general rule,
be considered as indicative of the degree of development of the osseous system of the child.*

In winter, from ten till one o'clock is very generally
the warmest and driest part of the day, and ought
never to be lost—as at that season the continuance of
favourable weather for two or three hours together can
never be relied upon, and the young soon suffer if
they are shut up even for a day or two.

But while inculcating the importance of abundant
exposure to the open air as a means of fortifying the
infant constitution, I would again caution parents
against sending their children out inadequately
clothed, or when really unseasonable weather or existing indisposition indicates the propriety of keeping

* See APPENDIX D.

them at home. As long as a child retains its natural
warmth, either from exercise or clothing, it may be
regarded as safe under almost any exposure; but if,
from deficient clothing, it becomes chilled, or even is
kept long cool, it will almost certainly suffer. In this,
as in other things, reason must be taken as our guide;
for it alone can ensure the infant's safety.

SLEEP.—The due regulation of sleep is another important consideration in early infancy, and, as such,
has been discussed at some length above (Chap. VIII.)
Here, however, it remains for me to point out the
propriety of weaning the child from sleep during the
day, as soon as he is sufficiently developed and vigorous to bear the change. This generally happens at
from two to three years of age; but in the case of
feeble children, and of such as are nervous and excitable, the mid-day sleep requires to be continued, and
even encouraged, much longer. In winter, the period
of sleep may be so arranged as to admit of the child
being taken out in the best part of the day.

As a general rule, the infant should not be left in
bed after it is once thoroughly awake. It is far better
to have him taken up and dressed, even if it should
be afterwards necessary to lay him down for a time on
the top of the bed. In infancy as well as maturity, it
is relaxing and enervating to lie in bed when nature
no longer requires the refreshment of sleep; and the
mother should be on her guard against encouraging
such a habit in her child, merely to suit her own temporary convenience. The sleep of a healthy child is

so sound and refreshing, that on awaking he almost
demands activity as a necessary of life; and the
shorter the time he spends in bed after awakening, the
better for his health and comfort.

As connected with this part of the subject, I may
here advert to the common practice of two or more
children sleeping in one bed. For many reasons it is
desirable that this should be avoided. It is far more
conducive to health that children should sleep in
separate beds, a little apart from each other. By
this means every child will breathe a purer air than
if they are placed together. Another obvious advantage is the smaller probability of partial exposure to cold from the bed-clothes being inadvertently pulled over to one side. After the age of
four or five years, it becomes, from moral considerations, still more desirable that every child should
sleep alone; and certainly bad habits have often
originated in the contrary practice, both in families
and schools. But as this remark applies much more
to a later period of life, not now under consideration,
I shall not here pursue the subject.

There is another custom connected with this part
of the management of infants, which cannot be too
soon given up after the first few weeks are over. I
allude to the practice of hushing the infant to sleep
in the nurse's arms or on her knee, before it is placed
in its cradle or bed. When a child is fretful or excited, it may be put to sleep perhaps a few minutes
sooner by this practice; but the advantage is pur-
chased at a much greater cost than it is worth, and is

often the first step to the loss, not only of its own,
but of its parent's health and comfort. Once let the
habit be established that the child is not to go to
sleep except on its mother's knee, and every time it
awakes in the night or in the day, it will compel her
to get up, no matter at what cost, and hush it to sleep
again ; and perhaps in the very act of laying it in its
cradle it once more awakes, and the whole process of
crying and hushing must be gone over again, and a
similar risk once more incurred. After all, the sleep
so induced is not so sound and refreshing as that
which speedily ensues when a child is laid quietly in
its bed and resigned to the influence of its natural
wants. The infant is thus converted into an uneasy
and restless tyrant, and the mother or nurse into his
almost sleepless slave, and all for no good purpose or
enjoyment whatever, even to himself.

Injurious, however, as this practice unquestionably
is, it is one of the most difficult for an over-anxious
mother to discontinue. When once accustomed to it,
the child necessarily remains sleepless, and cries, for
a short time when it is first broken off; and few
mothers are able to resist the cry of apparent distress
thus sounded in their ears, even when reason forbids
them to fly to his assistance. The fear of irritating
the child, and bringing on convulsions by continued
crying, too often overpowers all other considerations;
and yet the change, when firmly carried out, is much
more easily accomplished than many would expect,
and, with a little management and patience, is not
only wholly unattended with risk, but followed by

the best results so soon as to convince even the most
sensitive mother of its propriety.

MANAGEMENT DURING ILLNESS.—The occurrence of
measles, hooping-cough, and other infantile diseases,
is a source of great mortality during the second
year, which requires the serious consideration of
parents. I have no intention to say any thing here
as to the medical treatment of these diseases, because
that ought never to be conducted by the parent or
nurse. I refer to it merely to add, that the previous
good or bad management of the child has an important
influence on the progress and result of all infantile diseases. Even in the worst epidemics, a large proportion
of the children are restored to health; and experience
proves beyond a doubt that the recoveries occur chiefly
among those who are rationally treated, and favourably
situated as to external circumstances. So that, from
whatever point of view we regard the subject, every
thing tends to demonstrate the paramount influence
of the ordinary management.*

Domestic mismanagement during illness is so frequent a cause of death in infancy, that a few remarks
on it here will not be out of place. This mismanagement appears in a variety of forms, according
to the dispositions and external circumstances of the
parents. Many mothers and nurses are continually
administering medicines of one kind or another, and
thus deranging the healthy operations of the infant

* See observations on the preventible and other diseases of infants,
in APPENDIX B.

I 2

system. Instead of looking on the animal economy
as an organism constituted to work well under certain conditions, and having, in virtue of that constitution, a natural tendency to rectify temporary disorders if the requisite conditions of restorative action
be fulfilled, they seem to regard it as a machine acting
upon no fixed principles, and requiring now and then
to be driven by some foreign impulse in the shape of
medicine. If the child is convulsed, they do not
inquire whether the convulsions proceed from teething, indigestion, or worms, but forthwith administer
a remedy to *check the convulsions;* and as the medicine
used is most probably inapplicable to the individual
case, both the disease and the cause are left in full
operation, and so the danger is increased.

This is no imaginary case, but one of too frequent occurrence. Viewing disease as something
lodged in the system, the uninformed and anxious
mother hastens to expel it, and in so doing often
perils the life of her child. When the truth comes to
be more generally known, that disease is but an *aberration from the natural state of an organ or function,*
proceeding from some active cause, and not to be
remedied till the diseased organ is placed under the
conditions essential to its healthy action, then will
more attention be paid to seeking the co-operation of
Nature in our curative treatment, and much less
mischief be done by rash attempts to expel disease
by force. The physician, when in his right position,
is the "*servant and interpreter* of Nature," not her
ruler or opponent; and the same principle applies

ABUSE OF DRUGS. 203

with double force to the mother. I have therefore
no hesitation in expressing my conviction, that a
child cannot encounter many greater dangers than
that of being subjected to the vigorous discipline of
a medicine-giving mother or nurse. Wherever a
mother of a family is observed to be ready with doses
of calomel, cordials, anodynes, and other active drugs,
the likelihood is, that one-half of her children will be
found to have passed to a better world.

Even when the child is under the care of a professional adviser, it is by no means safe from the
risk arising from the giving of heterogeneous medicines. Whenever a child is seriously ill, there is not
only great anxiety on the part of the mother, but
much sympathy on the part of friends and neighbours,
each of whom has her own story of what was done
with such another child in the same situation, and
the great good obtained from such and such medicines.
In vain the mother may urge that the physician has
seen the patient, and already prescribed a different
course. Entreaties are poured in with an earnestness
proportioned to the danger, just *to try* the vaunted
remedy *without telling the doctor* or interrupting the
use of his medicines. Anxious for the relief of her
child, the mother often yields, before her better judgment can come into play to prevent her; and, in a
short time, the child suffers from this abuse of perhaps
incompatible or dangerous remedies, which aggravate the original disease. Those who are accustomed
to reflect before they act, would be amazed if they
were to witness the perilous follies sometimes per-

petrated in this way, and the perfect self-complacency
with which the promised results are expected from
the different medicines, no matter how much they
may counteract each other. Even if the consequences
are fatal, the self-satisfaction is scarcely impaired,
because supported by a false notion that *everything
has been done which could be done* to avert the
catastrophe. It would be a great mistake to suppose
that such conduct is to be met with only among the
uneducated poor. Even the middle and higher
classes are as yet so little instructed on the subject of
the human constitution, that although, from greater
general intelligence, they act more habitually under
the direction of a qualified professional adviser,
still, even among them, not a few instances occur
in which the child falls a sacrifice to the multi-
plicity of ignorant counsellors and excessive use of
drugs.

The habit of concealment from the family physician,
into which the adoption of "every body's" advice is
so apt to lead, is itself an evil of the first magnitude.
By inducing him to ascribe effects to wrong causes,
it necessarily tends to mislead his judgment, and may
thus render him also unwittingly an instrument of
mischief. The maternal anxiety which lies at the
root of the error is highly natural, and every sensible
practitioner will make allowance for its impulses, even
where they are ill-directed, and annoying to himself.
But the fair and proper way for the mother is, not to
act upon the suggestions of others without the knowledge of the medical attendant, but to state simply,

and in an honest spirit, that certain suggestions have been made, and inquire whether they meet with his approbation or not. If they do, then the measures recommended will be adapted by him to the necessities and peculiarities of the individual case, and the different parts of the treatment be carried on consistently and safely. If, on the contrary, they do not, he will have an opportunity of assigning a reason for his disapproval, and of pointing out the greater fitness of the means already employed. Should the mother be unsatisfied with this explanation, and still insist on the suggestion being tried, he can then either decline further responsibility, or take care that the trial be made with as much safety and prospect of advantage as possible.

So far from blaming the parents for calling the attention of the physician to any reasonable suggestion made by another, I acknowledge that even the most experienced may occasionally derive advantage from a hint thrown out by a casual observer. Something may escape notice during the shortness of a professional visit, which may be easily remarked at another time by a less skilful person, and by which some modification of treatment, not previously thought of, may be rendered needful. In like manner, useful practical suggestions may be thrown out, by which any medical man may profit without reproach to his skill. All, therefore, that I contend for is, that the physician in charge of the child should be consulted before any remedies unauthorised by him are tried; and that, where any are given against his advice, he

should not be kept in ignorance of the fact, but be
left to decide whether to administer them in the only
way which can be either beneficial to the patient or
satisfactory to himself, or to give up charge of the
patient altogether.

When a child becomes seriously indisposed, it
should, if practicable, be at once removed to a quiet
well-aired room, away from the noise and bustle of
the nursery. By this means the other children will
be more likely to escape if the disease should prove to
be infectious, and the patient will be benefited by the
change. The natural excitability of the infant constitution being always held in view, it is obvious that
the sick-room should be kept quiet, and nothing be
allowed to lessen the purity of its air. In a nursery,
quiet and order ought to be particularly enforced,
and no one should be allowed to remain in it except
the child and its nurse. Every unnecessary visitor
serves only to vitiate the atmosphere and disturb
the patient.* Pure fresh air, always important, becomes doubly so during disease: hence, the close
overheated atmosphere which some parents insist
upon from a morbid apprehension of cold, is often
productive of worse effects, especially in the febrile
complaints of childhood, than the evil which it is
sought to prevent. The same remark is applicable to

* In a small pamphlet by Dr West, senior physician to the
Hospital for Sick Children—entitled " How to Nurse Sick Children "—
will be found excellent directions for nursing children. And no family
should be unprovided with Miss Nightingale's comprehensive and
very judicious " Notes on Nursing," which apply even more to children
than to patients in general.

closely-drawn curtains, and the enervating quantity
of bedclothes occasionally heaped on the young suf-
ferers.

But it is in the mismanagement of diet during the
diseases of infancy that the physician meets with the
greatest obstacles to recovery, and in regard to which
he requires to be constantly on his guard, not only to
specify what he wishes to be given, but to make sure
that his wishes are understood and complied with.
Almost all the disorders of infancy, as might be inferred from the predominance of the nervous and
vascular systems at that age, are attended with more
or less of fever; as a general rule, therefore, a mild
and moderate diet is required, even when the strength
is much reduced. Stimulating or highly nutritive
food increases debility by aggravating the febrile
action; but, looking to the debility alone, many persons think they cannot give too strong or too much
nourishment. This is the source of no little mischief,
and of the occasional inefficacy of the best-devised and
most suitable treatment.

Another source of infant mortality is delay in sending for professional assistance, in the hope that some
domestic remedy will afford relief or effect a cure.
Some of the most serious diseases of infancy begin in
a very insidious manner, and can be effectually checked
only at their outset. When, therefore, a child com-
plains without any obvious removeable cause, the
sooner advice is sent for the better. If this plan
were generally followed, many children would be
saved who are now lost, and much professional at-

tendance be avoided which is now incurred to little
purpose.

There are one or two other points which, before concluding these cautions, I would earnestly impress upon
mothers. The first is, when the child is really ill, to
send for the physician *as early in the day as possible*,
instead of waiting, as is so often done through a spirit
of procrastination, till the darkness and solitude of
night work upon the mother's fears, and then sending
in great haste at a very late hour, when the difficulty
of procuring the needful remedies is greatly increased,
and the whole household is thrown into commotion.
Timeously warned, the physician would make his
visit at a seasonable hour, not only with more benefit
to the patient, but at far less expense of time, trouble,
and anxiety to all concerned; whereas, at night, he is
probably exhausted by the labours of the day, and of
course less fit for active usefulness.   In cases of acute
disease, above all, this rule should be scrupulously
followed.   To prevent mistakes from the bad memory
of servants, or from the physician's having more than
one patient of the same name, a *written note* should
invariably be sent, and the *address* be given.   It
should state also the *supposed seat and nature of the
ailment;* for this information will enable him, as he
goes along, to reflect on the constitutional peculiarities
of the patient and the probable influence of prevailing
epidemics, and to consider the precautions which a
knowledge of these may suggest in directing the treatment. This is especially of importance when he is sent
for in the night; because, from having some previous

notion of the case, he may carry remedies with him and give relief on the spot. But in all cases it is useful, by preparing the mind of the adviser in some degree for the investigation of the disease.*

The last point which I would strictly enforce is, that the medical attendant should never be made an object of terror to the child for the purpose of quieting it, or forcing it to submit to disagreeable remedies or the ordinary restraints required during both health and illness. The usefulness of the family physician depends in no small degree on his being on the very best terms with the children, and approached and welcomed by them as their steady friend. When he is viewed in this light, his presence soothes and tranquillizes them during illness, influences them to take the necessary remedies, and not only greatly promotes recovery, but even induces them to submit cheerfully to painful and disagreeable operations. Ignorant and thoughtless mothers employ threats of what "the doctor will do" if the child will not take medicine or submit to some other offensive prescription; till the very sight of him is sufficient to neutralize the effects of the best-devised treatment. The result of such folly is, that when the child is really ill, it is thrown into such agitation by his approach, that he cannot distinguish accurately how much of the disturbance is due to fright, and how

* These and some other hints are contained in a short paper on " Sending for the Doctor," contributed by the author to a newspaper, and reprinted in Chambers's Edinburgh Journal, Aug. 30, 1884.

much to disease; while, at the same time, it raises a
powerful moral obstacle to recovery.

Occasionally, the same ready method of reducing
the child to submission is resorted to by the attendants without the knowledge of the parents; and my
chief object in now directing attention to it, is to
put mothers on their guard, that they may not only
strictly prohibit all such proceedings, but take care,
by their own watchfulness, that their orders be fulfilled. By neither parents nor attendants ought the
physician ever to be spoken of in the presence of the
young but with kindness and respect. If he is a man
in whose character and skill the parents have confidence, he deserves this at their hands. If he is not,
the sooner they change him for another the better.
But under no circumstances can they be justified,
even in a selfish point of view, in converting him into
an object of terror to those whose health and well-
being are intrusted to his care. By judicious conduct
on the part of the parent, and a kind soothing manner
on that of the physician, the child will come to regard
him as its best friend, and the only one who can relieve
its suffering.

CHAPTER XIV.

HAVING discussed the physical management of infancy, I come now to consider the principles which
bear on the not less important subject of the moral
and intellectual training at this early stage of life.

Man, as he exists in this world, is a compound
being. We cannot conceive of him as either mind
alone or body alone. Living as he does in a material
world, surrounded by other organised beings like himself, and depending for his existence on material
objects, he would be as entirely out of harmony with
the rest of creation were his mind unprovided with
material organs, as an organised body would be
without a mind to direct its movements. To enable man, then, to fulfil the purposes for which
he was sent into the world, his education ought to
have constant reference to his *whole nature*,—to take
for its aim the *development of a sound mind in
a sound and vigorous body*. In whatever manner,
and to whatever degree, physical, moral, or intellectual

education falls short of the fulfilment of this aim, to
that extent it is defective.   To restrict it, as is usually
done, to the cultivation of a few—and these not the
highest—of the intellectual faculties, to the exclusion
both of the physical system and of the moral and the
higher intellectual powers, is to renounce the most
important advantages which education is capable of
conferring on man.   Not a year passes in which examples of this error do not occur in our universities—
of some highly-gifted but overstrained mind breaking
down in the hour of its greatest promise, and forfeit-
ing, when almost within its grasp, that prize for which
it has sacrificed everything, and which it has perhaps
the additional mortification of seeing carried off by
some competitor more remarkable for healthy, indus-
trious, and prudent mediocrity, than for either genius
or extent of acquirements.

In infancy the mental constitution presents the
rudiments, as it were, of the same external senses and
emotional and intellectual powers which characterise
the human being in mature age.   The senses of sight,
hearing, taste, smell, and touch, and the internal
faculties of emotion, perception, and thought, are all
essentially the same; but some are developed much
sooner than others.   At birth, indeed, the powers of
sensation alone are actively manifested, and even
they are at first very imperfect; for, during the
first week or two, the infant seems to have no distinct
consciousness of any kind.   The light may strike upon
the eye, or sound upon the ear, and yet no clear impression seems conveyed to the infant ; unless, indeed,

the impulse be of sufficient intensity to excite pain, in which case it will give unequivocal indications of uneasiness. As yet, one only of its actions seems to have a determinate end—that of turning the mouth to the mother's breast in search of the nipple, and of sucking when it is found; but even this is unattended with consciousness.

EXTERNAL SENSES.—A week or two after birth the eye begins to follow the light, and sudden sounds give rise to a start as if of surprise. By degrees, however, the senses become capable of receiving and conveying to the mind distinct impressions; but it is not till after the lapse of years that they attain their fullest vigour and capacity. In this respect man is remarkably different from many of the lower animals, which see and hear distinctly from the first, and not only at once distinguish and pick up the grain or insects which are their natural food, but move and act with almost as much unerring freedom and decision as at any subsequent period of their lives.

When we inquire into the cause of this striking difference, we have no difficulty in finding an explanation. In animals which are born with the different senses ready to start into action, we invariably find the corresponding organs of sense developed in a proportionate degree; whereas in man and those other animals whose senses are very imperfect at birth, the corresponding organs are still immature or imperfect in structure,—and each sense acquires power and facility of action, only in proportion as its organ becomes developed, and is duly exercised on the objects with which Nature has placed it in relation.

From this dependence of each of the senses on the condition of its special organ, two results necessarily follow, which should be kept in view in attempting to educate or improve them. The first is, that the different senses being connected with different organs, one or more of them may be developed before the others,—seeing before hearing, for instance, and taste before smell. The second is, that when we wish to call any one of them into exercise, we must present to it its appropriate object or stimulus. If we wish to improve vision, we must admit light, and present visible objects to the eye, in a manner adapted to the nature and delicacy of the organ. In the case of the ear, if we either exclude sounds altogether, or subject it to the impulse of loud and sudden noises before its structure is matured, we may impair or even destroy the sense of hearing; whereas, when we adapt the exercise of the organ to its structural delicacy, we promote its development and increase its power. The same principle applies to smell, taste, and touch.

Hence it is, that by well-regulated systematic exercise, the senses of hearing, seeing, and smelling, acquire, among some savage tribes, an intensity of action which would be incredible if the facts were not authenticated beyond the possibility of cavil. Taught by early practice, the savage can distinguish the tread, and track the route of an enemy or an animal, when no sound or trace is perceptible to the civi-

lised man. In our own pastoral districts, the shep-
herd can distinguish the individuals of a numerous
flock of sheep, while, to an unpractised observer, all
seem to be perfectly alike. From a similar training,
the senses of touch and hearing become remarkably
acute in intelligent and active-minded blind persons;
many of whom have been known to acquire, by constant practice, such a delicacy of touch, as enabled
them to distinguish by its means cloths of marked
shades of colour, and even true from false coins, in the
appearance of which there was so little difference as
almost to defy the scrutiny of an experienced eye.
The general quickness of hearing among the blind,
and their correct appreciation of sound, are too well
known to be dwelt upon.

For the production of this extraordinary acuteness
the method simply is, to exercise, from the earliest
youth, each organ of sense systematically, habitually, and energetically upon its appropriate objects, till acuteness is gained by dint of frequent
and attentive repetition. When a sound is made, the
ear is acted on whether we will or not; when light
strikes upon the eye, we cannot but see; and when
the air is impregnated with strong perfumes, smell
takes cognisance of their presence and qualities
without any exercise of volition. But when these
natural means of excitement are excluded, the organs
of the senses languish and become feeble from want
of exercise, and differences in impressions made on
them are unnoticed, which, in a more cultivated
state of the senses, would have been instantly and

accurately recognised. The infant, indeed, acts from
an early period in almost instinctive obedience to
this principle; for it delights to exercise its eyes
on brilliant objects and colours, to train its ear to
the discrimination of sounds by every variety of
noise, and to educate the sense of touch by feeling
and handling everything within its reach; and if it
does not seek the exercise and gratification of smell
in the same way, it is only because the nose is still
small, and comparatively unfit for its function. So
entirely, however, do many parents and nurses overlook the object and beneficial tendency of this employment of the senses, that when the child makes a noise
in the nursery, amuses itself in the playful exercise of
its voice, or lays hold of any object to examine it,
they are apt to regard only the disturbance to themselves, and to enforce silence and order; as if the
child were guilty of some mischievous folly, instead of
really performing a most useful and improving act of
self-education, which requires only to be well directed
to prove the source of important benefits. Even
among thinking and educated persons, the external
senses of the infant are treated with neglect. Notwithstanding their extreme value as inlets to the
storehouse of the mind, very little regard is paid to
their cultivation, or even to their preservation from
injury. At birth, the eye is often exposed to the
bright glare of day with as little consideration as if it
were not a most delicate organ. The ear, in like manner, is subjected to loud and sudden sounds, which, in
extreme cases, go far to destroy its delicate nervous

structure, and induce deafness for life; while no pains are bestowed in training the sense to finer and finer perception, by well-graduated exercise, according to the condition and development of its organ. Blindness and deafness are sometimes thus produced at the very dawn of existence, when a little knowledge and prudence would not only have preserved the sight and hearing, but have improved both in a remarkable degree.

As the senses are bestowed on us for use, and are so susceptible of cultivation, and as without them man would be shut out from every source of active and social enjoyment, it is surely worth our while to devote some attention to their preservation and improvement in infancy, when their organs are still delicate, and easily modified by the manner in which they are exercised. The very prevalence of short-sightedness among the young of the middle and higher classes may be received as a proof that some error in hygienic management exists, giving rise to this defect. Many reasons, indeed, concur to render it probable that the long confinement of the young within doors, at school and at home, has no small influence here. The eye, like every other organ, adapts itself in a great degree to its circumstances; and accordingly, while that of the seaman or wandering Indian is accustomed to scan distant as well as near objects, and so becomes adapted by exercise for its varied duties, the eye of the boy or girl confined within the four walls of a house or the narrow streets of a city, is exercised only on near objects,

K

and becomes unfit for the perception of those more distant—in other words, is rendered *short*-sighted. It is true that the original structure of the organ has a large share in the result; but it is not less true, that constant exercise upon near objects only, tends greatly to aggravate the defect.

On this branch of the subject I shall only add, that, to derive benefit from the exercise of any sense, the strength and continuance of the stimulus must be duly suited to the health, maturity, and condition of the organ upon which it acts.

THE MENTAL FACULTIES.—We come now to treat of what may be called the internal faculties of the mind,—namely, those included under the heads of EMOTION, OBSERVATION, and THOUGHT—constituting the basis of the moral, religious, and intellectual character. To the exercise of these, we shall find that the same principle applies as to that of the external senses. It will thus afford us a valuable guide in training the infant mind.

At birth, the brain is so imperfectly developed and so delicately constituted as to be unfit for active mental manifestations; and accordingly we observe none, except perhaps signs of the consciousness of bodily pain, and the desire for food. Beyond these, no trace of activity of mind can be detected; nearly the whole time is spent in sleep, which is the negation of mental action. The structure of the infant brain, being thus extremely delicate, is very easily disordered, and even permanently injured; and in-

juries sustained by it may, as in the similar instances
of the eye and the ear, impair the efficiency of its
functions to the end of life—may even induce permanent idiocy or imbecility.

Such is the state of the brain and mind for some
time after birth. By degrees, however, traces of
extended mental action begin to show themselves,
and the appetite for food is no longer the only instinct which seeks for gratification. The infant, by
its looks and smiles, gives indications of awakening
consciousness, long before it can conceive the nature
of the cause by which it is excited. In this way it
exhibits, even at a very early age, movements which
neither sensation nor experience can explain, and
which, as is happily remarked by an acute and elegant writer, are in truth the signs of its dawning
affections. "Even at the early age of six weeks,
when the infant is still a stranger to the world, and
perceives external objects so indistinctly as to make
no effort either to obtain or avoid them, he is nevertheless accessible to the influence of human expression. Although no material object possesses any
attraction for him, sympathy, or the action of a feeling in his mind corresponding to the expression of
the same feeling in the mind of another, is already at
work. A smile, a caressing accent, raises a smile on
his lips; pleasing emotions already animate this little
being; and we, recognising their expression, are de-
lighted in our turn. Who, then, has told this infant
that a certain expression of the features indicates
tenderness for him? How could he, to whom his

own physiognomy is unknown, imitate that of another, unless a corresponding feeling in his own mind impressed the same characters on his features? That person near his cradle is perhaps not his nurse; perhaps she has only disturbed him, or subjected him to some unpleasant operation. No matter, she has smiled affectionately on him; *he feels* that he is loved, and he loves in return."*

Here, then, is the true key to the right training of the infant mind. The internal emotions, like the external senses, being distinct from each other, and independent in their action—let the appropriate object of any one of them, the organ of which is already sufficiently developed, be presented to it, and it will start into activity, just as the eye does when the rays of light are directed on the retina. Look, for example, at an infant six months old, and observe the extent to which it responds to every variety of stimulus addressed to its feelings. If we wish to soothe it in a moment of fretful disappointment, do we not succeed by gentle fondling, and singing to it in a soft affectionate voice? If our aim is to rouse it to activity, are not our movements and tones at once changed to the lively and spirited? When an acrimonious dialogue occurs between the nurse and any other person in the presence of an infant, is it not common for the child to become as uneasy as if the angry expressions were addressed to itself, and forthwith begin to cry? If, on the other hand, an affec-

* L'Education Progressive, ou Etude du Cours de la Vie, par Mme. Necker de Saussure. Paris, 1836. Vol. I. p. 144.

tionate and gentle mother enters a nursery, and,
imagining the infant to be asleep, merely addresses
the nurse in the soft tones characteristic of her mind,
do we not see the infant waken up, and with a
placid smile look around to solicit the notice of its
parent? Or, to use one more example, if a disagreeable, coarse-looking person happens suddenly to approach an infant, are not the instantaneous results an
exclamation of terror, and a clinging to the mother's
bosom for protection? In short, to call out and give
healthy development to the kindly and affectionate
feelings of an infant, we must treat it, and every
person in its presence, with habitual kindliness and
affection,—the display of the natural stimulant to the
organs of such feelings. If, on the contrary, we present to an infant the stimulus of grief, discontent, or
bad temper, we call up in its mind, not kindliness or
affection, but the disagreeable feelings which we exhibit; and by the habitual exercise of the portions
of the brain with which these are connected, we promote their development, and thus run the risk of
giving permanence to such unkindly feelings for life.

It is astonishing, indeed, from what an early age
the mental faculties will respond to their respective
stimuli, whether these be direct or only from sympathy. Madame Necker de Saussure gives an affecting
example of this truth, which she witnessed in a child
nine months old. "The infant was gaily playing on
its mother's knees, when a woman, whose physiognomy expressed deep but calm sadness, entered the
room. From that moment the child's attention was

wholly fixed on the woman, whom it knew, but for
whom it had no particular affection. By degrees its
features became discomposed; its playthings dropped
from its hands, and at length it threw itself sobbing
violently upon its mother's bosom. It felt neither
fear nor pity; it knew not why it suffered, but it
sought for relief in tears."*   Facts like these show
how careful we should be in duly regulating the moral
as well as physical influences by which infancy is
surrounded.

The bearing and importance of these truths would
be at once perceived were parents acquainted with
the laws of the animal economy, and with the fact
that the mind acts through the medium of bodily
organs, and is influenced by the state of these during the whole course of life. The mind can see only
by means of the eye; and when the eye is injured
by too strong or too weak a stimulus,—namely, by
being exposed to a dazzling light, or kept in utter
darkness,—the mind no longer sees distinctly. It can
hear only through the medium of the ear; and when
that organ is either deranged by the impulse of too
violent sounds, or rendered obtuse by want of exercise, the mind loses the power of hearing and discriminating sounds. When, on the contrary, the eyes
and ears are appropriately exercised, in the degree
and with the attention which their delicacy requires,
the senses of seeing and hearing become acute and
active, and are ever ready at a call; because their
organs, strengthened by exercise, become fully de-

* Op. citat., vol. i. p. 179.

veloped, and ready to respond to their respective stimuli. And nobody ever dreams of attempting to
strengthen any one sense by exercising the organs
of another. In training these faculties, each must
be exercised on the objects related to the constitution which has been bestowed on it by the
Author of our being. We cannot improve vision
by reasoning, or educate the ear to the nice discrimination of sounds by scholastic precepts or metaphysi-
cal theories. We have no choice in the matter; our
only course is to exercise the eye in actual seeing, and
the ear in actual listening, or to remain contented
with the possession of imperfect senses. Our Maker
has assigned a distinct organ for the operations of
each; and if that organ be injured or destroyed, no
effort of ours will be successful in conveying to the
mind the impressions which it alone was specially
constituted to transmit.

Thanks to the invaluable discovery of Gall, we
are now in a position to explain why the past efforts
of mankind in the education of the *intellectual and
emotional powers* have been comparatively unsuccess-
ful; and we are in possession of principles, by the
judicious application of which a great and steady advance may be made, and by means of which a great
improvement has already been effected. By showing
that the various propensities, affections, and powers
of observation and reflection are independent, and that
each of them acts through the medium of an appropriate portion of the brain, commonly called its *organ;* that each is, by its natural constitution, related

to a certain class of objects, and starts into activity
when those objects are presented to it; and, lastly,
that we cannot cultivate the emotion of justice or of
pity, for example, any more than the sense of hearing
or seeing, by a mere intellectual exposition of moral
duty,—Phrenology has thus thrown upon the science
of education a flood of light, which will not be duly
appreciated for years to come, but for which posterity
will assuredly be grateful, when the benefits resulting
from it shall be widely felt.   To enter upon the consideration of all the applications that may be made
of Phrenology to the improvement of infant training
and general education, would lead me far beyond the
limits assigned to the present work.   But I should
be insensible of what I myself owe to its assistance
were I not to express in the strongest terms my obligations to its guidance, and to affirm, that, in the
hands of a rational and well-educated parent, it is
calculated to remove many a discouraging difficulty,
and to implant in the mind a profound, pervading,
and unshaken, because enlightened reliance on the
goodness, stability, and wisdom of the Divine arrangements, as the safest, clearest, and best which
can be followed in the training and education of the
young, as in all other cases in which man is to be
either influenced or improved.

I am quite aware that by many parents this estimate of the aid to be derived from the application of
Phrenology to the purposes of education will be regarded with suspicion, because it is a common though
unfounded and hurtful prejudice to consider its doc-

trines as hostile to religion. To my mind, on the contrary, its principal recommendation is, that it tends *necessarily* to bring us nearer to God, and to enforce a constant reference to the standard of His will as our surest rule of action, not only on great occasions, but in the daily and hourly business of our lives. In many instances, Phrenology reveals the finger of God in the clearest and most instructive light, where, but for it, His teaching would have remained unintelligible. As an explanation of God's highest work on earth—the mind of man—Phrenology tends to make religion part and parcel of our thoughts and feelings; and instead of causing us to lose sight of our Creator in the obscurity of a gloomy materialism, it renders His presence and power so palpable to reason, and almost to sense, that we can hardly shut our eyes to His manifestations even if we would. God himself is the source of truth, and if in any circumstances we turn the knowledge of truth to evil, the fault is our own, and we are making a wrong use of a thing good in itself. All truth being Divine, if Phrenology be true, it also must be of Divine origin, and therefore good. Its truths may indeed be abused by ignorant or perverted minds, as many other truths are; but this circumstance no more proves that in itself it is bad or dangerous, than that religion is bad because *its* truths are sometimes turned to evil purposes.

If it be thought that in forming this high opinion of the value of Phrenology I am blinded by partiality to a favourite study, I reply that we have similar and

K 2

even stronger testimony, though not so openly expressed, from men of extensive and successful experience in the moral and religious training of the young,
and who concur in regarding it as calculated in a
high degree to advance the diffusion and increase the
influence of religious truth.   As one example of this,
I may refer to the excellent practical work by Mr
Stow of Glasgow.*   The seminary over which Mr
Stow so long presided, and in which he still takes an
active interest, is acknowledged to stand high among
our educational institutions, for its success, not only
in giving intellectual instruction, but still more in
training its pupils in the principles and practice of
morality and religion.   So marked, indeed, has been
the success of the system in the great requisite of the
formation of character, that " of several thousands of
children who have attended the model schools of the
Normal Seminary, it is not known that any one has
been accused of crime, or brought before a magistrate.
This is particularly noticeable in respect of one of the
model schools, which for seven years was situated in
the Saltmarket, *the very centre of vice.*   On the contrary, a large number of these children are now grown
up excellent characters."†   Accordingly, Mr Stow's
school is supported with great zeal and energy by the
Free Church of Scotland, as a *model seminary for
religious and moral* as well as physical and intellec-

* On the Training System of Education, Religious, Intellectual,
and Moral, as established in the Glasgow Normal Training Seminary.
Eleventh edition.
† Page 16.

tual training. In the same spirit, the interesting
volume in which the principles and methods followed
in his seminary are fully explained, has been so widely
recognised as a safe and able guide, that ten large
editions of it have been exhausted. Everywhere
it has been cordially welcomed by those engaged in
the business of education; and not only has no whis-
per been ever heard against it on account of any danger supposed to lurk in its precepts or its practice, but
it has been prized in a special manner for the soundness and efficacy of its religious teaching.

Such being the admitted facts of the case, it will, I
think, be sufficient evidence of the perfect safety of
Phrenology to add, that the educational principles
which Mr Stow has adopted and acted upon with so
much success are strictly phrenological, and as such
are in perfect harmony with those inculcated in the
present volume. I do not mean by this to affirm that
the particular theological creed inculcated by Mr Stow
is deducible from Phrenology, or that I agree with him
in every point of religious faith. My present argu-
ment has reference exclusively to the best *methods
of training and developing the minds of the young*, and
not at all to the opinions or ideas which ought to be
taught. At the early age to which this book refers,
it is the former alone which is of importance; and it
is not till the faculties become more developed as
years advance, that the relative values of creeds and
doctrines can be understood or appreciated. To these,
accordingly, I make no reference whatever in the
present volume; and it is due to Mr Stow, no less

than to myself, to draw this clear line of distinction
between *methods* of training and instruction, and the
individual *facts and opinions* presented to the youthful
mind in the shape of general or religious knowledge.
It may be proper, also, to mention that Mr Stow himself makes no express reference to Phrenology as having afforded him any assistance.   But it is impossible
for any reflecting person who is acquainted with its
doctrines, not to recognise its guiding spirit in almost
every page of his work; and it would have been
equally impossible for Mr Stow himself to devise a
system of training so consistent in all its parts, and
so strikingly in harmony with nature, unless he had
extensively availed himself of the aid of Phrenology.

Even if Phrenology had done nothing more than
prove the specific or essential nature of the different
emotional and intellectual powers connected with
the brain, it would have rendered a signal service
to education, by strongly directing attention to the
principle, that to rouse any one of these powers
into healthful action, the surest and most successful way is to bring it WITHIN THE IMMEDIATE INFLU-
ENCE OF THE OBJECTS TO WHICH IT IS SPECIALLY
RELATED.   If we wish to train the sense of sight
to quicker perception, we employ the eye in the careful and rapid scrutiny of surrounding objects, of colour, magnitudes, and distances; if we wish to train
the sense of hearing to a nicer discrimination of
sounds, we exercise the ear in listening to and distinguishing them; and our success is in proportion to
the degree in which we have received form Nature

the endowment of the sense, and to the perseverance
and judgment with which we pursue its cultivation.
Precisely on the same principle, if, in our endeavours
to give improved action to the internal *sentiment* of
justice, we merely address to the *intellect* the precept
" Be just," we shall succeed no better than we should
do in trying to improve vision by the employment of
the ear in discriminating sounds.   To cultivate feelings of pity and devotion it is not enough to address
the intellect by eulogiums on their excellence, which
can act only on the reason.   We must also directly
address the feelings themselves, by showing sympathy
and respect, and by bringing them into contact with
suffering, which unfortunately is ever too abundant
around us.   If the *natural stimulant* to the feeling be
presented, the child will have no choice in the matter.
The feeling will start into activity, precisely as vision
does when the eye is penetrated by rays of light.   As
we cannot by an effort of the will cease to see or hear
while light and sound reach the eye and ear, so is it
impossible to prevent the internal feeling from arising when its object is present.

Of this truth I had a touching example many years
ago when in Italy, and in bad health. On calling one
forenoon at a friend's house which I was in the habit
of frequenting, I felt seriously unwell just as I reached
the door. My friends were not at home, but I walked
in and lay down on a sofa. Shortly a young girl,
eighteen months old, came tottering into the room
with a mirthful smile on its face. On seeing me in
that unusual position, she at once became grave, and

how erroneous is the opinion so commonly entertained, or at least acted on, that reason is the sole source of our conduct, and that hence it is useless to begin even domestic education till reason has developed itself sufficiently to understand all that is said. Whether we heed it or not, education—meaning thereby the formation of character, as well as intellectual instruction—commences for us WITH THE VERY DAWN OF LIFE. If we delay systematic education and training till the age of five or six, Nature will not remain idle till we are ready to begin. An unsystematic, irrational, and often hurtful education—namely, that arising out of the influences and circumstances by which every child is surrounded, and which never cease to act, for good or for evil, for a single hour of its life—will have taken the precedence, and raised up obstacles which may then render our best efforts fruitless; for it is not at school alone that a child can be educated. Habits of indolence and vice may be learned from companions in the streets and highways, and from immoral example in a vicious and degraded home, quite as readily and certainly as habits of order, activity, and virtue, may be acquired in our best-conducted schools.

Impressed by this great truth, Mr Stow insists strongly on the necessity of beginning moral—not intellectual—training at the very earliest age; and he says that eighteen years' experience has proved most triumphantly the advantages of doing so, and has demonstrated that " you increase geometrically in power as you descend in age, for if *training* at

twelve years of age be as *one*—at nine it is as *two*
—at seven as *four*—at five as *eight*—and at three
years of age as *sixteen*."* This is most instructive
and unexceptionable testimony, and I am convinced
that the same principle would apply at a still earlier
period; but no children being received by Mr Stow
under three years old, he, of course, could speak only
of his experience from that age upwards.

The PHYSIOLOGICAL LAW OF EXERCISE being the great
principle by which all our educational efforts ought
to be directed in the cultivation of the affections, and
the moral and religious feelings, as well as of the intellect, it is important that it should be rightly understood by parents and teachers. In my *Physiology
applied to Health and Education*, I have entered fully
into its exposition, and need only say here, that regular, suitable, and repeated exercise is the appointed
means by which to obtain development, strength, and
readiness of action of the *internal* mental faculties,
as well as of the *external* senses. But to succeed in
this to the utmost possible extent, it is clear that we
must know the nature of the different internal faculties, and the objects or qualities to which they are
respectively related, so that we may call each into
action by the stimulus of its own objects with the
same precision as is done in the case of the external
senses.

But it was precisely for want of this knowledge
that the difficulties of the parent and educationist
fairly began. Before the discovery of the functions of

* Page 6.

the brain by Gall, we were not in possession either of
any settled philosophy or theory of mind capable of
making us acquainted with the number and functions
of the primitive mental faculties, or of any principles by the application of which these might be
ascertained. Now, however, that Gall's discovery has
laid a solid foundation for a philosophy of mind in
accordance with nature, we enjoy greater facilities
than we ever before possessed, for rendering education practically useful in the improvement of man.
It would be out of place, in a work like this, to show
in what manner Phrenology has removed many of
the difficulties which have hitherto impeded the progress and success of our educational training.   For
detailed information on the subject, I must refer the
reader to the works of the discoverer and cultivators of
Phrenology.*   In regard to the mental faculties which
it assigns grounds, more or less conclusive, for re-

* Gall, "Sur les Fonctions du Cerveau;"   Spurzheim's "Phrenology," "Philosophical Principles of Phrenology," "Phrenology in
Connection with the Study of Physiognomy," and "Elementary Principles of Education;" George Combe's "System" and "Elements of
Phrenology;" "The Phrenological Journal," 20 vols., &c.

In the former editions of this work, an outline of the elementary
mental faculties was given in the text.   But it was so brief as to be
of little use to those who had not already studied Phrenology, and it
has therefore been omitted.   Those who desire to understand Phrenology, should study it in the works of Gall, Spurzheim, and George
Combe.   The author's earnest appeal in favour of Phrenology rested
on a deep conviction of its being the only well-founded philosophy
of mind, and on its paramount utility, notwithstanding its yet imperfect state, as a guide in the direction of education.   This conviction he arrived at after studying the work of Gall, and carefully
comparing the doctrine of that physiologist with the result of his
own observations.   See his "Life and Correspondence," by George
Combe, 1850.—ED.

garding as elementary, the important thing to remark here is, that in so far as any or all of them are
so, they may be possessed in different degrees of
relative strength by different persons, and may also
be called into action separately or together, as is the
case with the external senses.   Thus, a man may
be benevolent, and yet have a defective sense of
justice, precisely as one may hear acutely, and yet
have indifferent eye-sight.   In like manner, we
may have lively sentiments of hope and veneration,
while benevolence remains unmoved, just as wo may
smell without seeing.   On the same principle, a person may be a quick and accurate observer of facts or
phenomena, and yet a bad reasoner upon them; or
an excellent reasoner, but an inaccurate observer.
And one gifted with high talent for geometry, or
drawing, or languages, may be incapable of learning
music, and even of appreciating it when performed
in his hearing.

From the similarity of constitution, which, in this
respect, exists between the external senses and the
internal faculties of the mind, the sentiment of cautiousness, for example, may start singly into action
at the sight of danger; benevolence, at the appearance
of suffering; attachment, at the approach of a friend ;
just as the sense of hearing does on the occurrence of
a sound, or that of seeing on the admission of light.
Hence it follows, that, in cultivating the internal
faculties of the mind, we ought to act upon the
principle which proves so successful in the education
of the external senses, namely, that of EXERCISING

EACH FACULTY ON THE OBJECTS DIRECTLY RELATED TO
IT. In reality, it is just as absurd to attempt to train
the moral faculties to activity by lessons addressed to
the intellect alone, as it would be to try to improve
hearing by the exercise of smell or of vision.

So also, when we wish to weaken or repress any
mental faculty, we must endeavour to remove it from
the influence of all objects that naturally excite it;
in other words, we must be careful to "*lead it not
into temptation.*" If we act on this principle, we
shall succeed in so far as the nature of the original
constitution will permit. If we disregard it, failure
and disappointment will follow our best exertions in
education, simply because we shall then be labouring
in opposition to the laws of the Creator. Except,
indeed, for the ready response of the faculty to the
stimulus of its objects, *temptation* would be a word
devoid of meaning; but the object being presented,
the faculty starts into action even against the efforts
of the will

CHAPTER XV.

ASSUMING, as I may now venture to do, that whatever tends to modify the corporeal or mental constitution of man, tends to have a permanent influence upon him for good or for evil, it follows that although education, technically so called, is generally delayed till the age of five or six years, real education, or the influence of surrounding circumstances, begins at birth, and often lays a durable foundation for the future bodily and mental character, even before the dawn of distinct consciousness. From the moment, indeed, that the young being can express a want, and derive enjoyment from its gratification; from the moment that its bodily comfort is visibly increased or impaired by judicious or injudicious treatment—from that moment, although the intellect may still slumber in comparative inactivity, and be unable to generate one well-defined idea, intellectual and moral education has commenced, and, whether recognised as such or not, will continue to impress its effects on the constitution so long as the individual continues to exist.

If, bearing this important truth constantly in mind, the mother be careful to direct her training in harmony with the laws of nature, she will reap her reward in the continued improvement and happiness of her child. But if she act otherwise, much mischief may be done, not only before the child can think or reason, but even before it can speak. It is a common excuse with over-indulgent mothers for omitting to correct any even glaring impropriety of feeling or of conduct in a child, that it is still " too young to listen to reason," and that it will be time enough to check such aberrations when the child is older. This is a great mistake. In infancy we are governed not by reason, but by the well-directed affection and kindness of our guardians ; and to wait till the development of a child's understanding before we commence its moral training, is to wait till years of unregulated indulgence shall have cultivated and strengthened its more selfish and powerful appetites and passions—to wait, in short, till the weed has grown and ripened and shed its seed, before attempting to extirpate it from the soil.

So entirely is the infant under the influence of this natural parental ascendency in the early period of its existence, that it seems almost as if instinctively conscious that its safety and wellbeing lie in its very dependence ; for, powerless in itself, it is ever ready to yield implicit obedience where it has experienced consistent sympathy and kindness. This

is so true, that when a child *habitually* disputes
or rebels against the authority of its guardian, we
may be sure that it is either suffering from physical
discomfort, or fretted by injudicious management.
At that early age, habitual peevishness and discontent indicate the existence of some real grievance,
and not of mere wilful perversity; and whatever
the evil may be, every means should be used for
its removal before it shall have taken root, and
have left in the system traces which may never be
effaced.

As, then, the feelings or emotions come into play
long before the intellect is sufficiently developed or
enlightened to assume their direction or control, it
is obvious that if their proper regulation by the
parent be unduly delayed by waiting for the dawn
of reason, the character and happiness of the child
must remain meanwhile very much at the mercy
of accident.　If the circumstances by which it is
surrounded should happen to be unusually favourable, comparatively little mischief may ensue from
the absence of systematic moral training.　But if,
besides wanting proper guidance, the child should be
exposed to the contaminating influence of bad-tem-
pered, selfish, or ill-disposed guardians, or companions
of its own age, its character may sustain more serious
injury than years of subsequent care will be able to
compensate.　It is from the lasting impression which
may thus be made on the infant constitution, even at
a very early age, that the influence of the mother and
nurse on the dispositions of the child is more powerful

than any other single cause to the operation of which
it is subjected.

Of the errors committed in the management of
early childhood, the two which are perhaps the most
common may be said to arise from the tendency of
human nature to go to one extreme while seeking to
avoid the other. The *first* error consists in allowing the
will of the child to have almost unlimited sway, and
consequently permitting the unregulated and unlimited
indulgence of every wish as it rises in the infant mind.
The *second* and opposite error consists in substituting,
on all occasions, the mother's feelings, inclinations,
and judgment for those of the child, and regulating
even the minutest and most unimportant details by a
rigid adherence to rules, which is not less at variance
with their spirit than destructive of the comfort and
dispositions of the child. By the former of these
methods, selfishness is so directly and systematically
cultivated, that in most instances the child becomes
thoroughly "spoiled." By the second, the child finds
itself so continually thwarted that its spirit is broken,
and it is made to lead a life of fretting and wretched-
ness. A third error, far from uncommon among weak-
minded but over-anxious mothers, consists in asking
and acting upon the advice of every visitor who happens to cross the threshold. The parent's only safety
in all these circumstances is to be found in making
herself acquainted with the nature of the infant constitution. Were the guardians of the young more
deeply impressed with the advantages to be derived

from assuming this standard for their rule of action
in regulating the details of infant management, they
would be more distrustful of substituting the blind prejudices of the nurse or of bystanders for the rational
advice of the experienced and enlightened physician.

In early childhood, as well as in maturer age, spontaneous, varied, and harmonious activity of mind and
body, elicited by objects calculated to rouse without
exhausting our faculties, constitutes our highest enjoyment, and indolent inactivity about the lowest.
Sprightly animation and idiotic apathy thus represent
the two extremes; the one accompanied by a pleasing
consciousness of happiness, and the other by a dull
and gloomy dissatisfaction. As a natural consequence
of this part of our mental constitution, the highest
and purest enjoyment which we experience is that
springing from the gratified activity of our higher sentiments—benevolence, veneration, conscientiousness,
hope, wonder, and ideality—regulated by a well-trained
and well-furnished understanding. Whereas, when
it is chiefly the lower and more selfish propensities
that are roused into action, and the moral and intellectual powers are either outraged or left in abeyance,
the pleasure experienced is not only inferior in kind
and in degree, but also greatly impaired by the consciousness of wrongdoing, which, in a well-constituted
mind, never fails to accompany it.

Here, then, we have three distinct principles for
our guidance in promoting the health and happiness
of the young. The first is, that the system of management shall be such as to afford ample opportu-

nity for the due and appropriate exercise of *all* the
bodily and mental functions. The second is, that
while fulfilling this aim, we shall not allow the mental
activity to be carried to such excess as to exhaust or
weaken the faculties exercised. The third is, that
while affording due scope for the gratification of the
propensities and affections which fit us for the domestic relations of life, we shall carefully prohibit
every indulgence at variance with the dictates of the
moral sentiments and intellect.

In all cases, adaptation to the wants, feelings, and
nature of the infant—so different in many respects
from those of the adult—ought to be made the leading principle of our management; and accordingly
the child ought, as far as possible, to be allowed
the choice of its own occupations and amusements,
and to become the chief agent in the development
and formation of its own character. So long as
it manifests feelings, desires, or intellectual wants,
which are in themselves right and proper, we cannot
in any way contribute to its welfare and happiness so
much as by allowing it due scope for their gratification.
In this respect the lower animals teach us a valuable
lesson. The young kitten gradually developes its
own muscular powers, and peculiar instincts and qualities, by their free and playful exercise according to
its own wishes and desires; but it does so under a
vigilant maternal guardianship, which, while leaving
it ample liberty of locomotion and amusement, is yet
ever ready to interfere in case of danger. If, however,
the cat were to insist on prescribing to the kitten in

L

what manner it should amuse itself, when it should
begin and when it should leave off its frolics, the harmony and affection between them would speedily
come to an end. Under the guidance of an instinct
which supplies the place of reason, the cat allows the
kitten to pursue its frolic in its own way ; and if she
does not always take an active share in it, she at least
never puts a stop to it unless her interference is required by an adequate cause. When there is such a
cause, her authority is promptly and vigorously exercised, and the interference is never resented. The
kitten feels, even when suffering from its effects, that
it was prompted by kindness ; and the danger once
over, both parties continue as loving as before.

Precisely the same principle ought to be followed
with the child. Let it be left free to feel and act
according to its own inspirations, so long as its feelings and conduct are physically harmless and morally
proper. But let the parent be at all times watchful
and ready either to check or give a better direction
to its activity when prudence requires it. Improper
conduct and unreasonable demands should at once
be checked with a kind and gentle but firm hand,
and the child be made to feel that the denial, being
dictated by love, is unalterable by entreaty. In this
way implicit obedience will soon be secured. To the
young being, the harsh or vacillating exercise of mere
authority, unguided by reason, and uninfluenced by
kindly affections, is as grating and disagreeable, and
as provocative of resistance, as it is to the adult. Even
in its earliest months the infant learns to distinguish

and appreciate genuine and rational kindness, and, when managed with a little tact and good sense, yields willingly to the benignant influence. In most cases, therefore, it is the parent rather than the child that is in fault, when irrational and vacillating over-indulgence brings forth the natural fruit of selfishness, peevishness, and caprice.

From the preceding view of the sources of enjoyment in infancy, it is obvious that the best thing we can do is, to afford the child all due facilities for the wholesome and appropriate exercise of its various functions and faculties, according to their actual state of development, and to encourage rather than supersede its efforts to entertain itself. It would serve no good purpose, even if we were able, to convert the infant into a puppet moved only by our will. A child thus trained, and discouraged from the free exercise of its own faculties, and from placing the slightest reliance on its own caution and foresight, by being taught to trust to another's prudence for its security and direction, may seem at first sight to be less wilful and more amiable, than other children of the same age who have been more independently trained. But in after life, especially when the temperament is low, the child thus trained to act only at the bidding of another will be found to display a feebleness and indecision of character, in strong contrast with the promptitude and energy manifested by those who have been trained, from an early age, to think and act for themselves, under the superintendence and correction, but not the dictation, of their natural guardians.

From the difference between these two modes of
training not being generally understood, the young
are often treated as if it were equally advantageous
to render them the *passive* instruments of another's
feelings and ideas, as to enable them to become the
active agents in their own guidance by the exercise
of their own faculties. But no reflecting person can
have much experience in observing and directing the
youthful mind without becoming fully alive to the
superiority of the latter method. .Indeed, the greatest
improvements effected of late years in scholastic education have mainly proceeded from acting on the
principle of direct exercise to a much greater extent
than formerly, and making the pupil the active instrument in the development of his own mind, and in
the acquisition of his stores of knowledge ; and it is
the extension of this principle to the NURSERY, in common with the school, that I now earnestly advocate.
In the Normal Training Seminary of Glasgow, which,
as we have seen, is distinguished for its success in
forming the character as well as developing the intellect of its pupils, the practical importance of this
principle is thoroughly understood Common sense itself may teach us that if, from misplaced and ill-judged
tenderness, we contrive with over-watchful care to
forestall every wish and gratify every feeling of the
child, without allowing it the satisfaction of actively
contributing to its own gratification,—and try at every
moment to draw its attention from what pleases itself
to what we consider a better source of entertainment,—
we not only deprive it of the higher pleasure of grati-

fying its spontaneous activity according to its natural
wants and inclinations, but deprive it of the proper stimulus to the very form of mental exercise which is best
calculated to develop and improve its various mental
powers. The instinctive readiness with which a child,
on seeing anything done, cries out, " Let me do it
too ! " might have suggested the propriety of making
a more extensive use of the same tendency in conducting its education.

Another evil inseparable from the method of doing
everything for a child, instead of allowing him, to the
greatest possible extent, and even at the occasional
cost of a little temporary suffering, to be the agent in
his own education, is, that when trained to act only
under surveillance, he becomes useless and bewil-
dered, or falls into mischief, whenever the watchful
eye is withdrawn, as sooner or later it must be. He
is trained, in short, to regulate his conduct by the
uncertain will and feelings of another, and not by a
standard which is at once known and always accessible to him. In other words, he is trained to *moral
slavery;* and the more perfect the discipline, the more
will his mind partake either of the feebleness consequent on entire subjection, or of the disappointed
and rebellious perversity which fits him for becoming
in his turn the tyrant of others.

In the moral management of infancy, then, the
great aim of the mother ought to be, to call into due
and direct activity the various feelings or emotions,
as well as intellectual powers ; since it is on the well-
regulated and harmonious operation of all the mental

faculties that the future character, usefulness, and happiness of the child chiefly depend. But in fulfilling this object parents ought carefully to cultivate the power of *self-action* and *self-regulation*, by inducing the infant, even from its earliest days, to minister, as far as possible, to the gratification of its own wants, instead of growing up wholly dependent on the services and forethought of others. It is, of course, not meant by this that the infant should be encouraged or allowed to follow every whim, whether right or wrong, or well or ill timed. On the contrary, *obedience* and *self-denial* ought to be among the earliest of its lessons ; but the requisite discipline should be enforced by *insensibly* and *kindly* giving a right direction to the impulses and desires, rather than by meeting them with a rude denial.

CHAPTER XVI.

HAVING thus stated my views concerning the nature
of the mental constitution in infancy, and expounded
some of the principles by which we should be guided
in our endeavours to promote the welfare and improvement of the young, I now proceed to offer some
additional remarks, illustrative of the application of
those principles to the ordinary management of the
nursery and domestic circle.

From the many examples which are continually to
be met with of the influence exercised by the mother
over the mental condition of her offspring, it has
often been affirmed that bad temper, strong passions,
and even intellectual peculiarities, are communicated
to the infant *through the medium of the mother's or
nurse's milk,* and that hence it is of great consequence, in choosing a nurse, to select one of a cheerful
and amiable character. But in all the cases of this
kind which have come under my observation, the
supposed influence of the milk on the dispositions of

the nursling, was much less evident than that of the
moral infirmities and defects of temper in the parent,
in exciting, and educating to frequent and vigorous
action, the corresponding passions in the child. Many
sensible people imagine that they may say or do anything in the presence of an infant, because it is too
young to observe or to be affected by it. But, according to the principle explained in a previous
chapter, this is a great mistake. It is true that an
infant is unable to form a sound intellectual opinion
of any occurrence ; but it is not less true that from
a very early period, as shown by the case quoted from
Madame Necker de Saussure,* its feelings respond to
the calls made upon them, and thus give a bias to
the mind long before the child can exercise any act
of judgment. From the natural relation which exists
between the different faculties and their stimuli, it is
thus most important that the circumstances in which
the young are placed during the impressionable period
of infancy, should be such as tend to call into fit and
habitual action the best feelings and faculties of our
nature. Keeping in view that the best cultivation
we can give to the moral and intellectual powers is
that which secures their regular and reiterated exercise, it follows that the character and dispositions of
the child will in no small degree be influenced by the
character and dispositions of those to whose care it is
confided, and in whose society it spends the earliest
years of its existence.

It is, moreover, a common and pernicious error in

* See above, pp. 219, 221.

modern education, to imagine that the passions and moral emotions implanted in the human mind *are the results of intellectual cultivation*, and that intellectual discipline, and storing the mind with precepts, will suffice to regulate them. Under this mistaken notion, parents are often disappointed and displeased with a child, when, after a full explanation of the impropriety of the feeling or passion, it still, on the recurrence of the temptation, gives way to it as much as before. Fortunately for mankind, however, morality and religion have a much more solid foundation than if they were but the deductions of an erring intellect. They are based on feelings implanted in the very nature of man, which mere intellectual cultivation or neglect can neither generate nor destroy, and the real strength and authority of which will not be fully recognised till they are cherished and developed in more strict accordance with their natural constitution. Like the external senses, the mental faculties must be habitually exercised on their appropriate objects, before they can attain their due influence over the character, and their full power in regulating the conduct. From almost the first hour of existence, this principle should be systematically acted on, and the utmost care be taken to secure at all times a healthy moral atmosphere around the young. To do perfect justice to the infant, there is required, on the part of the mother, a combination of cheerfulness, good sense, knowledge, readiness of resource, and unfailing kindness and impartiality, which is not often to be met

2 L

with. But, by aiming at a high standard, we shall
make a nearer approach to what is required, than
if we quietly rest satisfied with whatever occurs.
It is lamentable to reflect how numerous are those
mothers, who, from indolence or other causes, leave
the entire control of their offspring to unqualified
attendants, and even themselves give way to expressions of anger or caprice, which never fail to act
injuriously upon the infant.

Let us, then, not deceive ourselves, but ever bear
in mind that WHAT WE DESIRE OUR CHILDREN TO BE-
COME, WE MUST ENDEAVOUR TO BE BEFORE THEM. If we
wish them to grow up kind, gentle, affectionate, just,
and truthful, we must habitually exhibit the same
qualities as regulating principles of our conduct,
not only towards them, but towards all; because
these qualities act as so many stimulants to the
corresponding faculties of the child, just as light to
vision, and odours to the sense of smell. If we cannot restrain our own passions, but at one time overwhelm the young with kindness, and at another surprise and confound them by our caprice or deceit, we
may with as much reason expect to gather grapes
from thistles, or figs from thorns, as to develop moral
purity and simplicity of character in our children.
It is in vain to argue that, because the intellect is
feeble, it cannot detect the inconsistency of our conduct. The feelings and reasoning faculties, being
perfectly distinct from each other, may, and sometimes do, act independently;—the feelings may at
once condemn, although the judgment may be unable

to assign a reason. In many instances, indeed, we are impelled to act before having time to think deeply about the best course to be pursued. In such cases, it is feeling which takes the lead, and in a well-constituted mind it rarely prompts to a course which reason would have refused to sanction had it been duly consulted. In this result we have another example of the admirable harmony which prevails in the moral as well as the physical arrangements of the Creator, and which renders it impossible to pursue a right course without also doing collateral as well as direct good, or to pursue a wrong course without producing collateral evil. If the mother, for example, moved by affection for her children, endeavours to keep any infirmity of her temper in subjection, and ultimately succeeds in placing herself under the habitual guidance of her higher and purer feelings in her general conduct, the good which results is not limited to the improvement of the child. She herself becomes healthier and happier, and every day adds to her influence and enjoyment. If, on the other hand, she give way to fits of passion, selfishness, caprice, and injustice, the evil is by no means limited to the suffering which she brings upon herself. Her child also suffers both in disposition and in happiness; and while, in the one case, she secures the love and regard of all who come into communication with her, in the other she rouses only their fear or dislike.

It is a grave mistake to imagine, that it matters little whether the person to whose guidance

the infant is entrusted be an active-minded and
amiable woman, or one whose good-nature is the
passive product of a vacant and indolent mind. If
the mother be a right-minded woman, and acquainted
with the nature of the being committed to her charge,
she will understand how important it is that during
infancy her child should be surrounded by persons of
intelligence, refinement, and morality; and that it is
a gross dereliction of duty to devolve her trust on
incompetent substitutes. The mother is the natural
guardian of her infant's happiness; and if she is fit
for her duties, and yet neglectful of them, is it
to be expected that any substitute, however well
qualified, will be able fully to supply her place ?

In thus attaching a high value to the mother's
influence, in preference to, or along with, that of even
the best-qualified attendants, I have no wish to speak
lightly of the services of a kind, intelligent, upright,
and experienced nurse. So far from this, I have
great pleasure in stating that I have met with some
whom I considered evidently better qualified for their
duties, by temper and knowledge, than the mothers
whose place they supplied; and that I have often
witnessed as much self-denying and unwearied devotion on the part of nurses to the welfare of their
little charges, as it is possible for any human being
to manifest towards the offspring of another. The
deficiencies with which many of them are chargeable
are almost inseparable from their position in society,
and their very imperfect education; and if, in their
ignorance of the laws of the human constitution,

they sometimes do positive mischief when their aim is good, this is what happens almost as frequently with the mothers in whose service they are placed. In pointing out errors, therefore, my object is simply to secure and advance the welfare of the child, and not to throw blame on the nurse for defects which it is impossible for her to be without.

But it is not merely the behaviour of the mother and attendants to the child itself which ought to be under the habitual influence of our best feelings. It is equally important that the same right feeling should predominate in the behaviour of the attendants to each other. I have already instanced the effect upon the child, of an angry scold conducted in its presence, although not addressed to itself. The harsh tones grate upon its feelings, and are direct stimulants to its fears, without even the perception, on its part, to whom the scold is meant to apply.

Infant-schools have been strongly objected to, because two years of age is considered too early for commencing the business of education. As, however, practical education and emotional training really begin at the dawn of consciousness, the true question comes to be, whether the child will derive more advantage from the education of chance, or from an education adapted to its natural constitution. Nobody has condemned more strongly than I, the establishment, under the name of infant-schools, of places of confinement, and intellectual and theological cramming; and nobody can have a clearer perception of the evils they inflict on the young. But such establish-

ments are mere perversions and abuses of a thing
really good in itself. Indeed, a fitter instrument for
the physical, moral, and religious training of infancy
can scarcely be imagined, than a seminary in which
the young are brought together, and their affections
and nobler feelings called into habitual and pleasing
exercise in the regulation of their conduct towards
each other in their sports and general conduct, while
their physical energies are developed and strengthened
by inspiriting and social exercise. In a well-conducted infant-school, intellectual tasks and close confinement are unknown, while the senses and the observing powers are agreeably employed in the gratification of the strong curiosity so natural to that period
of life. Objects, or images of objects, should be placed
before the child, and its attention be directed to the observation of their colours, forms, properties, and uses ;
exactly on the principle, already so strongly insisted
on, of presenting every faculty of the mind with its
direct stimulus, when we wish to excite it to activity.*
But if, instead of thus following the footsteps of Nature, we attempt to convey instruction by language
merely, we must beware of regarding the accurate
and ready repetition of a sound, as in itself a proof
that the object or idea represented by it is understood
by the child. The quick imitative faculty of a child
may seize in a moment the sound made by its teacher

* By means of cheap but elegant pictorial and other works of art,
the sentiment of the beautiful (Ideality) may be usefully cultivated in
schools. When well directed, this feeling promotes refinement and
purity in its possessor. Its ameliorating influence is not sufficiently
attended to in the education of the young.

or companions, and yet its mind may be wandering
during all the time of the lesson. I have again and
again seen this truth exemplified in infant-schools,
where the proper word was uttered in a sing-song
tone at the right place by a child in the act of drop-
ping from its seat asleep ; and I have satisfied myself,
by varying the question a little, that few even of those
who were wide awake and ready with their answers
had the slightest conception of the idea that the
words were intended to convey. When children so
taught are examined out of the regular order of
routine, their readiness and self-possession forsake
them, and their stock of ideas is found to be much
smaller than the sample educed by the teacher
would lead us to expect. All this, however, is no
proof that a proper system of infant training is bad.
It only shows that many things which are done in
the manner of infant training, are, in reality, at variance with sound principles ; and that, even when a
right system is professedly adopted, it is far from
being always carried efficiently into practice. It
shows also the necessity of attending more to the
state of mind of each individual child than is done at
present, and that TEACHERS MUST THEMSELVES BE
TRAINED FOR TEACHING before their services can be
productive of every possible advantage to the pupil.

The public mind has been so long accustomed to
associate education exclusively with the idea of intellectual *teaching*, and parents in general attach so
little value comparatively to the influence of good
training in the formation of character, that I cannot,

even at the risk of wearying the reader, abstain from
repeating once more that infant-schools, and the habitual society of other children, are, in my opinion, to
be prized chiefly for the advantages which they afford
for the development and due regulation of the emotional part of our nature. Our affections and moral
emotions have direct reference to other human beings,
and in solitude cannot find objects to excite or
gratify them. We must feel attachment *to some
one*, act justly or kindly *to some one*, fear *some
one*, be angry *with some one*, and seek the esteem *of
some one*. To develop the powers which God has
given us, and turn them to purposes conducive to our
happiness, we must therefore associate with our fel-
lows, and, in our intercourse with them, bring into
active and habitual exercise the sentiments of justice, kindness, forbearance, and mutual regard. In
solitude, on the other hand, the various faculties have
self alone for their object; the beings on whom we
should pour out kindness and affection, and towards
whom we should practise patient forbearance and
justice, being absent, the higher and more disinte-
rested faculties, which contribute so largely to our
happiness, are necessarily deprived of their legitimate exercise and enjoyment. This forms one of
the most serious objections to private education.

Before taking leave of the subject of infant-schools,
I must refer briefly to what I cannot help considering
as a serious mistake, which threatens to convert many
of them into sources of positive injury to the young.
I allude to the subordinate importance which their

managers attach to that physical and moral training
which ought to be their primary object, and to the
prevailing tendency to convert them into ordinary
seminaries for scholastic teaching, and for the inculcation of abstruse points of faith which no infant can
comprehend. I am quite aware that, in most instances,
these changes have been made under the influence of
the highest and purest motives. But the course pursued is too palpably in opposition to the order of
development of the human faculties, as arranged by
the Creator, to succeed in effecting its aim—that of
early implanting a sense of religion in the infant
mind. Were the subject to be inculcated any other
than religion, should we not act very differently?
Suppose that the happiness of a man's life were to
depend, not on his religious character, but on the
extent of his mathematical knowledge, and on his
success in applying it to the regulation of his general conduct. The question would then be, How
shall we proceed in educating him so as to secure,
to the greatest possible extent, that knowledge which
is so indispensable to his welfare? Ought we to
begin in infancy by drilling him to repeat the rules
of arithmetic, and by teaching him the propositions
of Euclid? Should we not rather follow the more
rational course of first promoting the healthful development of his bodily and mental constitution, and
cultivating his senses and perceptive faculties in the
observation of the objects around him; and proceed
to the study of numbers and mathematical relations
and proportions, only when the corresponding intel-

lectual faculties had become sufficiently developed to appreciate them and their applications? Every one will agree that the latter would be the proper course, and that to trouble a very young child with rules of arithmetic and propositions from Euclid would only weary and disgust him. The words of the rules might, indeed, be impressed on the memory, and for a time be repeated with parrot-like accuracy; but not being understood, they would prove utterly barren, and soon fade from the recollection. If, however, following the order of Nature, we let the earlier years of the child be employed in gaining an extensive and accurate acquaintance with the objects around him, and their properties and phenomena, we shall thereby lay the surest foundation for his future success in receiving instruction in arithmetic and geometry; because then not only will he possess the facts or elements to which the scientific principles are to be applied, but his maturer faculties will be more able to trace the relations among them, and to appreciate the practical value of the knowledge he has gained.

Now, the same principle applies to the religious education of the young. Believing, as I do, that no form of human happiness can be relied upon which does not rest on a sound religious foundation, I am as desirous as any one can be to imprint on the youthful mind, at the earliest possible age, such a sense of our immediate dependence on God as it is capable of receiving. But, looking to the feeble development of the *intellect*, and to the activity of the *feelings*, in childhood, it seems to me as hopeless a task to attempt to render a child religious by teaching it to repeat theological dogmas which it cannot understand, as to make it a skilful mathematician by merely teaching it to repeat the rules of arithmetic, or the terms of a geometrical proposition. The result, however, will be widely different, if, again following the order of Nature, we *begin* with the careful training of the *feelings* and *affections*, and the direction of the *observing faculties*, which are early in activity; and delay, till a maturer age, the inculcation of creeds and dogmas, which address themselves to the *intellect.* In this way we may succeed in gradually forming those pure and virtuous habits which constitute the best ground-work for the superstructure of a true and improving religion. If, indeed, religion consisted wholly in certain outward forms of worship, and in the belief of certain abstruse doctrines, there might be an excuse, although still an unsatisfactory one, for attempting to reverse the order of Nature. But, however important creeds and dogmas may be for our guidance in maturer years, or for holding men together in ecclesiastical sects, a knowledge of them is far from constituting the most essential part of personal religion, and they are precisely those portions which are least applicable to the period of infancy and childhood. Instead of promoting peace and good-will among men, they have been in all ages the chief sources of that fierce and bitter strife which has so often disgraced the Christian profession,—and they will, I fear, con-

tinue to be a fruitful source of contention as long
as Religion shall be made the arena for displays
of mere intellectual gladiatorship, and the subject
of deep and abstruse speculation. Viewed in its
true light, Religion addresses itself directly to our
highest and purest emotions. In the teachings of
Jesus himself, it is always the keeping of "*the
heart*" that is emphatically spoken of as its vital
essence; and at no period of life can that object be more successfully prosecuted than in infancy. Religion, then, not only may, but ought to be
taught even from early infancy; but it is with the
religion of the heart or affections that we must begin.
The obligations to honour father and mother, to do
justly and love mercy, to forgive injuries, to do
good to those who hate us, and to abstain from all
envy and uncharitableness, are as integral parts of
true religion as the duty to worship the only true and
living God. The habitual fulfilment of most of these
obligations depends, however, much more on the proper discipline and regulation of our moral nature, than
on intellectual eminence or attainments; and hence,
our success in performing them in mature life will
depend, in no small degree, on the extent to which
we have been trained to practise them in childhood,
when the feelings can be easily bent in a right direction. We have the assurance that if we " train up a
child in the way he should go, when he is old he will
not depart from it;" but the promised result is to be
consequent on *training the child*, and not on merely
teaching it either doctrines or forms. Let us not,

then, be alarmed by the frivolous and yet common
objection, that religion would be endangered if infant-
schools were limited chiefly to their proper objects of
physical and moral training. The very reverse is the
truth; for the surest basis on which religion can rest
in early life, is the lively existence of its practical
spirit in the love and affections of the child. For fostering this spirit, there can scarcely be a fitter means
than a well-conducted infant-school—except, indeed,
the habitual and varied intercourse of a large and
well-regulated family and social circle, in which the
young are brought together, and their affections and
nobler feelings are called into frequent and pleasing
exercise, both by the habitual example of their parents
and associates, and by their own direct employment
and training for the ordinary duties of social life.

If the reader should think that I have condemned,
without sufficient reason, the kind of religious teaching pursued in some of our infant-schools, and that it
is by no means so much beyond the reach of the child-
ish intellect as I have represented, I would solicit a
perusal of the subjoined extracts from a little work
published since my remarks were written, and which,
I think it will be admitted, bear out those remarks to
the fullest extent. The work referred to is entitled
"THE HEART; Lessons for the Young, by J. Fergu-
son, Teacher of the Model Infant-School, Edinburgh."
In a preface dated February 1847, the author states
that the directors of the school recommended it
"as a useful guide in infant education," and that he
himself has found it "pleasant and profitable" to his

little pupils. To avoid any risk of unfairness I shall quote the first and last lessons entire, and only add that the first is rather a favourable specimen. Let the reader peruse them carefully, and consider as he goes along what kind of meaning children of three, four, or five years would be likely to attach to them.

The first lesson is entitled *The Heart*, and its text is, " *The heart is deep.*" The child is then asked—

1. Who speaks in the text ?—God.

2. Who is spoken to ?—Every person.

3. What is spoken of ?—The heart.

4. What does God say to every person about the heart ?

"The heart is deceitful above all things and desperately wicked ; who can know it."

5. What are all God's sayings ?—True. (Titus i. 2 ; Psalms xiv. 7.)

6. For what purpose does God tell us that our hearts are so bad ?

That we may desire a new heart. (Rev. iii. 17, 18; John iv. 7, 29.)

7. Can you repeat a verse in which God has promised a new heart to all who are willing to receive it?

"A new heart also will I give you, and a new spirit will I put within you ; and I will take away the stony heart out of your flesh, and I will give you an heart of flesh.—(Ezek. xxxvi. 26.)

8. When does one begin to be happy ?

When he receives a new heart.

9. Why does one begin to be happy on receiving a new heart ?

Because he begins to love God.—(Rom. vi. 5.)

The 24th and last lesson is entitled *A weapon*, and the text which it explains is, "Death and life are in the power of the tongue." On this the child is asked—

1. What weapon did Delilah use deceitfully to overcome Samson ?

Her tongue.

2. When did he tell her all his heart ?

" When she pressed him daily with her words, and urged him so that his soul was vexed unto death."— (Judges xvi. 16, 17.)

3. What does Solomon, speaking by the Spirit of God, say of such an one as Delilah ?

" I find more bitter than death the woman whose heart is snares and nets, and her hands as bands."— (Eccles. vii. 26.)

4. Can you repeat a prayer suited to these exercises on the deceitfulness of the heart ?

" Create in me a clean heart, O God, and renew a right spirit within me."—(Psalm li. 10.)

Such are two of the lessons written for and taught at this Model Infant-School. Appreciating, as I do, the earnestness and zeal of the teacher, and the excellence of the motives which have inspired him with the desire to instil such lessons into the minds of the children under his care, it is with great reluctance that I venture to utter one word of doubt or discouragement on the propriety of the course he has

pursued. But a deep sense of the important interests
at stake prevents me from remaining silent regarding
what I believe to be a very serious error of judgment,
both on his part and on that of the directors who have
sanctioned his *Lessons* by their approval.*   I have no
doubt that a large proportion of the children at an
infant-school may be taught to *repeat the words* of
such lessons; but when we consider not only the extent of knowledge of the Bible, and of human nature,
but also the power of thinking, and actual experience
of the world, which are required, even in a person of
mature mind, fully to understand the last lesson for
example, it seems to me nothing less than a delusion
to expect that the mere repetition of the words—dry
and meaningless as they must appear to the infant
mind—can in any way, or in any degree, profit the
child who is made to learn them. In fact, the time
and pains sacrificed in the attempt are worse than
lost. If any intelligent person will only try the ex-
periment of teaching that lesson to a child of even
double the age of those usually attending infant-
schools, and ascertain, by a careful and candid examination, how far it has succeeded in extracting from
the words the meaning which they really embody,
and which he himself perceives in them, he will require no arguments to satisfy him that it is not by
such means that little children are to be brought
under the influence of true religion. In childhood

* Since this was written, the school here remarked upon has passed
into other hands, and no longer professes to be a Model Infant-School
The observations in the text continue, however, to apply in substance
to not a few of our seminaries for young children.—ED.

the domestic example exhibited in the habitual regulation of the feelings, character, and conduct of all around, in accordance with the dictates of a pure and elevated religion, will, when occasionally accompanied with a simple explanatory remark or anecdote, do more to stamp a similar character on the impressible mind of a child, than the learning by rote of the whole creed and doctrines of the Church. All experience shows that the infant is easily touched by a simple and direct appeal to its feelings, but remains unmoved if addressed only through the medium of words which its unformed mind is incapable of understanding or appreciating.

From the exposition which has been given in the preceding pages, it will now, I trust, be evident, that whatever acts upon the senses of a child, interests its feelings, or attracts its observation, necessarily influences its mental state, or, in other words, becomes a means of education. Even the locality and climate in which a child lives, the objects by which it is surrounded, the ordinary occurrences of the nursery, the spirit which they exhibit, and the very toys with which it amuses itself, exert an influence on its constitution, and, under the direction of an enlightened mother, become a means of educating its feelings and its intellect. "In caressing a dog or a cat in the presence of a child," says the acute observer already frequently quoted, "we develop that sympathy which the young so easily experience for animals; by showing him a beautiful object, and getting him to look

M

at it in detail, we both strengthen his attention, and
excite in him admiration, which is one of the most
exalted movements of the soul; by placing imita-
tions or pictures before him, we awaken his imagination; and so in a thousand different ways we may
appeal to his dawning faculties. When once the
mind has been put in play by some impression, he
associates it with himself, and acquires clearness and
precision of perception by occupying himself with
it. It is thus that he exercises and forms himself.
To vary, without excess, the sensations of the infant, always embracing his moral nature at the same
time to the utmost possible extent, constitutes the
real education of the intellect in early infancy. It
is also the best education for the moral feelings,
which at that age ought to be most assiduously
cultivated."*

In the preceding pages I have dwelt on the much
greater facility with which the mental faculties are
called into action by presenting to them their own
direct objects than by any other means. But obvious
as this principle is when broadly stated, and beauti-
fully as its influence in strengthening the faculties,
by exciting them to lively activity, is illustrated in
the above quotation, it is surprising how little it is
generally appreciated or intentionally applied by parents, or even by professional educators. Thus, I
have seen parents deliberately encourage the pigmy
passion of an infant against some unhappy animal or
plaything, because it amused them to contrast the

* Necker de Saussure de l'Education Progressive, vol. i. p. 158.

violence of his rage with the impotence of his efforts
to give effect to it—without entertaining a suspicion
that, in so doing, they were assiduously cultivating
his worst passions.

From all this it may be concluded that the first step
toward improving the moral training of the young
must be, to IMPROVE THE EDUCATION AND ENLARGE THE
KNOWLEDGE OF THOSE TO WHOSE CARE THEY ARE IN-
TRUSTED.

.

Another rule arising out of the natural constitution
of man, and which is important in the moral and intellectual management of infancy, is, TO GIVE DUE
EXERCISE TO ALL THE FACULTIES, AND NOT TO CULTI-
VATE ANY TO EXCESS, WHILE OTHERS ARE ALLOWED TO
LANGUISH FROM INACTION. It is the more important
to bear this rule in mind, because it points to an error
very frequently committed. I have no hesitation in
saying, that if the moral faculties were as assiduously
called into exercise in infancy as the feelings of
vanity, self-esteem, cautiousness, secretiveness, and
wonder, there would be a much more rapid advance
than there is in the morality of mankind.* In in-

* The sentiment of justice (conscientiousness) is active in many
children at an early age, but is often blunted before maturity by the
outrages to which it is exposed in ordinary life, more frequently
from its nature not being recognised by the parent than from any
intentional breach of morality. Hence the prevalence of fraud, falsi-
fication, and deceit in every trade and profession, notwithstanding the
checks imposed by municipal inspectors, and by all the custom-house,
excise, and other regulations which have ever been, or ever will be,
devised. This sentiment stands more in need of improved domestic
and social training than any other.

fancy, the moral feelings respond readily to any call made upon them; and if children were not so habitually perplexed by the contrast between the *precepts* and the *conduct* of those around them, those feelings would become daily more influential over them, and at last gain paramount power in regulating the ordinary actions of life. Of this truth, the works of Wilderspin, Stow, Barwell, and others, on infant education and training, afford numerous instructive examples; and I regret that my limits preclude me from doing more than referring to the pages of these writers.* To the parent, their perusal and study will be highly instructive. It is gratifying to see sound educational principles at last applied so intelligently and successfully to moral and religious, as well as to intellectual training. The former, although in reality the more important of the two, was long unaccountably overlooked; and it is one of the many services rendered by Phrenology to the cause of human improvement, that it places the necessity of moral and religious training, and the means of conducting it, in a clearer and more practical light than they were ever placed before.

It is of much importance to begin the moral training of the young by suitable exercise of the different feelings and emotions FROM THEIR EARLIEST DAWN;

* Wilderspin on Infant Education.—The Training System of Education, Religious, Intellectual, and Moral, as established in the Glasgow Normal Training Seminary. By David Stow, Esq.— Simpson's Philosophy of Education.—Warne's Phrenology in the Family.—Mrs Barwell's Nursery Government.—Bray's Education of the Feelings.

and not to allow any of the propensities to gain an unduo ascendency by habitual indulgence, while the kindlier feelings remain weak from inactivity. Knowing from experience how susceptible the infant is both of physical and mental impressions, we ought to be the more careful about the proper treatment of its moral nature; for just as certainly as the sight or hearing may be cultivated, by reiterated exercise, to the nicest, quickest, and most accurate perception, or enfeebled and blunted by inaction, so may the feelings be modified in strength, rapidity, and precision of action by habitual use or disuse.

VARIETY OF OCCUPATION is another important means of success in infant education. In early life, the nervous system is too mobile and excitable to admit of long-sustained effort in any one direction—a fact of special moment in the education of children in whom the mental powers are feeble. The very restlessness and impatience which ensue when we attempt to fix the attention of a child for a long time on one subject, afford a clear indication that variety of occupation and amusement is the means intended by the Creator for ensuring that scope and exercise for all our faculties which is so essential to our progress and improvement. Even so early as the fifth or sixth month, the child, when awake, is always looking, listening, feeling, moving, and giving expression on its ever-changing features to a variety of mental emotions. At one moment we see the smile of affectionate recognition on the entrance of its mother; at another, the playful enjoyment of mus-

cular motion in its limbs; at a third, the delight
of gratified wonder and curiosity, arising from the
handling or tasting of some new object; at a fourth,
peevish dissatisfaction from being thwarted in some
wish; at a fifth, gratified affection, roused by the
unexpected appearance of a little brother or sister;
and at a sixth, the fear of some unprepossessing
stranger, from whose approach it shrinks in alarm.
True, it cannot express its feelings in words, and thus
prove to the uninterested or unobservant bystander
the rapidity of their succession; but to the intelligent
mother every emotion is as perceptible as if uttered
in the plainest language.   And if it be granted that
such really is the variety of active feelings in the infant mind, can any one maintain that the right or
wrong direction of these feelings, or the means by
which a right direction may be most certainly given,
is a matter of little importance to the future welfare
and happiness of the child?   It ought, therefore, I
repeat, to be constantly borne in mind, that the due
exercise, upon their appropriate objects, of all the
affections and moral emotions, is as indispensable to
their development and strength, as exercise of the
intellectual powers is to intellectual proficiency; and
that harm must result when the mode of life or
management is such as to keep a few only of the
mental faculties in preponderating activity, to the
necessary repression of those which are not exercised.   This result is most likely to ensue where a
child is without companions, and without variety in
its daily life; consequently, every care should be taken

to guard against these evils, particularly in the case
of private tuition.

Progressive Development of the Mental Faculties.—In exercising the different powers of the mind,
we require to attend to the *degree* in which they are
respectively developed at the different stages of infancy and childhood, and to adapt our management
to their relative maturity.   Every one is familiar
with the fact that the external senses are not all
equally developed at the same time, but appear in
succession.   The same thing holds with the mental
faculties: they also are developed in succession, and
arrive at maturity at different ages.   This is too much
overlooked in practical education.

In the case of the EXTERNAL SENSES, the power of
sensation is observed to be directly proportioned to
the degree of maturity of their respective organs.
Such animals as both see and hear perfectly at birth,
do so simply because the respective organs are already
fully developed.   Others remain blind for several days,
and acquire by slow degrees the power of distinguishing objects.   So also the human infant feels before
he sees or hears, and both sees and hears before he
seems to smell.   These results are always in harmony
with the state of the respective organs.   The nerves
of feeling are well developed before the eye or ear is
matured; and the eye and ear are already well or-
ganized while the nose remains flat and small, and
the nostrils limited in extent.   If, however, light
were shut out from the eyes, and the other senses

were never exercised, the development of their organs
would be greatly retarded, and their vigour considerably impaired.   Hence, both conditions must be
taken into account in our educational proceedings ;
and the exercise of the sense ought always to bear a
relation to the condition of its organ.

On observing the operation of the MENTAL FACUL-
TIES generally, we find that they also are developed
in succession, and that the organs of those of them
which are manifested earliest arrive at maturity
sooner than the others.   The child observes long
before it compares and reasons, because the organs
of the perceptive are matured before those of the
reflecting faculties.   For a similar reason, it feels
and appreciates affection and kindness before it ex-
periences the sense of justice, the love of praise,
or the desire of gain.   From a very early age the
infant shows an irresistible tendency to IMITATION,
or to do as those around it do; and if this be not
rightly directed, it becomes as active an instrument
in the formation of bad, as it may be made one of
good habits.

As pleasure always accompanies the legitimate exercise of a faculty, the natural way to procure healthy
enjoyment for a child, is to allow the different faculties
to work upon their appropriate objects.   Not aware
of the real constitution of the human mind, many
parents act in opposition to this principle, and seek
to amuse the infant at one time by exciting its external senses, at another by dandling, and at a third
by some vivid appeal to its wonder.   As already re-

marked, most parents are too little alive to the value of SELF-ACTION and SELF-REGULATION as the grand means in the formation of character. They are apt to be too officious. They generally do too much, and cannot make up their minds to leave Nature to do her part. "I believe that we often agitate infants too much," remarks, most justly, Madame Necker de Saussure: "we ought not to let them weary, it is true; ennui is a lethargy of the soul; but what constantly brings on this malady is the very excess of distractions with which we think it right to overwhelm the infant. The contrasts are reproduced by each other; and the less excited state is the only one which can be indefinitely prolonged. The more serenity an infant has enjoyed, the more will he afterwards have. That disposition may be rendered permanent, but it is far otherwise with excited gaiety. Even with the children who are fondest of it, gaiety is but a fleeting visitor. It ought always to be welcomed, and sometimes gently invited; but, once present, it ought not to be continued to excess. Immoderate, it is followed by tears, and shakes the delicate nerves, which soon oscillate in the opposite direction."

These judicious remarks are particularly applicable to the case of children of a naturally nervous, excitable temperament. I have often observed the injury inflicted by the restless over-anxiety of parents to excite and amuse very young children, and am convinced that, in many instances, it is the cause of that nervous susceptibility which forms a prominent feature of the constitution, being often continued through the re-

muinder of life, and ultimately becoming the source
of great distress of both mind and body. Morally,
also, it inflicts an injury, by the real though unin-
tended cultivation of the selfish feelings. When a
child finds itself unceasingly the object of the exclu-
sive attention of those around it, it comes, in time, to
rely wholly upon them for its comfort and entertainment, and to regard them as present for no other
purpose than to gratify its desires and devote themselves to its caprices. Its self-esteem, thus early and
assiduously fostered, becomes daily more dominant
and exacting; and, in proportion as the infant feels
its power, it becomes a tyrant in its own petty sphere.
The mother who, in the mean time, lavishes all her
affection upon its gratification, in the hope of a rich
return of love and regard, is wounded and disappointed
in reaping only coldness and indifference. And yet,
keeping in mind the principle that every faculty is
strengthened by exercise on its proper objects, what
other result could reasonably be hoped for? The
practice pursued towards the child, of yielding everything to its wishes, is naturally a source of future
unhappiness, and not of enjoyment. It cultivates self-
esteem and love of power, and blights rather than
fosters affection. No wonder, then, that the selfishness of pampered pride, instead of the expected beam-
ing of affection, should be eminently the characteristic of spoiled children. The sentiment of self-esteem,
in due proportion, is essential to dignity of character
—pride and arrogance are its abuses. In some children it is so weak that they need to be encouraged

and brought forward; but in general it requires judicious training rather than cultivation.

When, again, in our whole intercourse with children, we occupy ourselves exclusively with their feelings and doings, their dress and appearance, but make little or no effort to draw forth their kindness and good feeling towards others, or to teach them the pleasure of fulfilling duties even at the cost of present self-denial, what can we expect but that they should become the constant subjects of their own thoughts, and the slaves of a contemptible vanity? We educate them to selfishness, self-conceit, and a passion for admiration, and are disappointed at the success of our efforts!* By nature, however, a child is by no means exacting and selfish. It feels its dependence from an early age, and, rightly treated, it will not only repay kindness with kindness and gratitude, but be ready to sacrifice its own wishes for the purpose of gratifying those who have established a claim upon its affection. But where the good feelings of an infant

---

* Most young children are peculiarly sensitive to praise and blame, and this feeling may be made the means of much good, as well as of much harm, according to the good or bad training of the child. In domestic management the sentiment of love of approbation is more abused, because more easily acted on by the means at hand, than almost any other faculty we possess. When well directed, it gives a desire for the *deserved* good opinion of others. When in excess, it leads to vanity and an insatiable love of distinction, without much regard to merit or the honesty of the means employed to attain it. In schools and families it is greatly abused in the shape of a vicious emulation in the former, and the lavish praise of dress, personal beauty, cleverness, or accomplishments in the latter. The natural consequence is the tendency now so prevalent, to consider *what people will say or think* of our conduct, rather than *what is in itself right and proper.*

are not called into play by genuine maternal benignity,
and its will is yielded to simply from weakness, and
in order to obviate discontent, the amiable emotions
necessarily languish for want of exercise. Here, then,
we have the selfish feelings actively strengthened,
and the higher feelings indirectly weakened;—and
what can be the fruit of such treatment but general
deterioration of the infant's dispositions, and that perversity of character of which we hear the parents,
whose conduct has fostered it, so pathetically complain?

Contrasting such management with that of an infant treated from the first with the same kind intentions, but directed with greater intelligence and
higher moral principle, how different do we find the
result! Let the mother exercise a salutary control
over the manifestation of the selfish desires, and
steadily oppose what she feels to be wrong, while, at
the same time, every means of legitimate gratification
are kindly, cheerfully, and ungrudgingly bestowed;
and the child will display in return, not only affection, but a *confidence* in its parent's kindness, which
is never shown in the other case, and which affords a
striking indication of the accuracy with which even
an infant can discriminate the natural language of
human feeling.

To enter fully into the subject of the moral and intellectual management of infancy and childhood would
require an extent of detail sufficient of itself to fill a
volume. All that I can do on the present occasion
is to direct attention to *principles* by which those

may profit who are engaged in this most interesting and important occupation. If these principles
be kept in view, intelligent parents and teachers,
who know something of the constitution of the human
mind, will experience many facilities in soliciting the
activity of the different faculties, and directing them
in their natural channel, and will soon, by repeated
observation, discover the appropriate stimulus to
each.*

The only other principle in the education of infancy to be noticed at present, is one upon which I
shall touch very briefly, both because it is in some
measure implied in those already considered, and because it is treated of more at large in the work referred
to below. It is simply, that THE DEVELOPMENT OF THE
HUMAN FACULTIES, AND THE FORMATION OF HUMAN CHA-
RACTER, TAKE PLACE ACCORDING TO FIXED LAWS, imposed by the Creator for the regulation of both mind
and body; and that, to be successful, our endeavours
to modify either must be made in conformity with the
Divine arrangements. By realizing the conditions
under which any organ or function is fitted to act,
we may modify or improve its action; but in no case
can we alter the nature of the function itself. We
may modify, but we can neither annul nor create.
Accordingly, it is indispensable to success in educa-

* In my work on *Physiology applied to Health and Education*, I have
entered more deeply into the general subject of the training of the
young than I could properly do in the present volume; and to its pages
I refer the reader for further suggestions.

. tion that we ADAPT OUR MEANS IN SUCH A MANNER TO
THE NATURE OF THE BEING TO BE EDUCATED, AS THAT
THEY MAY BE IN PERFECT HARMONY WITH THE LAWS OF
ITS CONSTITUTION, so that these laws may themselves
become the instruments, as it were, of attaining the
desired result.

In ordinary life, this principle, chiefly from ignorance of the human constitution, is often wholly overlooked, and we hear even sensible men talking habitually as if they could implant or eradicate any quality
of the mind at pleasure, while at the same time they
employ the most heterogeneous methods to accomplish their purpose.

Each of our faculties is implanted in us by the
Creator, with a definite constitution and a definite
function ; and we can no more add a new feeling or a
new power, by education or other means, than we can
cause apples to grow on one branch of a fig-tree and
plums on another. Man will never stand in a right
position towards God or towards his fellow-creatures,
till he regard himself and the world around him as
placed from the beginning in definite relations to
each other, and governed by laws emanating from a
Wisdom and Beneficence which it is impossible for
him fully to scan, but which he ought humbly to
study, and gratefully to venerate, admire, and obey.
If he do this, and seek, in the simple spirit of faith
and truth, to fulfil the plan marked out in legible
characters by the finger of Providence in the laws of
the animal economy, he will assuredly reap comfort
and improvement from his endeavours. But if he

presumptuously step beyond this, and attempt to fashion himself or others according to laws and fancies of his own, he will not less assuredly and deservedly reap pain and trouble for his reward.

Before concluding, I ought perhaps to apologize for some repetitions into which I have been led by an earnest desire to render this work available to parents as a practical guide in the discharge of their important but difficult duties. I am aware that in some places I have insisted with perhaps wearisome iteration upon truths and principles which, when broadly stated, meet with almost universal assent, and which therefore may seem to be familiar to the public mind. But I have done so intentionally, from having often observed with pain, how wide a difference there is between merely knowing a thing as a fact, and being fully impressed with the importance of *turning it to practical account* in the affairs of life. By a common error in education, we are led to estimate the mere *possession* of knowledge as all that is required of us, and to overlook the still higher interest attaching to its *uses* and *applications*. Hence, in one sense, we may be said to be familiar with many things which, strictly speaking, we know but very imperfectly; because, looking upon them simply as isolated objects, we remain blind to the reality of their influence. In practice, examples of this are of daily or hourly occurrence; and it is with the hope of rousing the attention of my readers to the necessity of a more comprehensive study of the subject, that I have ventured upon repetitions which I should otherwise have considered unnecessary. In a work not to be merely read and thrown aside, but to become the nursery companion of the mother, a degree of completeness in its separate parts was required, which occasionally called for repetition of what had gone before. But as UTILITY has been my aim throughout, and everything was to be risked to secure it, I trust that the fault will be excused if in any instance repetition has been carried to excess.

APPENDIX.

Appendix A, p. 10.

The results of marriages of consanguinity in the United States of America have been made the subject of special investigation by Dr M. S. Bemis, who writes in the *North American Medico-Chirurgical Review*, vol. i., 1857; and by Dr Devay, in an article entitled "Hygiène des Familles," in the *American Journal of Insanity*, 1859. The following are the results of Dr Bemis's observations:—Marriages between first cousins, 28; between second cousins, 6. Of these, 27 were fruitful and produced 192 children, 7 were sterile. Of the 28 marriages between first cousins, 23 were fruitful, 5 sterile; of the union between second cousins, 4 were fruitful, 2 sterile. Of the 192 children born, 58 died in early life. In 24 of these the causes of death are stated as follows:—Spasmodic diseases, 8; hydrocephalus, 1; consumption, 15.

Of the 134 surviving children, 46 arrived at maturity, apparently healthy; 32 in deteriorated health, but not diseased; 23 scrofulous; 4 epileptic; 4 idiots; 2 insane; 1 chorea; 2 mutes; 2 blind; 2 deformed; 5 albinoes; 6 with defective vision; 9 undescribed. Thus, of 134 children, 46 only reached maturity in health.

Dr Devay's observations are divided into two categories: the first, amounting to 39 cases, were partly collected within the circle of his own acquaintances, partly furnished to him by patients, and obtained from other authentic sources. The marriages were mostly between first and second cousins; two were between uncles and nieces.

The second series consists of 82 cases, collected and the

facts verified by himself. These alliances, with the exception of four uncles who espoused their nieces, were between
cousins and the children of cousins. Of these 82 marriages
14 proved sterile, which, added to 8 of the previous series of
39 cases, makes 22 instances of sterility in the whole 121
cases. Of these 22 cases, 16 were absolutely sterile—that is,
conception did not take place; while in the 6 others, abor-
tion occurred in the first months of gestation. The result of
Dr Devay's observations is, that consanguineous marriages
are either sterile, or the issue are affected in health or
structure. He considers idiocy, mental alienation, and deaf-
mutism frequent coincidences; congenital malformation,
and even blindness and hæmiplegia, he also states to be
not unfrequently observed in the issue of such marriages.
Of the abnormal deviations, he noticed superfluity of fingers
or toes as the most frequent.

That under very favourable circumstances of good constitutions and judicious management of the health after marriage, the union of blood relations is not always attended
with such disastrous consequences, may be very true; but
the general result of such unions is nevertheless well authenticated. And if such consequences follow these marriages
when they take place between relatives in good health,
how much must the case be aggravated when one or both
parents are in delicate health, or suffer from hereditary taint;
or, as not unfrequently happens from the social intercourse
of cousins in early life, marriage takes place when the parties
have scarcely arrived at maturity. The subject deserves
the earnest consideration of parents, who may often use their
judgment in guarding their children in time from forming
unions which are too likely to blight the prospects of their
married life.

APPENDIX B, pp. 65, 163, 176, 201.

Although it is true that the great mortality of children
under five years of age is mainly owing to the deteriorating

influence of crowded unhealthy localities and ill-ventilated dwellings, together with the injudicious management of their parents, the immediate cause of death is often acute disease. It is of great consequence, therefore, that parents should be made acquainted with the exciting causes and nature of those diseases which prove most fatal in infancy and early childhood, in order that they may adopt measures for their prevention ; and, when these fail, that they may have their attention directed to the disease at its outset, the time when remedial measures are most likely to be efficient.

Mr Simon states that the deaths which occur in excess within five years of birth are mainly due to two classes of diseases :—

1. To the common infectious diseases of childhood,—measles, scarlatina, hooping-cough and smallpox, prevailing with unusual fatality.

2. To the endemic prevalence of convulsive disorders, bowel-complaints, and inflammatory diseases of the lungs.

We shall notice only the second class.

How much yet remains to be done in the management of children, appears from the fact that *convulsive diseases, diarrhœa, and inflammatory diseases of the lungs*—which are all preventible diseases—destroy by their conjoint operation 72,000 children a year, thus causing about a sixth part of the total annual mortality of England !

Nervous Diseases.—Two-thirds of the mortality just stated are registered as *convulsions.* The most powerful cause of this class of diseases in infancy has been shown to be breathing a confined and vitiated air; and how much may be done to diminish this frightful mortality was shown by the experience of the Dublin Lying-in Hospital, cited at p. 51, where 19 out of every 20 deaths within the first fortnight occurred from convulsions. That this mortality was caused by the vitiated air of the hospital, was evident from the fact that the mortality diminished in proportion as the ventilation was improved.

Breathing an impure air being thus found to be the chief

APPENDIX.

cause of convulsive diseases in infancy, the slightest threaten-
ings of the disease should attract the immediate attention
of the nurse, and no time should be lost in improving the
ventilation of the nursery and bedroom of the child. This
constitutes the most essential part of the treatment; and
without attention to it, remedies will prove of little avail in
the cure of disease. It is during the night that the greatest
care is necessary to maintain a pure state of the air in the
nurseries and bedrooms of children at all times, but more
especially when they are labouring under diseases of the
nervous system.

Diarrhœa and Dysentery.—More than 11,000 children die
annually in England of bowel-complaints. Where these
diseases prevail with unusual severity or frequency, we are
almost sure to find the house-drainage bad, and the non-
removal of animal refuse from the vicinity of the dwellings
and the sources of water supply. "Cases of infantile dysentery," observes Dr West, "are most numerous and severe
wherever these noxious influences are most abundant."*
The same causes are found to exist, also, where diarrhœa
prevails among adults. Until these silent but continuously
active sources of disease are removed, or the patients removed
from their influence, medical treatment will be powerless.
The medical attendant, under such circumstances, may do
much good by impressing this truth on the minds of the
parents, who will be more ready to listen to him while suffering under anxiety for their sick children.

Pneumonia, Bronchitis, Croup.—By the returns of the
Registrar-General for 1856, the deaths of children under
five years of age from these diseases amounted to 28,763.
The immediate or exciting cause of inflammatory diseases of
the respiratory organs is exposure to a cold or damp and
chilly atmosphere. It is not so much, however, the breathing of the cold or damp air, as the chill produced on the
sensitive and feeble system of the child by exposure to a
chilly atmosphere, or to a current of cold air, which acts more

* Diseases of Infancy and Childhood. Edition 1859.

rapidly in lowering the temperature. But although exposure to cold air is the exciting cause of the inflammatory attacks on the lungs, the pernicious in-door influences
give the predisposition to these diseases, and are the chief
obstacles to their successful treatment. The child is too
often in a feeble unhealthy state when attacked by the
malady, and easily sinks under it, the powers of the system
to resist disease being at the lowest ebb.—The period of
infant life at which pulmonary diseases are most frequent is
during dentition, when, as Dr West well remarks, the susceptibility of all the mucous membranes is at its highest point,
and when, moreover, diseases of the nervous system are
most easily excited. During the first six months of infant
life, the mucous membrane of the air-passages is endowed
with but little susceptibility, and therefore diseases of the
lungs are less frequent at this early age than during the succeeding eighteen months; while after the second year, and
the completion of dentition, they continue to diminish in
frequency and fatality up to puberty. "We are thus
taught," Dr West observes, "that a catarrh is a much more
serious thing in infancy than in adult age, and also that it
is a more serious thing at one period of infancy than at another. They warn us to guard a child, during the time that
the process of teething is going on, with double care against
all causes that are likely to excite inflammation of its respiratory organs."* He further observes, that the susceptibility of the respiratory organs appears to increase in exact
proportion to the frequency with which they have already
suffered by previous attacks. It must also be borne in mind,
that bronchitis is apt to occur in the progress of other diseases of childhood, such as *measles* and the *hooping-cough*,
and adds greatly to the danger. This is more especially
the case in the latter disease, the chief danger of which
arises from this complication. To prevent such an untoward occurrence, the child, when it first exhibits symptoms
of hooping-cough, should be kept in the house, and as quiet

* West, op. cit.

as possible, both mentally and physically, for the first week
or ten days, even in summer, and much longer in winter.
The diet also should be of the mildest kind. By judicious
management in this way, hooping-cough may be rendered
much milder and of shorter duration than it is by the usual
treatment. Should the disease occur during dentition, the
utmost vigilance and care will be required in the management of the child.

For the greater part of the statistical information contained in this note, we are indebted to the Introductory
Report of Mr Simon, and to Dr Greenhow's Papers on the
Sanitary State of the People of England, referred to on page
58. That Report and those Papers contain much valuable
information on our most prevalent and fatal diseases, more
especially on the causes and means of prevention of *preventible diseases*—that is, of diseases producing nearly one
half of the mortality of this country.

Appendix C, pp. 96, 107, 149.*

To enable the reader more fully to understand the principles laid down in the text for regulating the diet of infants,
it may be useful to append a few details on the composition
of substances used for food, especially milk.

All aliment capable of permanently supporting life must
contain elements fit to supply the waste of the tissues, and
to maintain the temperature of the body. With reference
to this double object, food is considered as *nutritive* or as
calorific aliment, according as its sole or chief use is the
nourishment of the tissues, or the support of the temperature.

Heat is a result of the combination of oxygen with hydrogen and with carbon; and hence, any substance containing hydrogen and carbon, in conditions in which they are
capable of combining with oxygen in the body, may serve
as calorific aliment. Accordingly, sugar, starch, and fat,

---

* This Note was appended by Dr James Coxe to the eighth edition,
which was edited by him. ▶

which are so constituted, combine, when used as aliment, with the oxygen inhaled in respiration ; and the products—water and carbonic acid—pass off almost entirely by the skin and lungs, without having entered into the composition of the solid tissues of the body.   Their sole office is the generation of heat.

For the nutrition and growth of the tissues of the body, more complex material is needed.   The muscles, and animal tissues generally, are composed of oxygen, hydrogen, carbon, and nitrogen ; to supply their growth and waste, therefore, substances containing all these elements are required.   Starch, sugar, and fat cannot nourish the muscles,—for the simple reason, that they are altogether deficient in the important element, nitrogen ; which, on the other hand, abounds in albumen, gluten, and fibrin, and in all other animal and vegetable principles capable of repairing muscular waste. It is a remarkable fact, that all these principles, wherever found, and whether of animal or vegetable nature, are almost identical in their ultimate chemical composition.   Thus the gluten of wheat, the legumin of peas, the fibrin of muscles, the casein of milk, and the albumen of eggs, contain very nearly the same proportions of oxygen, hydrogen, carbon, and nitrogen.

	Carbon.	Hydrogen.	Nitrogen.	Oxygen, &c.
Animal fibrin contains, .	52·5	7·	10·5	24.0
Vegetable fibrin, . . .	53·28	7·01	10·41	23·35
Albumen (white of egg), .	53·14	7·10	15·77	28·99
Vegetable albumen, . .	57·74	7·11	15·65	25·60
Casein of cow, ...	53·50	7·05	15·77	23·68
Vegetable casein, . . .	53·40	7·13	16·04	23·87

On the other hand, substances containing these elements in other proportions are incapable of repairing the waste of the tissues, and of permanently supporting life.   From this it appears, that the complex nutritive principles must be ready formed in the food, from which, by the process of digestion, they are extracted and conveyed to the fluids and tissues, where they undergo those changes on the occurrence of which the continuation of vitality depends, and which consist in the gradual resolution of complex organic atoms into the more simple atoms of the inorganic kingdom.

The term *albuminated aliment* is frequently applied to all the varieties of food capable of repairing waste, albumen being considered as the representative of nutritive material; and the same aliment is also occasionally termed *plastic*, from its giving form to the body. It must not, however, be supposed that albuminated aliment nowise contributes to the support of the temperature of the body. Being destitute of nitrogen, calorific (called also *respiratory*) aliment assists only indirectly in nutrition; but albuminated aliment, from containing carbon and hydrogen in a condition capable of uniting with oxygen, undergoes oxygenation in the body, and thus contributes to the support of the temperature.

The food of man unites calorific and albuminated principles; and these we naturally expect to find associated in MILK, from its constituting for several months the sole food of the infant. In this fluid the curd forms the albuminated aliment, while the sugar of milk and butter are the calorific principles.* According to the analyses of MM. Vernois and Becquerel, the mean composition of human milk is—

Water,	880·08
Solids,	110·92
	1000·00

These solids are composed of—

Sugar and soluble salts,	43·64
Casein and extractive matter,†	39·24
Butter,	26·66
Salts,	1·88
	110·92

* Fat, though in one sense a plastic element, is still essentially merely calorific aliment, which is stored up in the body when the supply is greater than the demand.

† The term *extractive matter* is applied to some ill-defined animal principles, which, in minute quantity, are associated with the casein.

Thus the quantity of respiratory aliment it contains is nearly
double that of the plastic aliment.

We must however observe, that this result is the mean
obtained from 89 observations.   In individual specimens the
amount of solid constituents varies greatly, as well as the
proportion which these constituents bear to each other.
Thus the maximum of solids found was 147·70, and the
minimum 33·33, in 1000 parts; while the quantity of sugar
varied between 59·55 and 25·22, that of casein between
70·92 and 19·32, and that of butter between 56·42 and 6·66.

The following table presents a comparison of the average
composition of human milk with that of several of the lower
animals, and shews at a glance the modifications of composition which would be necessary to assimilate the milk of
the latter to that of the human female, supposing the average
composition given by MM. Vernois and Becquerel to be the
normal composition :—

Animals.	Water.	Solids.	Sugar.	Casein and Extractive Matter.	Butter.	Salts by incineration.
Woman, . .	889·08	110·92	43·64	39·24	26·66	1·88
Cow, . . .	864·06	135·94	88·08	55·15	36·12	6·64
Ass, ...	890·12	109·88	50·40	35·06	18·58	5·24
Goat, . . .	844·90	155·10	36·91	55·14	56·87	6·18
Mare, . . .	904·60	95·70	32·76	33·85	24·36	5·23
Bitch, . . .	772·08	227·92	15·29	116·88	87·95	7·80
Ewe, . . .	832·32	167·68	89·43	69·78	51·81	7·16

According to Dumas, the milk of carnivorous animals is
totally deficient in sugar, and this opinion is probably correct
when animal food constitutes the sole aliment.   When this
is not the case, however, the milk of the carnivora contains
also sugar, though in quantity much inferior to that contained in the milk of the herbivora, as appears on comparing,

N

in the above table, the quantity in the milk of the bitch with that in the milk of the other animals. Upon the whole, the milk of the ass approaches nearest in composition to that of woman; but it is evident from what has already been said as to the varying quantity of the solids, and especially as to the disappearance of sugar from the milk of the carnivora, that the composition of the milk does not so much depend upon the species of the animal as upon the diet on which it is fed. This fact MM. Vernois and Becquerel further illustrate by analyses of different specimens of human milk, which show a great difference in composition between the milk of mothers who were well nourished, and that of mothers who were ill nourished; the latter being more watery, and containing considerably less than the normal proportion of curd and butter.

In practice, it is occasionally found that the milk of a perfectly healthy nurse disagrees with the infant. In such a case, when there is no urgent necessity to change the milk, it is probable that a radical alteration in the diet of the nurse, by either increasing or diminishing her allowance of animal or vegetable aliment, and by changing the hours of meals and exercise, will be followed by the best results; but where the health of the infant will not allow of any delay, the milk should at once be changed. The effect of diet in altering the composition of the milk will be evident from the following example. The milk of a goat, fed on straw and lucerne, was found to contain—

Water, . . .	824·67
Solids, . . .	176·38

the solids being composed of—

Butter, ...	70·01
Casein and Extractive Matter. . .	57·50
Sugar, ...	85·98
Salts, ...	5·84

When fed on beet-root, the composition was—

Water, . . .	887·74
Solids, . . .	112·26

the latter being composed of—

Butter,	31·60
Casein and Extractive Matter.	30·26
Sugar,	38·85
Salts,	0·05

The investigations of MM. Vernois and Becquerel lead them to think that the most frequent cause of the milk of a healthy woman disagreeing with the infant is an excess of solid matter, arising principally from an augmentation of butter, and, in a minor degree, from an increase of casein. It is not however asserted, that an excess of butter must of necessity operate injuriously on the child; they merely maintain, that when an infant does not thrive, an excess of butter will generally be found in the milk. In normal milk, the average quantity of butter is 26·66 parts in 1000; in the milk of nurses whose infants did not thrive, it amounted, on an average, to 33·22 parts. Guided by these indications, we should, in such cases, place the nurse upon a less nutritious diet, by substituting vegetable for animal aliment, and thus seek to supply the infant with a watery but digestible milk, in the place of one which, from its richness, proves too heavy for its digestive organs. In this way a mother whose milk disagreed with her first infant, may be enabled, on future occasions, to nurse with perfect success.

In the text, reference is made to cases in which angry passions or distress of mind produce a change in the milk, most prejudicial to the infant. Whether this effect is due simply to an alteration in the proportions of the constituents of milk, or whether some peculiar poisonous animal matter is generated, cannot easily be determined. However, there is no doubt that the constitution of the milk is, on such occasions, greatly modified, and this fact was demonstrated by chemical analysis in a case which fell under the observation of MM. Vernois and Becquerel. A nurse in the hospital St Antoine lost her only infant by an attack of pneumonia. Before its death her milk was analyzed, and found to consist of—

Water	889·49
Solids	110·51

the solids containing—

Sugar	.	.	.	.	41·52
Casein and Extractive Matter		.	.	44·02
Butter	.	.	.	.	23·70
Salts .	.	.	.	.	1·18

At the moment of its death she was attacked with violent
hysterical symptoms, followed in a few hours by intense
fever. The milk rapidly diminished, and was found on
analysis to be composed of—

Water	.	.	.	908·98
Solids	.	.	.	91·07

the solids containing—

Sugar	.	.	.	.	34·92
Casein and Extractive Matter		.	.	50·00
Butter	.	.	.	.	5·14
Salts .	.	.	.	.	1·01

It is, of course, impossible to say what effect this altered
milk would have produced upon the infant; nor, had symptoms of disease followed, could we with certainty have
affirmed that the alteration of composition was their cause.
Still, as the alteration proves that the quality of the milk is
affected by the condition of the nervous system of the
mother, the prudent course, in cases of anger or mental distress, is to abstain from offering the breast to the infant for
a day or two, until the milk has had time to regain its
normal composition.

In the adult, the functions of digestion are carried on by
the action of the salivary, gastric, and intestinal juices.
During mastication the saliva is mixed with the alimentary
bodies, and it exercises an important influence on the digestion of farinaceous substances. The investigations of MM.
Bidder and Schmidt have, however, shown that the salivary
secretion of infants, during the first months, acts very feebly,
if at all, on farinaceous substances. Hence, when these form
part of the diet of the infant, they are received into the
stomach in a condition unprepared for undergoing the digestive process, and are consequently very apt to produce
unpleasant symptoms. During the first period of life, then,

the digestive organs are adapted for the perfect digestion of
milk only, and all deviations from the natural food of the
infant are calculated, on physiological grounds, to produce
indigestion.

When, from any cause, it becomes necessary to substitute
the milk of one of the lower animals for that of the mother,
care should be taken not to supply the infant exclusively
with the milk which is first or last drawn. In the udder of
the cow, for instance, the milk is not of homogeneous composition; for, exactly as in a dish, the cream rises to the top,
so that the milk last drawn is always the richest. The difference in the quantity of butter in the first and last portions
was found by MM. Vernois and Becquerel to be in the cow
as 25 to 60, and in the ass as 6 to 36; while the proportions
of sugar and casein scarcely underwent any variation. In
woman, from the position of the breasts, the first and last
portions of the milk show no difference of composition; but
the caution just given may be useful when the milk is supplied to the infant directly from the animal.

The following tabular statements exhibit more distinctly
than those already given the relative amount of each ingre-
dient in woman's milk, as well as in that of those animals
whose milk is sometimes used as a substitute for human
milk. The ingredients are arranged in the order of their
relative abundance:—

1. Woman.			2. She-Ass.		
Sugar	. .	43·04	Sugar	. . .	50·46
Casein	. . .	80·24	Casein	. . .	35·65
Butter	. . .	26·66	Butter	. . .	18·58
Salts	. . .	1·88	Salts .	. . .	5·24
3. Cow.			**4. Mare.**		
Casein	. . .	55·15	Casein	. . .	83·85
Sugar	. . .	88·08	Sugar .	. . .	82·76
Butter	. . .	80·12	Butter .	. .	24·36
Salts .	. . .	6·64	Salts .	. . .	5·23
5. Goat.			**6. Ewe.**		
Butter	. . .	56·87	Casein	. . .	69·75
Casein	. . .	58·14	Butter .	. .	51·31
Sugar .	. . .	36·91	Sugar .	. . .	80·43
Salts	. . .	0·18	Salts .	. . .	7·16

As a general rule, the solids of the milk increase in quantity from the first to the fifteenth day. They are at their maximum during the first two months, and then slightly decrease.

The occurrence of pregnancy or menstruation does not, unless in exceptional cases, interfere with the quality of the milk. Neither does the age of the nurse appear in any particular way to modify its composition. The best age, however, is, on general physiological grounds, between twenty and thirty.

The milk of brunettes contains a greater quantity of solids than that of blondes, and is in general to be preferred. It is also worthy of remark, that when the milk is abundant and flows easily, it is richer in solids than when it is scanty and flows with difficulty. In conclusion, MM. Vernois and Becquerel remark that it is only by chemical analysis that the composition of milk can be ascertained. The determination of the specific gravity leaves the proportion of the different ingredients uncertain, while the microscope is here equally at fault.

We pass over the modifications produced in milk by disease in the mother, as in all cases of illness nursing should at once cease. The medical reader may consult the work of MM. Vernois and Becquerel, *Du Lait chez la Femme* (Paris, 1853).

APPENDIX D, pp. 111, 180, 197.

The period and progress of dentition demands our attention, not only as regards its influence on the immediate health of the child, but as a visible indication of the child's present constitutional development, and even of its future constitution.

Dr Whitehead of Manchester, who has evidently devoted much attention to this subject, and by whom statistical data on a large scale have been collected, has arrived at the following important conclusions :*—

"That in children possessing the advantages of mature intra-uterine growth, untainted parentage, proper nourishment, and healthy locality, the teething process ought to commence at from five to eight months.

"That at the age of fourteen months a child should have ten teeth or more, and that six teeth are the minimum number compatible with good development and favourable prospects at that age.

"That the teething process should, as a rule, be completed in healthy children at the age of two years.

"That *precocious dentition*—that is, the irruption of the *first* teeth before the fifth month—has not in every case a favourable significance, but that, on the contrary, the *precocious irruption* of *all* the twenty teeth is the constant attribute of an excellent state of development. Not a few children who accomplish the teething process at sixteen or eighteen months, or earlier, are able to walk freely at nine months, and are exceedingly strong in all their physical faculties." (Pp. 25, 26.)

The inference drawn by Dr Whitehead from his observations is, that the retardation of teething, and its concomitant ailments, depend more upon the faulty state of the developmental processes generally, than upon local irritation.

Another indication of good or bad development having a close relation to dentition, is the progress of the ossification of the *fontanelle*.

"As a rule, a child of good development, with closure of the fontanelle at fourteen and a half months, has usually at the same time (or ought to have) about fourteen teeth, and has been able to walk firmly several weeks or months; while in one having at this age the fontanelle largely open, it frequently happens that not more than two to six teeth have appeared, and he is unable to walk; and even at the

* Third Report of the Clinical Hospital, Manchester. 1859, by James Whitehead, M.D.

age of two years, when the teething process should be completed, the fontanelle being still open, there are generally
not more than eight to twelve teeth.

"The closure of the fontanelle, therefore, gives a fair indication of the state of the developmental processes, being
accompanied generally, with the exception of a few cases of
irregularity, by a corresponding condition of dentition, of
the faculty of walking, and of the whole physical frame."
(Pp. 30, 31.)

"Deviations from the general rule do not unfrequently
occur in children of good development, but without a bad
significance. The most frequent of these irregularities is
retardation of the teething process, sometimes to a considerable extent; but, in such cases, if the fontanelle be early
closed, and the faculty of walking duly advanced, there is no
need to fear about the after progress." (Pp. 50, 51.)

These observations of Dr Whitehead are very valuable,
both in a physiological and therapeutic point of view, and
deserve the attentive consideration of the medical practitioner called on to direct the management of infancy. The
whole Report merits a careful perusal, on account of both its
practical and suggestive bearings.

APPENDIX F, p. ix.

MEDICAL OPINION ON THE IMPORTANCE OF TEACHING PHYSIOLOGY
AND THE LAWS OF HEALTH IN COMMON SCHOOLS.

In order to remove all doubts as to the usefulness of an
elementary knowledge of physiology and the laws of health
being made a part of general education, and as to the possibility of its being taught "with the utmost facility and propriety in ordinary schools," the following conclusive document, signed by sixty-five of the most eminent physicians
and surgeons in London, including the Professors of Ana-

tomy and Physiology, was addressed some time ago to Lord
Granville, as Lord President of the Council, with the object
of inducing his lordship to require the teachers of schools
under Government inspection to possess such a knowledge
of physiology as would enable them to communicate it to
their pupils :—

"Our opinion having been requested as to the advantage
of making the elements of human physiology, or a general
knowledge of the laws of health, a part of the education of
youth, we the undersigned have no hesitation in giving it
strongly in the affirmative. We are satisfied that much of
the sickness from which the working-classes at present suffer
might be avoided; and we know that the best-directed
efforts to benefit them by medical treatment are often greatly
impeded, and sometimes entirely frustrated, by their ignorance and their neglect of the conditions upon which health
necessarily depends. We are therefore of opinion, that it
would greatly tend to prevent sickness, and to promote
soundness of body and mind, were the elements of physiology,
in its application to the preservation of health, made a part
of general education ; and we are convinced that such instruction may be rendered most interesting to the young,
and may be communicated to them with the utmost facility
and propriety in the ordinary schools, by properly instructed
schoolmasters.

"LONDON, *March* 1853."

Here follow the signatures.

The original document is deposited in the Council Office.

INDEX.

www.ingramcontent.com/pod-product-compliance
Lightning Source LLC
Chambersburg PA
CBHW021123270326
41929CB00009B/1011